CASTING SEAWARD

CASTING SEAWARD

*Fishing Adventures in Search of
America's Saltwater Gamefish*

STEVE RAMIREZ

Illustrations by Bob White

Foreword by Kirk Deeter

Essex, Connecticut

An imprint of Globe Pequot, the trade division of
The Rowman & Littlefield Publishing Group, Inc.
4501 Forbes Blvd., Ste. 200
Lanham, MD 20706
www.rowman.com

Distributed by NATIONAL BOOK NETWORK

British Library Cataloguing in Publication Information available

Library of Congress Cataloging-in-Publication Data
Names: Ramirez, Steve, 1961- author. | White, Bob, illustrator,
    illustrator. | Deeter, Kirk, writer of foreword.
Title: Casting seaward : fishing adventures in search of America's
    saltwater gamefish / Steve Ramirez ; illustrations by Bob White ;
    foreword by Kirk Deeter.
Description: Lanham, MD : Lyons Press, an imprint of Globe Pequot, the
    trade division of The Rowman & Littlefield Publishing Group, Inc.,
    [2023] | Includes bibliographical references.
Identifiers: LCCN 2022040529 (print) | LCCN 2022040530 (ebook) | ISBN
    9781493070985 (hardcover) | ISBN 9781493070992 (e-book)
Subjects: LCSH: Saltwater fishing—North America.
Classification: LCC SH457 .R36 2023 (print) | LCC SH457 (ebook) | DDC
    639.2/2097—dc23/eng/20220928
LC record available at https://lccn.loc.gov/2022040529
LC ebook record available at https://lccn.loc.gov/2022040530

Author's Dedication

To my father, Stephen J. Ramirez, who through hardship and heartache, raised me as a single parent and taught me how to be a man of honor, courage, humility, love, and compassion. My dad was born into poverty but raised with a wealth of love by his immigrant mother who overcame her lack of education to raise her children to be "Good Americans" one and all.

Born on December 26, 1931, and leaving this life on July 28, 2016, Dad served as a Staff Sergeant in the U.S. Air Force during the Korean War. He chose to enlist as a medic because he wanted to serve his country but did not want to hurt anyone in the process. That was my dad. He was a man of peace, and yet, the bravest man I've ever known.

My father saved my life, in many ways. He taught me to love and connect with nature and find solace in its beauty and honesty. He taught me to play my first chords on the guitar and thus began my passion and appreciation for music. That guitar soothed my soul many times. He shared his love of the sea with me, and we made many wonderful memories together riding across and diving below its surface. Dad loved the ocean so deeply that my sisters and I always referred to him as "The Captain." But most of all, dad taught me what unconditional love is, and he did so by example.

When he died, I cried. Then, I picked up my guitar and played the Jimmy Buffet song titled, "The Captain and the Kid." After, I sat the guitar down and did not play it again for three years. Well, Captain, I'm singing again. After all, you taught me to find joy, even in the darkest storms. Fair Winds and Following Seas Captain . . . I love you.

Illustrator's Dedication

I am deeply humbled to have been asked by Steve Ramirez to include a dedication to my father in this, his third book. While I had nothing to do with the writing of Steve's book, I was honored to have contributed some of my artwork as illustrations. The pencil drawings in this book are dedicated to my father, Richard Allen "Dick" White.

My father was born on December 31, 1930, and crossed his last river on August 6, 2018. While in some regards he was a complicated man, in other more important matters, he was quite straightforward. I believe there were four aspects of my father's life by which he defined himself and taught me to be a man.

His marriage was his first and foremost duty. He loved my mother deeply, and it was by their example that my four sisters and I learned the value of love, dedication, and a strong marriage. All of his children were loved and cherished, and it was through this experience that we learned to be parents. My father was a man of conscience and faith, and by this example we learned to believe in something larger than ourselves.

And last, but not least, my father was a United States Marine, and it was the lessons he learned about himself as a Recon Marine that gave him the depth of character and internal strength he needed to succeed in everything else: as a husband, a father, a neighbor, and a friend.

While growing up, my father may not have always told me what I wanted to hear, but I knew that he was telling me what he believed to be true. He was always true—true to his beliefs, true to his wife, true to his family, and true to his friends. Semper fi, Dad.

You have to carry the fire.
I don't know how to.
Yes, you do.
Is the fire real? The fire?
Yes it is.
Where is it? I don't know where it is.
Yes you do. It's inside you. It always was there. I can see it.
—CORMAC MCCARTHY, THE ROAD

CONTENTS

FOREWORD

IT ALL TRENDS TOWARD THE SEA.

That starts with the water itself. It's pretty darn cool to straddle a tiny ribbon of water and think, "some of these molecules may just end up in the Gulf of Mexico and the Atlantic Ocean . . . or the Pacific Ocean." I live for the headwaters. The cold, clean brooks that spring from the earth, or collect snowmelt and raindrops from the glades of rocky slopes or Midwestern marshes—places where trout typically live—fuel my angling soul.

I am hardly alone in that respect. The fly-fishing world, for better or worse, spins on an axis of trout, as evidenced by the fact that three-quarters (at least) of all the gear sold in the fly-fishing market is trout-centric. But my dirty little secret is that, while I often daydream about trout rising to a dry fly, my *night dreams* inevitably—and I mean *always*—revolve around tarpon, bonefish, permit, sharks, stripers, redfish, and other species native to salt water.

Any angler may indeed start fly-fishing on a creek or bluegill pond, a bass river in the Texas Hill Country, or any number of other waters and then stretch herself or himself to the big brawling rivers. Some may be perfectly content operating in that realm for an entire lifetime. And that's just fine. But, in my experience, if you fish long enough, you're going to at least sniff the salt. You're gonna wonder. You're going to feel the pull. And when you go there, it will change you and also change everything you've ever thought about fly fishing. After all, 71 percent of our earth's surface is covered by water, but less than 3 percent of that is fresh water.

The salt is where the real action abounds, and where you really stand to evolve as an angler. It's harsh. It's honest. It's all about tricking a raw, predatory instinct. You must know how to cast a fly rod. You must know how to fight a fish. There's no day trip, instant gratification, "feel the tug for fun" happening in the oceans. The fish are often bigger, and smarter, and they'll beat you up if you don't know what you're doing. Moreover, Mother Nature plays no favorites on the flats. It is what it is . . . wind, rain, ripping tides, whatever, that's what you get, and you deal with it. You cannot force the matter in the sea. I can't count the days I've spent shucking oysters and drinking beer on the dock in Louisiana because it "just wasn't right." That's all part of the game and perfectly fine. I wouldn't trade any of it for the world.

To the real point . . . I also wouldn't have traded anything in the world for the chance to write this foreword for my brother-from-another-mother Steve Ramirez, because I am so damn proud of him for following the fly-fishing path full course. He started at home in the Hill Country of Texas with *Casting Forward*, which I thought read like a fly-fishing troubadour ballad. I actually got to fish with Steve and straddle some of those high-country brooks in the Rockies (and also fish for Guadalupe bass in Texas) as he worked on his second book, *Casting Onward*. Now, I think he's closed the loop and established himself as one of the most honest and talented writers in the modern fly-fishing era with this one. He nailed it. Of course. Read on, and you will see.

Kirk Deeter, Editor-in-Chief, *Trout Magazine*, Trout Unlimited

PROLOGUE

Where there is no hope, it is incumbent on us to invent it.
~ ALBERT CAMUS

THIS IS A STORY ABOUT CREATING REASONS FOR HOPE IN AN ALL TOO often seemingly hopeless world. It is a reimagining of how nature and humanity can live together, from this moment onward. And it is an attempt to shake us free of our illusions so that we might confront and overcome the many challenges that have been the natural outcomes of our individual and collective choices. This is a hopeful plea that "We the People" will choose to demonstrate the courage and wisdom required to give humankind and our beautiful blue planet the best chance of surviving and thriving.

This is also the story of a man dealing with the consequences of aging and loss. Sometimes it's hard to out-survive many of the people and places that I've loved. I once heard it said that the older we get the more life takes from us. Perhaps this is true. Still, it is incumbent on us to adapt to our new surroundings and find joy—wherever it lives. During my time living in Africa, I learned a saying that is as wise as that continent is old. In the Zulu language it is, "Guka 'mzimba, sala 'nhliziyo," which means, "The body grows old but the heart stays young." With each rotation of the Earth, I remind myself to live those words.

As I watch our society becoming increasingly dysfunctional and disjointed and our planet becoming alarmingly endangered, I refuse to surrender all hope. This is because I know that no one and nothing has any power over me unless I choose to give that power away. (The same is true for us all.) And I choose to do whatever I can do to be a trim-tab for the vessel that often feels lost in a sea of apathy and despair. I will not surrender . . . will you? There is hope, and that hope resides within each of us. As an aging man, I know that words and ideas outlive us.

It is important to realize and remember that everything is created twice: first in our imaginations and then in our realities. Once we can imagine and envision the way the world "should be" and "can be," we can act on that vision, like raindrops on limestone, drop by drop, building a canyon and filling a sea. Nothing is as powerful as an idea whose time has come. It is almost past time for us, to change direction.

In my first book, *Casting Forward*, I wrote of my love for my Texas Hill Country homeland and home waters, and of my determination to find the best in human nature within myself and others. I wrote of my concerns for my homeland, community, and world, and of my hopeful optimism about the resilience of nature and humanity. I wrote of the healing and teaching powers of nature and the need for all of humanity to reconnect with our one and only true home.

My second book, *Casting Onward*, was a continuation and expansion of my first work. When I set out to write this book, my original plan was to travel across North America, connecting with and learning about these native gamefish within their historical range and natural habitat. I planned to learn about them and their watersheds and what that could teach me about the state of our nation's environment, both human and nonhuman. And I decided that I would tell these stories through the eyes of the people who live within the watersheds where each native fish originates, and currently clings to existence.

In *Casting Seaward*, together we will take the next logical steps in the adventure by following the rivers and fish toward the sea, and then following them once again, from the sea to the rivers. Water imitates life just as life imitates water. They both travel in timeless circles—flowing through each other. Our finite bodies contain the lifeblood of the oceans. We are all simply animated and temporarily rearranged bits of stardust and seawater. We are drawn to the ocean in part because it is the original home from which we first sprung. We are also drawn to the ocean because it calls to us, lives within us, and if we choose to harness the right wind, it brings us together. Our understanding and perspective determine the seas we sail upon and our ultimate destination.

It doesn't matter if you're an angler, hunter, hiker, naturalist, birder, kayaker, rockhound, mountain climber, scuba diver, gardener, or just someone who enjoys a walk on the beach at sunrise—this is your book. I hope you will join me on this adventure around the varied coastlines of America the Beautiful. As long as we keep *"casting"* together, we can *"turn the wheel"* and begin to move in a more sane, healthy, and happy direction.

Namaste, Y'all . . . Keep Casting Forward!
Steve Ramirez, Comfort, Texas

CHAPTER ONE

First Cast—Native Guadalupe Bass and Stocker Rainbow Trout

Crabapple Creek, Texas Hill Country

I wanted you to see what real courage is, instead of getting the idea that courage is a man with a gun in his hand. It's when you know you're licked before you begin but you begin anyway and you see it through no matter what.

~ HARPER LEE

WHEN I TURNED SIXTY, I WENT FISHING. I WENT FISHING NOT BECAUSE I was searching for some form of wisdom or enlightenment, and I wasn't trying to escape from anything, anyone, or any place. I went fishing because after six decades of living I had finally learned that most human endeavors are the equivalent of building sandcastles at low tide, and almost none of them were half as much fun as angling. And I went fishing because life really is just a flicker of light, and we never know when the wind will pick up and blow out our candle.

It's important to not look back and not look forward but rather, just cast, and see what's biting. Instead, we must simply accept whatever the rivers, seas, or life itself chooses to give us, and then adapt to the prevailing currents. We need to play it out, and in the end, let it swim free without expectations, conditions, or regrets . . . allowing life to flow naturally, even as we set a hopeful course. After all, we aren't going anywhere in particular. We're just traveling in the here and now. We're all treading water, as the sea moves us. "Time and tide wait for no man."

The drive up to Crabapple Creek was a familiar one through my beloved Texas hills, across the wine country vineyards that line the

Pedernales River and up into the Llano Uplift where the rocks are enchanting and the songs of canyon wrens warble hypnotically. It was my birthday, and I had arranged to meet my friend Sue Kerver, who had invited me up as her guest on a trout lease operated by the Hill Country Fly Fishers Club. It was a wonderful birthday gift for my friend to give me because although the area was familiar, the creek was not. Up until this day I had never been offered access to the creek that passes through private ranchland. And although there are a few road crossings where I could wade in, I had never done so until this day, my sixtieth birthday.

Crabapple Creek is a lovely little ribbon of Texas Hill Country water. It's the kind of stream that people drive over while crossing a low bridge and they never give it a second look, but they should. It rises up out of the granite rock of the Llano Uplift and tumbles down into the ancient limestone seabed of the Balcones Escarpment until it empties itself into Pedernales Creek and onward, down the Colorado River to Matagorda Bay and the Gulf of Mexico. I smiled as I thought of the water drops of Crabapple Creek tumbling over the stones on their way to the sea. I envisioned them rising up into the clouds and falling back down as rain only to be sipped from the palm of my outstretched hand—temporarily becoming part of me.

We are nothing more than ephemeral streams that briefly contemplate their own existence. I wonder if Crabapple Creek ever lies awake at night wondering about mortality. Creeks like Crabapple are drying up all over the world as temperatures rise and thirsty sprinklers water worthless lawns that scar the landscape. If only we'd kill the lawns and revive the creeks—imagine the world we might know.

Sue is, among other things, a proud veteran of the U.S. Coast Guard who rose from the ranks of enlisted to officer, earning two master's degrees in the process, including one from the famed military college of the south, The Citadel. She cares for a young dog named "Meatball" and an old dog named "Odin," whom she loads into a red Radio Flyer wagon so that he can go on walks too. And she took good care of this old "Devil Dog" on his birthday, although she did not offer me a ride in her little red wagon.

One thing I've learned about Sue is that like me, she enjoys taking her time gearing up, pulling on waders, stringing up rods, and tying on flies. As we slowly gathered our gear we talked about life and love and living a life we love, out in nature. We talked about its challenges and rewards, and how quickly it all seems to pass, like an autumn leaf on Crabapple Creek. And we watched the water as it moved from somewhere to somewhere else . . . from creek to river to bay to sea to sky and ultimately back to the creek again. It's a cycle and a circle, just like life. Sue and I know this, and we enjoyed talking about it as we walked up and waded into the cold, flowing water that once created us and currently saves us. The water was lovely, clear, and filled with stocked rainbow trout of admirable size and unusually nice color for stockers.

I always have mixed feelings about "stockers." I mean, it's not their fault that they are raised in stainless steel tanks like cattle in a feedlot, only to be dumped into foreign waters, where, in the case of Texas, they never belonged and have zero chance of long-term survival. Their hearts beat just as hopefully as mine, and my only consolation is, for a small space in time, they live in the illusion of freedom, also, just like me. I do catch them, but I don't try too hard to catch them, and when I do, I treat them with all the respect that any living creature is due, including the Earth itself. That's how I see the Earth. It is a living being, complete with wounds and healing and the constant threat of being wounded so deeply that healing becomes impossible.

Sue walked down to a nice pool just downstream of where we crossed the creek, and I took one farther upstream. We were both tossing streamers, small olive buggers with golden-colored beads that proved a little too lightweight, and a hint of flash that proved to be just flashy enough. I cast into my pool and immediately got a follow and refusal from a chunky rainbow that looked to be about sixteen inches or so. All of the trout stocked here are at least that big.

To me, this kind of fishing is a bit like casting into a koi pond at the zoo, but I did not let it spoil the beauty of the place or the good fortune of investing time in nature with a friend. In short order my friend started catching one trout after another from the bottom of her deep, clear, fishy-filled pool. For a while it seemed like she was hooking a fish every other cast. Sue was showing off, I guess. I smiled, happy for my friend.

"Come on down here!" she called out to me over the sound of rushing water. "You need to catch your first 'birthday fish'!" I did, and while she remained at the head of the pool, I positioned myself at the tail and began working the streamer across the current. I caught a nice trout on my second cast which gave me a brief but beautiful battle that included a couple of jumps that would make a Romanian gymnast envious. Once in the net I quickly slipped out the barbless hook and was happy to watch him swim away, seemingly no worse for wear.

He was so damn beautiful that it was almost heartbreaking to know his fate. I hoped that he did not know what was coming next. None of us do, really . . . but I knew that he was either destined for a frying pan or the belly of any number of predators in and along this creek. I knew that soon the bluebonnets will bloom, and the days and water will grow warmer. By the end of April, the water will grow so warm that he and his kind will lose the light in their eyes and the color on their sides. His fate was sealed the moment he was spawned in that hatchery runway. In time he will return to the creek, river, and sea, which I guess also makes him just like me. Impermanence is life; life is impermanence.

Sue moved upstream to a new spot where the current ran beneath a rocky ledge and a couple of big fish were milling about as if they were waiting for something. As I walked away, I was hoping that my friend had just the right "something" tied to her tippet to bring their waiting to an end. I switched to a soft-hackle wet fly that just felt right when I looked at it in the box. There was nothing more scientific to my choice than the recognition that it seemed "buggy," and that I liked it.

I went prospecting downstream, looking long and hard into a pool that appeared to be empty, and then finding another that was teeming with trout from one side to the other. A massive head and shoulders rose from the surface. That rainbow looked to be eighteen to twenty inches long as he slid into the deepest pool like the Loch Ness Monster, or at least, that is how he seemed, on such small water. I waded in and set up my cast, allowing the wet fly to swing with the current. I received a quick tug and hook up with a fish that leapt three times before I brought him to the net, slipped out the hook, thanked him, and sent him back to the stream. Two more casts brought two more trout, all about sixteen inches long and brightly colored. The monster eluded me.

Every one of these fish jumped once I set the hook, and every time they did, they seemed to be shaking off water-colored diamonds. The slanting sunlight caught them perfectly in midair as each rainbow defied gravity and their own need for oxygen in an attempt to be free. For a moment I wondered what right I had to catch them, and then I remembered that there is no such thing as "rights," or "morality," or "justice" or "fairness" in nature. All are human constructs, unknown outside our own imaginations. But there is nothing wrong with imagining a kinder, better, more decent world. Ideals such as kindness and respect are not things we can realistically expect from the world, but they are things we can choose to give to the world.

Don't get me wrong, I am an angler and I have been a hunter who has no regrets about the animals I have killed and processed into food and textiles. I do not regret a single fresh fish shore lunch or the kudu steaks we roasted on an open fire under a blanket of African stars. I recall every catch and kill as being my contribution to the true circle of life, and I treated each creature with respect and gratitude. Hunting and gathering are the natural way of things for Homo sapiens. I doubt that any trout feels regret about swallowing a mayfly. But I have thought of these things as I catch fish, however ethically I do so, for the sheer joy of it. I have asked myself, "Is this right?"

Each of us comes to our own ethical conclusions in life, and mine tend to change as I learn new things. But I have decided that angling, like so many human interactions with nature, is vital to keeping people connected to fish, streams, rivers, and oceans. It's easy to care about songbirds because we see and hear them every day. But fish live in a hidden world. We must find them in order to know them, and we must know them in order to love them, and we must love them in order to save them—from us. Ironic, huh?

As my buddy Bob White might say, "fish were caught," with my friend Sue jokingly pointing out that she "out fished" me, and me seriously pointing out that, "I couldn't care less." As it turns out, the sixty-year-old man was quite like the six-year-old boy who caught tiny bluegills on a cane pole while never caring a lick that his dad was catching the "big fish" on his spinning rig. I'm not hardcore at angling. I don't keep count and don't care if I catch a trout that is six pounds or six ounces. I only care about being truly alive and fully connected in the moment. I don't expect anything in particular, so I am seldom disappointed in the outcome. I just keep casting forward, just as a trout keeps rising. And like the trout, I wait to see what the river might bring. Uncertainty is the essence of adventure; certainty is a myth that breeds boredom.

The fish in the upper pool proved to be the shy type, so I told Sue she should try the one downstream of me, and once she did, she immediately began to catch fish. I was happy for her. As for me, I felt content. I had found another deep pool that surrounded three sides of a granite boulder that was about the size of a minibus. It was full of surprisingly big trout, stacked up like lumber at a sawmill.

I tossed a streamer in there and they flashed at it and turned away, but that was fine for me, because, quite like these fish, my heart wasn't into it. I had caught enough, and all I really wanted to do was listen to the birds and the sound of the rushing water as it and time passed me by. So, I sat on a rock, between two waterfalls, in the middle of the creek, my rod across my lap, and I watched and listened and felt everything around me and inside me. I watched Sue casting and catching with a three-quarter moon suspended above her in the clear, blue sky. I watched some deer as they foraged among the junipers and oaks on the bluff above us, and I felt the coolness of the breeze and the warmth of the sunlight. And although I tried not to think, I did think, a little.

When we got back to our trucks we sat on the tailgates and Sue ate her soup while I enjoyed my chili and tortillas. At one point she mentioned that she saw me sitting on the rock in the middle of the creek just watching the water falling all around me. She asked, "Were you thinking about turning sixty?"

"A little," I replied.

"How do you feel about that?" She asked.

After a pause I said, "I feel fine about that."

Then, after a moment, I added, "After all, there's not a damn thing I can do about it! Sure, I'd love to go back thirty years with all I have learned along the way and try the whole ride once again, but I have no regrets and besides, regrets are a waste of time. I rarely look back except to recall something I have learned, and I never look forward except to set a general direction—all the while knowing that I'm liable to end up someplace else. Life happens as we plan. Still, I am planning to make this decade of my life, the best decade of my life. So . . . I feel fine about turning sixty."

The chili tasted good, and the tortillas tasted good enough, and I thought about my younger friend as she drove back toward Austin and I drove back toward San Antonio. I was feeling that sleepiness that comes after a peaceful day in the outdoors, and I needed to keep my eyes open for the long drive home. Thankfully, the coffee in my insulated cup was still warm enough to drink. It tasted wonderful and lifegiving. I had enjoyed a good day on a nice creek with a friend who, like me, was in transition.

It's kind of ironic that we humans are always wanting to "get back to normal" when the only thing that is normal in life is change. Living authentically is all about being the best version of ourselves, in the moment. That's a much better path than whining about "lost youth." In my heart I am still the boy of six with my cane pole in hand and a "lifetime" of living yet to do. In "real time," I am a man of sixty casting graceful loops toward the progeny of those first fish, many generations removed. Nothing lasts forever, even as life on Earth outlasts any one lifetime. Even the sun will sleep—in time.

——◆——

Every moment of value I have ever experienced was the result of choosing to ignore the voices of limitation and fear. Life is a series of choices, and I genuinely believe that we must choose to live many lives, now. When we stop learning, we stop growing. When we stop growing, we are by definition—dead. Why do so many people choose to be the living dead?

When I got home from Crabapple Creek, I stowed my fishing gear before dropping to the floor and knocking out one push-up for every year of my life, just because I could. I guess some people might say that it was a childish thing to do, but I saw it as the childlike thing to do, and there is a big difference. Sometimes children choose to run fast, simply because they can. I guess quite like the character Rocky Balboa, I wanted to prove to myself that I still have "stuff in the basement." I wanted to remind myself that no matter what comes my way, I can choose to keep casting onward. I hope you remember that too.

—◦—

When I was a young Marine, I had two best friends, both of whom I loved like brothers. Dave, Monty, and I were the three amigos. We were different in so many ways, and yet the same in the ways that mattered.

Dave was the ultimate boisterous bad-boy Marine who seemed to do his best to hide his great intellectual and spiritual depth, turning every eventuality into an opportunity for laughter and lighthearted rebellion. He was always getting into trouble, breaking the rules, and walking on the edge of disaster. Dave died almost twenty years ago, and part of me died with him. He was forty-one years old when he crossed that river. I was the only person who openly cried at his funeral. I'm not ashamed of that.

Monty was quiet, intellectual, and seemed too gentle to be a warrior. Yet he served his country as a U.S. Marine and then as a twenty-year Parks and Wildlife law enforcement officer. Three days after my sixtieth birthday, I got the call from Monty's life partner, Ginny. At sixty-one years of age, Monty was gone. My heart broke a little more at the tragedy of his declining health and ultimate passing. And now with them both gone, I am the lone survivor.

Dave died at forty-one and Monty at sixty-one . . . would I live to be eighty-one? There's no telling. All I know is, I want to keep living as long as I live. All I know is, I'm going to keep casting until there is no more river left in life.

It was comforting to read the many heartfelt messages from friends across the country when I shared of the loss of my second Marine brother. Speaking of spiritual brothers, Bob White wrote me a private message that was so brave and beautiful that it brought both a smile to my face and a few tears to my eyes. I told my daughter Megan about Monty's passing via a video call, and she cried. I knew it was because she felt her dad's pain. My wife Alice was kind and oh so understanding with my constant need to talk it out and my need to sometimes be silent with my memories. And then I received a message from my friend Sue that simply asked, "Do you want to return to Crabapple Creek for one last fishing trip before I leave?" (Sue was moving to Montana and a new life adventure at the end of the week.) I read the message, smiled, and replied, "Let's go!"

There was so much kindness sent my way, all I could think of was something Monty once said, "When times get tough, you don't lose any friends; you just find out who your true friends are and who never really was a true friend." I found out what I already knew. I found out that I'm a lucky man.

<hr />

When we arrived back at Crabapple Creek, everything seemed in flux. The water was still cold enough to keep the doomed stocker rainbows alive, but the air was almost too warm to wear waders comfortably. The trees were still mostly winter bare, but the first tiny green buds were opening cautiously, hoping for spring. And Sue seemed a bit troubled, mulling over the seemingly big leap of faith that she needed to make, that same day. You see, this was the day she needed to resign from one job and finalize the acceptance of another. This was the day she had to commit to selling her house in the hope of creating a new home in the mountains of Montana, so far away. We talked about it a little bit as we strung up our rods, and then we let it go for a while and went fishing. That's what fly fishing allows us to do—let go. Mulling over things can drive us mad, but letting them find their own drift, can carry us home. It was like that, on this day. A homecoming of sorts.

We walked upstream and I stood on the banks of a lower pool as Sue continued toward the next. At first I saw a single trout as it held in a foam line just below a small waterfall. I knew to keep looking, silently and patiently. Fishing begins long before the first cast. This wasn't something casual; it was courtship. As with a beautiful woman, I needed to respect the stream and get to know her, before I asked her to dance.

I always find it magical how the invisible can become visible if we are patient and open both our eyes and our mind's eye. In time, one trout became two, and two became six, and six became a dozen, all jockeying for space in a couple of pretty runs and a few lovely pools. I had tied on a small wet fly, just because I felt like it. I was matching my mood, not any particular hatch. I cast once, let it swing and drift and then began a halting retrieve and I felt a bump, but no solid take. I could not see the fish that bumped the fly as it passed through the bubbles below the falls. I cast again and this time felt a take which I returned with a hook set that resulted in a spectacular leaping rainbow that soon was brought to hand, revived, and released. Sue saw me land it and she cheered me on over the sound of the rushing, tumbling, gurgling stream.

These trout were educated after months of being bombarded by the fishing club membership, and once again, I almost felt guilty trying to catch them. But it wasn't easy fishing, because the water was clear, the current was modest, and the trout had learned to resist impulsive eating and to inspect everything that floats, swims, or skips by them, in or on the water. We changed flies again and again without much luck. I caught another rainbow fair and square, hooked another in the lip but lost it halfway through the fight, and somehow accidentally managed to foul hook one in the tail as it rejected and turned from the fly, just as I was raising my rod tip. I landed that fish and released it, but it was a surreal experience to play a fish backward!

That was about the time I looked upstream and saw my friend sitting in the middle of the creek on a big rock, just staring at a couple of waterfalls, quite like I had done on our first trip to this place, on my birthday. I could see that she was deep in thought, not about the passing of another year, but about the uncertainty of choosing a vastly different venue for her next chapter in life. I reeled in and walked up along the shore until I was within view, and I called out, "You've found a nice place to sit out there! I'd come join you, but the water is a bit deep between you and me . . . how did you get out there?"

"I swam," she replied.

"You swam?"

"Well, first I fell in, and then I swam. I'm soaked all the way down to my socks!"

I smiled. "Want to swim back and have lunch?" I joked.

She laughed and began working her way across the stream at a slightly shallower crossing.

We'd agreed to have a tailgate lunch and then go back to fishing for these reticent rainbows, but that never happened. Instead, we spent a long time with Sue sitting on her tailgate and me on mine, just chatting about life and living and the struggles of two military veterans who carry both wounds and wonderful memories from our time of service. We talked about her ruminations over resigning from her job and moving into another one, thousands of miles away. And I listened, as any good friend must do. And once I felt the time was right, I said, "Every adventure contains uncertainty. Every life, is a brief moment in time, filled with choices that define us. How do you want to be defined?"

"I want a big life," she replied.

After a moment of silence I said, "Then just go, and enjoy this adventure without any expectations, except that you will have new opportunities to practice living a big, beautiful life."

In the span of two fishing trips to a pretty little ephemeral stream, fish were caught, a friendship was grown, and cares were released along with the fish. In the span of two fishing trips, my last Marine brother had died, my new friend had decided to make a bold leap that any trout would envy, and we managed more laughter than tears, although both became part of this journey. And a beautiful journey it was, complete with all the challenges and rewards that come whenever we do as author Richard Bach once wrote and "run from safety."

Every great thing I have ever done in life, I have done by ignoring the voices of limitation and fear and leaping into uncertainty, just because I felt that failing to do so would be more dangerous than anything I'd face along the way. Life is a series of choices. I genuinely believe that we must choose to live many lives, now.

Driving home, once again I imagined the faces of many friends, old and new, as I listened to the Steve Miller Band playing, "Space Cowboy," and watched the Texas Hill Country rolling south toward the Texas scrub country, coastal plains, and ultimately, the Gulf of Mexico. I sang along with the song of my youth, and I thought about the water drops of Crabapple Creek as they traveled south from their fresh spring water source to their saltwater destination in Matagorda Bay. Water flows like life, never-ending, always changing. Everything is connected to everything. I keep reminding myself that I am the ocean, not the fish.

However hapless or happy this adventure might be, I've made my choice for this, my sixtieth year of life. This year, I am taking a new leap of faith, living life big and finding out what's biting, and what's not. This year, I am going to seek out more of the best in nature and the best of human nature. And this year, I'm choosing to keep casting seaward.

I wonder what I'll discover. I wonder what we'll discover. So much can be pondered and understood while wading a sand flat, walking a sandy beach, or chatting with a friend from the back of a tailgate. Let's go fishing for answers—together.

Part I

The North Atlantic Ocean

Chapter Two

Bluefish and Striped Bass
The Estuaries of Eastern Long Island, New York

We have only this moment, sparkling like a star in our hand . . . and melting like a snowflake. Let us use it before it is too late.

~ Marie Beyon Ray

The thing about life is that you just never know how many sunrises, sunsets, moonglows, moments for memories, smiles and belly laughs, breaths and heartbeats you have remaining. And it's not "time" that gets you; it's the Second Law of Thermodynamics. I can go back in clock-time if I get on a plane and chase the rotation of the Earth while flying at supersonic speeds toward the setting sun, but it won't make me one day younger or cause me to live one day longer. Entropy rules, Camus's absurdity exists, and there isn't a damn thing any of us can do to change that, nor should we if we could. All of life is now.

I thought about this as I flew forward in time from my home in the Texas Hill Country toward the home of my friend David Blinken on New York's Long Island. David and I turned sixty within thirty-five days of each other, and although he shared with me that he didn't much like "looking down that tunnel," neither of us is looking back or forward . . . much. Instead, we get up each morning and seek moving water, moving winds, and moving moments with as much grace and gratitude as we can muster. Every cast counts, and we know it.

When I arrived at the house I was slightly awestruck by its grandeur as I drove through the gate, past the sign that reminded me to "please drive slowly" because "grandchildren play here." David's wife Cathy, and Hana the pup who owns them, came out to greet me. Hana is a magnificent standard poodle with black curly hair, an efficient yet aristocratic trotting gait, and a disposition made up of boundless playfulness and love. Cathy showed me to my room for the next few days on the east end of the main house and invited me to walk down to the cottage by the water for some tea as we waited for David to return from a fishing charter. (I was soon to discover his client had a great day that included a dozen striped bass and some bluefish for extra measure. Things looked promising.)

My new home away from home included ceiling-to-floor windows with a view of the bright green lawn, dark green trees waving in the oceanic breeze, and Georgica salt pond that emptied into the Atlantic Ocean. From the open window I heard both the songs of birds in the trees and the rush of waves against the sandbar just beyond. It was perfection in a moment, and it was then that I first saw him sitting under a tree, immovable, stone-faced, and seemingly timeless. It was Pablo Picasso, or at least, it was a seated concrete statue of the master, bald-headed, cross-armed, and emotionless, looking out to sea . . . like me. I walked across the lush, perfectly clipped lawn and up to Picasso and in that moment, I was struck by a sense of recognition that went far beyond the artist's intentions. I could not place the where or why of it, but I knew it was real. I had been in the presence of this likeness before. Somehow, I had to remember when we last met . . . stone-faced Picasso and me.

<hr />

The night was soft, starlit, and filled with the songs of spring peepers and the aroma of black locust blooms. The morning was cool, damp, and filled with the sounds of the ocean colliding with the near-distant sand bars and the bleating of invasive mute swans as they flew and fed in the nearby salt pond. Picasso remained motionless, cross-armed, and sullen, and still looking unblinkingly out to sea as if he knew something about the universe and wasn't going to share it.

I've always wanted to be able to see through the eyes of Picasso and Van Gogh, so I walked across the lawn with my coffee in hand and sat beside him while looking outward and inward, trying to recall where we had met before. In time, I turned to him and said aloud, "You've got a nice spot, my friend." I half expected him to reply. It was a bit unsettling, so I left Pablo where I found him and met up with David to help load up the skiff and soon, we were headed off toward the launch site while listening to the Grateful Dead singing "Ship of Fools." The song was either prophetic or simply amusing. We had yet to find out.

There are few things in life that I enjoy as much as I do when I'm skidding across some salty flat, bay, or shoreline at first light. My mind drifts briefly to all those golden-edged mornings when I would sit on the bow of my father's boat, feeling the salt spray against my face, watching the flying fish fly and porpoises porpoise. And every now and then when he ran up onto a swell the bow rose up into the sky as if suspended and then fell with a crash into the sea, my dangling young legs would be soaked to the knees, and my smiling young face, dripping and wonderfully salty. This is the magical imaginary time travel that I experienced as we raced across Sag Harbor Bay toward Northwest Creek. All at once, I was a young man, sitting on the front of my father's old boat, and a much older man, sitting in the back of my friend David's brand-new skiff. These moments are timeless.

When we arrived at our first little backwater cove, not far from Sag Harbor, David cut and raised the engine. I grabbed an eight-weight with a sinking-tip line and a brown, shrimpy-looking fly at the end of the tippet. The water was motionless, the air was imitating the water, and David began poling us across the edges of a slight drop-off that was about twenty feet from the grass-covered marshland. Sea robins seemed to be everywhere on the muddy bottom of this cove, and although David said that they were tasty and would take a fly, these were not the fish of my dreams. I had come here, in part, to chase striped bass in the shallow backwater flats from the Peconic River to Montauk. And I had come here to battle bluefish in the slightly deeper waters of the bays, but like life and any fishing trip, you cast out and discover what's out there.

The water here was shallow, slightly stained, and seemed to have little current. The marshland looked healthy, and that pleased me as I cast casually and methodically toward "eleven o'clock" off the port bow, into the deeper water, counting down a few digits to allow the fly to sink into the feeding lane, and then stripping it in so as to make it appear as brown and shrimpy as a pinch of fur and feathers can seem. It was about then that I felt the first bite. We were being swarmed by no-see-ums. David stopped to put on his bug net, and I pulled up my buff, and we went on fishing. It's all part of the adventure.

No-see-ums or biting midges have over 5,000 species that range across every continent except the Arctic and Antarctic. The adults spend most of their lives feeding on flower nectar as sweetly as any butterfly. But when the adult females require protein and other nutrients to produce eggs in the act of reproduction, they ingest the blood of various animals before laying their eggs in moist soil near water. Mostly, their bite is simply annoying, but like mosquitoes, they can be vectors for disease-carrying pathogens. In nature, everything is feeding upon everything and the larvae of no-see-ums are eaten by microbic predators in the soil while the adults are eaten by dragonflies and damselflies. I love the irony of nature. We are feeding the creature that is feeding something else, and we help reproduce the source of our brackish bayside torment.

Anglers are optimists. If we're honest, we'd admit that we expect a fish at the end of every cast and are somewhere between surprised and dumbfounded when our expectations are foiled, again and again. But fortunately for us, fly-fishers are also quite frequently practicing "Imperfect Buddhas" and as such, we are doing our best to live in the moment, so that each cast is our first cast. That way, the imperfect part of us keeps expecting a fish while the Buddha in us is not attached to any expectations, and so we cast again. Every cast is our first cast, just like life. In the vast view of things, I am casting a circle, not a line, again, also . . . just like life.

We worked our way around the edge of the cove while the no-see-ums worked their way along the edges of our clothing. Not a single fish rose to the occasion and so we decided to move out into the harbor away from the bugs and hopefully toward the stripers. It felt good to feel the breeze again and breathe fresh ocean air that didn't smell like mud.

The skiff bounced along past Shelter Island and the Nature Conservancy's Mashomack Preserve, down the Peconic River, across Noyack Bay, and into the backwater coves of Little Peconic Bay. Here the breeze was moving and the shoreline was a mix of estate-like homes, docks, and marshland grasses. We drifted into a smallish cove and immediately saw the swirling, syncopated action of "bunker" as they were being chased and eaten by something. David returned to the poling platform to work his alchemy, and I began casting the eight-weight into the cove, again, half expecting a strike on the end of every cast. After half a dozen hopeful tries, a striper flashed up from the dark bottom, smacked the fly, and returned to the deep. Expectation became excitement and I worked that spot in the bay with all the repetition of Ravel's *Boléro*, to a now silent audience below. We moved on.

Just across the little cove we noticed the baitfish swirling again, and I realized that being a "bait fish" was as sorry a fate as wearing a red shirt on an away team in the original *Star Trek*. Sooner or later, you're dead meat. I guess in a way, everything and everyone becomes poop for something else. Billionaires and bunker fish all end up where they started billions of years ago, in the guts of a microbe. Again, nature is ironic in its apathy.

David moved the skiff closer to the commotion and poled me within striking range of whatever was causing the bunker such consternation. We were hoping for stripers but could not yet see the source of their terror. I cast toward the edges of the troubled waters and in an instant had a vicious strike, brief tussle, and then nothing. No fish. No fly. No tippet. It was a bluefish!

I racked the eight-weight and grabbed for a ten with a sixty-pound shock tippet already set up for blues. Adjusting to the new rod took a moment but in a brief time I was enjoying its extra punch and dropping the fly into the melee. It took no time at all to notice the circling and slashing images of bluefish, with their sickle-like tail fins, slicing the water. I almost felt sorry for the baitfish, but this was no time for sentimental emotions. This was a battle. A bluefish seized the fly, I strip set the hook, and the fight was on!

David knows more about angling than I will ever know, and I was grateful not only to be sharing this moment with him, but also to have his expertise giving me helpful encouragement as I fought this fish that I had already come to love. I have caught bluefish once before when I was with my friend Ted Williams off the coast of Cape Cod. But that was deeper water and open ocean, and the fish routinely sounded downward, bending the heavy rod, and straining my arms and shoulders so thoroughly that I would have to take a moment between catching and casting just so I could get the blood circulating again in my aching arms. But this was shallow water, and the fish fought accordingly as he twisted, pulled, and leaped, with his angry head shaking and his dark eye seeming to stare directly at me. We made eye contact, and that is the same as recognition. I'm not sure what the bluefish saw in me, but I saw a magnificent warrior in him, and I felt respect and joy and something almost like regret as I pulled left as he pulled right, and right as he pulled left. And in the end he was boat-side, and David reached down and seized his tail, and I relaxed a little too much and allowed the leader to slip from the corner of his toothy mouth, and in that instant he bit down, snipping the sixty-pound shock tippet as if it were the easiest thing in the world to do, and then he kicked his mighty tail fin and swam away. Silence is deafening in moments like that. It was as if all of time stopped, as my mind looped through that last image, like a scratched vinyl record.

I felt bad for him and proud of him all at the same time. I had visions of the *Old Man and The Sea*, and I loved him for the way he never gave up, but I wished he had not left with my hook in his lip. To that end, David ties his flies with barbless hooks that are designed to eventually rust and remove themselves . . . hopefully. I thought of that fish many times since then, and every time, I wished him well.

Don't get me wrong, I am a predator too. I have no problem with purposely killing a fish, deer, or radish and making it part of my sustenance. But I respect every living thing and the Earth itself. And I kill nothing without a reason. Perhaps someday I will evolve to the point where I fish with hookless flies, just to feel the initial tug . . . but I'm not there yet. I'm still a caveman who needs to know that I can hunt or gather my own food, if need be.

There were more fish in that cove and so we kept casting and drifting with both David and me hooking a few and landing fewer. It felt like catching lions while they were on the hunt. Hunting the hunters and trying to beat them at their own game. The only difference was I wasn't casting zebras, and the bluefish weren't charging the boat. Still, just like lions, whenever they flipped their tails, they meant business, and interesting things were bound to happen. In time, the bunker stopped swirling and the bluefish stopped slashing and there was nothing left on the water's surface but the inquisitive heads of diamondback terrapins and the occasional cry of an osprey. Again, we moved on.

Ever since I was a boy, I had always wanted to see a diamondback terrapin in the wild. I have looked for them along the mangroves of the Florida Suncoast and among the spartina marshes of the Texas Coastal Bend, thus far, to no avail. But now I found myself seeing them swimming and sunning by the dozen along the marshlands of Sag Harbor, Little Peconic, and Northwest Creek, and it gave me a feeling of hope because after all, this was New York, and if they can make it here, they can make it anywhere. Then and there I decided that I would seek to find more of them as I traveled the American Atlantic and Gulf Coastal waters connecting with gamefish and good friends.

The diamondback terrapin, *Malaclemys terrapin*, is native to the coastal, tidal marshes from Cape Cod to Florida and around the Gulf of Mexico to my home state of Texas. Seven subspecies are recognized, including Northern, Carolina, Mississippi, ornate, mangrove, East Florida, and Texas. These are beautiful creatures with ornate diamond patterns on their carapaces and artful zigzag patterns on the gray, tan, yellow, or even white skin. They have webbed feet for swimming and strong jaws for crushing the shells of the snails, clams, oysters, and crabs that make up the majority of their prey. And they even have adapted to find fresh drinking water by sipping the surface film after a heavy rain or opening their mouths during a rainstorm.

In the latter part of the nineteenth and early twentieth century diamondback terrapins were hunted nearly to extinction for the delicacy of turtle soup, and none of the populations have fully recovered from these decades of slaughter. Now over 70 percent of American coastal marshlands have been lost to human development and nesting sites are being lost to seawalls and other erosion controls. Thousands of terrapins drown each year in active and abandoned crab traps, and more are lost to everything from boat propellers, car tires, and predation from the exploding populations of invasive rats. With all this pressure and the impacts of climate change, these little turtles are up against it! And yet, here they are, swimming past me, probably laughing at the ridiculous primate swinging that stick in the humid air. And the mere fact that these creatures are still here is reason enough for me to feel a little hope for America's estuaries.

It's not that a world without diamondback terrapins is a world in collapse. But as I will say again and again . . . everything is connected to everything. The turtles, spartina grass, no-see-ums, menhaden, seagulls, striped bass, and me, are all joined at the ecological hip. As an angler, hunter, hiker, paddler, and human being, I need to understand this and act accordingly.

─◦~

After a spirited time of catching and releasing and more often losing bluefish after bluefish, David indicated it was time to move on to new waters and another chance to find the striped bass we were seeking. We skidded across the water past palatial homes and mega-yachts and the remnants of ancient estuaries. We took a few casts just beyond the "Buffet House"—Jimmy, not Warren—and then moved on across Noyack Bay, and into the expanse of water known as Little Peconic Bay. To the starboard I saw Shelter Island with the Nature Conservancy's Mashomack Preserve, and it was easy to see why David and so many others had come to love this place, its culture, and its beauty. In time David guided the boat into a cove that contained a few promising flats, surrounded by narrow marshlands, and guarded by a sandbar that was covered in shorebirds.

Massive great black-backed gulls that looked as if they could eat small children patrolled the muddy edges, while midsized herring gulls did the same in the skies above them. Osprey sailed overhead, periodically propelling themselves like javelins toward the water, eyes focused and talons at the ready. Tiny common, least, and roseate terns fluttered along the shallow mouths of creeks, their deeply forked tails and slow, shallow, rapid, wingbeats often being the only way to tell them apart from one another. Death from above and below . . . baitfish beware!

David cut the engine and began to pole the skiff along the shoreline of the cove as I cast repeatedly into the slightly deeper water just beyond. At times he would allow us to drift and we'd both be casting, me on the bow and David at the stern. It was wonderful fun in a flats-filled cove that looked perfect for stripers. If only the stripers knew this, we would have been bending our rods instead of just stripping our lines. We circled around and tried the flats one more time, because it just looked so perfect, but the result was the same. No stripers. No blues. No reason to try a third time, and so we sought new waters.

I was having a great time, but I could tell that David was less than thrilled that we'd seen and missed exactly one striped bass all day. We had already covered a lot of water hopping from cove to cove, poling the flats and drifting the edges, and although we did experience some luck on bluefish that should not have even been way back in these shallows, we had no luck finding the stripers that should have been there. I guess angling and living are both full of surprises. That's what makes them both adventures.

When I relive the simple lunch we had that day, drifting across the little cove, watching terns fluttering over grassy shallows and listening to red-winged blackbirds calling out from the breeze-bent reeds along the shoreline, I cannot think of any time in life that was more simply perfect. We sat there sipping cool water on a warm day and talking about life and love and living. We talked about our families and our failures that taught us things we will never forget. We talked about David's love for these waters and my newfound love for his homeland. And just when the conversation had meandered to its most philosophical level, I leaned forward and "poked the bear" by adapting a line from the movie, *Jurassic Park*. "Ah, you are planning to have striped bass on this striped bass tour someday . . . aren't you?" I laughed . . . not sure if my friend did. Then I reminded him that all was well; this southern boy loves the blues.

Long Island Sound is massive, extending across 1,320 square miles of shallow water habitat with an average depth of only 63 feet, and containing an estimated 18 trillion gallons of salt and brackish water. In other words, it has almost as much life-giving water as the United States has soul-sucking national debt. Almost ... but not quite. Pure water and perceived wealth are both transitory, finite, and conditional. Investment is not the same as spending. I wish we'd invest more in places like these estuaries and spend less on the concrete caves that surround them. I, for one, prefer bluefish to blue chips.

The three major gamefish of this region are bluefish, striped bass, and false albacore, all of which have been in decline and fluctuate between moderately stable and extremely overfished status. But it's not just overfishing that is getting them down, it is a barrage of barriers from the destruction of spawning habitat, the obstruction of spawning rivers with often outdated dams, and the massive reduction of prey fish like menhaden, sardines, herring, anchovy, and shad due to the activities of the commercial fishing industry that collects them by the millions each year and turns them into Omega-3 pills, farm animal feed, and fertilizer.

We've had a long history of this cavalier behavior toward "bait fish" that existed before the arrival of Europeans. In fact, the name "menhaden" is thought to be an anglicization of two Algonquin words that in essence mean "fertilizer." The words we choose change the way we respect or disrespect anything or anyone. We have used words like "savage" and "slave" to marginalize other humans and legitimize how poorly we treat them. Imagine if we designated an entire race of people as "fertilizer." Words matter.

Perhaps menhaden should be called "platinum fish," because they are truly valuable to everything that lives along the American coast from the Atlantic and Gulf to the Pacific, where several different species fill the same niche. They are a "double keystone species," meaning that they are "key" to the health of these water in two ways. As filter feeders they provide ecological services by eating phytoplankton and zooplankton, controlling algal blooms that reduce oxygen in the water. In addition, they are an important food source for gamefish, shorebirds, and seals that all fit together in the web that makes this place so special.

As an angler and outdoorsman, I need to understand these things and care enough to act upon that caring. Words do matter, and it is no accident that the vast majority of these fish are regulated by the U.S. Departments of Commerce and Agriculture. Commerce and conservation are not the same thing.

—❦—

I was watching some cormorants fishing in the large, shallow cove that David held in his back pocket of go-to places for bluefish. By this time in the day, we were holding out only a glimmer of hope of seeing any striped bass, and so we decided to go with the prevailing flow, switch to the ten-weight rods with sixty-pound shock tippets and focus soulfully on the blues. I had a brown-white-silverish minnow-looking thing that David had tied for me the night before, and he decided to spice things up a bit by tying on a big, splashy popper. We could see the boiling of bunker all across the surface and between watching the birds overhead and the bunker down below, we were able to locate what I'd describe as a mob of bluefish, circling around and crashing through the source of their early supper. We both cast in unison, and the game was on!

In shallow water bluefish appear to me like a pack of aquatic wolves. I almost felt sorry for anything they could get into or chop up with their toothy mouths. We watched them swimming toward us, their fins slicing the water, their teeth no doubt slicing into the bunker in an ancient ritual of eat and be eaten. Only humans seem to think they are the center of the universe, granted some divine place of prominence on Earth, when all we really are to nature is a collection of temporarily underused protein. Bunker and bankers all end up as poop for microbes and mushrooms. If we understand nature, we remain humble.

David tucked his rod under his arm and began stripping hand over hand as fast as he could, and I tried to do as well as I could, by wearing out my stripping arm and holding my rod in the other hand. We could see them coming, fighting over the fly and popper, smacking the water, and missing, twisting and turning in a battle to outcompete their schoolmates for the food that wasn't really food. My rod bent, I strip set the hook, and soon I had a nice-sized bluefish leaping and spinning and ultimately trying to keelhaul my line as I switched from starboard to port. David was getting hit after hit on the popper but no hookups, and as I brought a bluefish to the boat I wondered if he was going to switch back to a streamer, but he seemed to be determined to make the popper work and witness the thrill of a solid surface take. I admired his determination but was happy to keep casting the much lighter collection of feathers and fur.

As the action would die down in one area we'd look to the sky and surface to see where the bunker and bluefish were, then move the skiff in their path and either wait for the current to drift us toward them or drive them to us. We never had to wait long as these fish were aggressive and hungry. The water boiled with menhaden and seethed with their tormentors. And for now, David and I were at the top of that particular food chain, casting to the predators who were eating their prey, as the prey sought to escape them, so that they could in turn swim peacefully open-mouthed, consuming even smaller prey. Everything alive seeks to live forever. I doubt that cuttlefish ponder an afterlife, but I do wonder if zooplankton feel fear.

David snipped off the popper and tied on a streamer not unlike the one he had given me, and we cast simultaneously into the churning mass of bunker and bluefish, stripping the line as fast as we could, strip setting the hooks the instant they were seized, and in no time at all we had a double hookup! David got his in quickly, being the more skilled angler by a long shot, but I was having a blast working my fish left and right, watching him leap into the air and crash into the bay as if he expected to fly. Once I wore him down and brought him boat side, David tailed him and reached for the tiniest set of forceps I could imagine using on a bluefish. Upon contact, the fish bit, creating a sickening, metallic sound that was something like you might hear in your head when the dentist has hardware in your mouth and you bite down when you should have said, "Ahh." David looked up at me and smiled saying, "You can see why we have to be careful with these things." Being a bluesman myself, I'm hoping to keep all my fingers and made a mental note to get a bigger hook remover.

After catching a few and losing a few more, things began to slow down, and I took that moment to get the blood circulating in my arms again. It's funny how when you're in the heat of battle you feel no pain, but when you're sitting calmly on the boat, sipping some water, and scanning the horizon for more fish, it quickly comes back to you that your bad shoulder feels worse and your good arm doesn't feel so good. But everyone should embrace their scars and realize that our wounds give us texture and form. I consider my PTSD a tough gift that not everyone gets to carry. I learn from adversity and hardship. As we said in the Marines, I "Embrace the suck!" I guess that's why I've never had a bad day of fishing. I don't step into the water with any expectations except to be there. Life and fishing are neither good nor bad; they simply are as they are. Acceptance is freedom. Freedom is joy.

The Peconic Estuary is identified by the Nature Conservancy as "one of the last great places," and I agree. It provides habitat and nursery grounds, waters, and systems for many aquatic and terrestrial species of plants and animals. I was happy to see how healthy much of these salt marshes seemed, but also concerned to see the buildup of algae that is a sure sign of too many nutrients being washed into the water from storm drains, farmers' fields, and manicured lawns.

This is a stunningly beautiful place. It is home to striped bass, bluefish, flounder, and false albacore. Farther out it teems with seals, sharks, whales, and pelagic fishes of many kinds. These waters give life to an abundance of birdlife, reptiles, amphibians, and the all-important insects upon which almost everything else relies. And it is all too easy to miss or dismiss these pieces in the puzzle, until it's too late and the entire picture is gone. I don't want to live in that world, and chances are, none of us can.

As we started back across the Little Peconic, past Shelter Island and onward toward the docks, the road home, a warm shower, and a hot dinner . . . I did as I always do and tried to burn this beautiful place into my mind as if saying goodbye to a true love before going off to war. I watched as an oystercatcher waded in the shallows, plying his trade. His striking black and brown back over his soft, white underbelly were offset by his almost ridiculously long, orange bill that seemed too big for such a little bird. As it turns out, it's exactly right for shucking oysters. Knowing that it is common for the male oystercatcher to have two females at a time, I wondered if there is anything to that old fishwives' tale. I'm not sure, but as I watched two pretty young females toddling up behind him I couldn't help but think, it's worth investigating further.

I'm not going to forget that little black-and-white bird. Even from the boat I could tell that we were making eye contact, and in the eyes there is life. His life is not unlike mine. He was born, struggled to reach maturity, will hopefully procreate, and will ultimately return to the Earth . . . just like me. And for me, his life has value. Something beautiful animates those feathers, and inside that chest beats a small but significant four-chambered heart. Do shorebirds fall in love?

As a naturalist who is also an angler, these questions call to me. I don't want to miss the trees while walking through the forest, and I don't want to miss the seabirds while bouncing across the sea. It's too easy to focus on fishing and forget what really makes it special. It's the sound of blackbirds among the wind-bent reeds. It's the sight of marsh grass from dune to shoreline. It's the smell of salt water and marsh muck and chicken salad sandwiches made with fresh-baked bread. It's the taste of white wine upon our return as we sit around the back porch table recalling the day's adventure, and then I ask, "What's for dinner, y'all?" David pours me a little more wine, smiles and says, "Do you like oysters?" I smile back. "Yes," I say. "It just so happens, that I do."

CHAPTER THREE

False Albacore—Three Days in Montauk

Montauk, Long Island, New York

The Sea . . . Will be the Sea
Whatever the drop's philosophy.

~ ATTAR OF NISHAPUR

THE FIRST DAY

Montauk sits on the end of Long Island like a finger pointing across the sea. It's the kind of quaint, seaside place where I'd love to live out my retirement, fishing and hanging out in the many little cafés and coffee shops—if only I were a multimillionaire. But I'm not, so I won't. Instead, I will visit my good friend David Blinken, who lives part of his life in a small town in New Jersey and the other in a cottage built within sight of the ocean behind his mom's beautiful home in the Hamptons.

If I were to paint a picture of the idyllic backyard, something worthy of Claude Monet or Cézanne, I'd paint David's mother's house as it looked when I first saw it, dripping in purple wisteria and surrounded by green trees, multicolored gardens, and the deep blue sea. And even if

I wasn't a very good painter it would end up on some art museum wall with a security guard standing solemnly by, just to ensure that no one tried to touch the paint or jump into the painting. It's that dreamlike. In the morning the songbirds serenade you in a multitude of dialects. Mute swans drift peacefully by on Georgica Pond and skeins of Canada geese career across the pond and over the treetops, honking, as if they are going somewhere, but they're not. These geese knew a good thing when they found it; they're not migrating anywhere.

My first morning in Montauk began with a quick stop at Goldberg's Deli, where locals stand patiently in line for the community experience of pastrami, corned beef, and smoked whitefish that's "to die for." This Texas boy wanted a true taste of New York for lunch so it was pastrami on rye, no cheese, just out of respect. David once told me, "No self-respecting Jew puts cheese on pastrami." I'm not Jewish but at least for my first day, I wanted to dive into the local culture. It didn't last. By the second day I was getting a corned beef Reuben—the full dripping in delicious dressing, cheese, and sauerkraut-covered catastrophe. What can I say? I'm a weak-willed sinner, addicted to cheese.

Montauk Harbor is as quaint as Montauk, save for the slightly threatening and cultlike nature of some of the local sailors who flew banners from their boats declaring their allegiance and who looked askew at anyone daring to wear a mask during a global pandemic. One rust bucket of a trawler boat was named after the self-declared leader of the movement, and I watched as it spewed black smoke from its groaning engines on its way out to drag the sea floor until it was devoid of any living thing. It seemed tragically ironic. It also felt out of place in such a beautiful, peaceful, land and seascape. It was like a wart on the face of a fashion model. Why would anyone be proud of willful ignorance, selfishness, and ecological profiteering? We're all in this together. The ship sails or sinks with all hands on deck.

Today we'd be fishing with my newest friend, Luyen Chou. He met us at David's boat, and in no time I knew that this was going to be a wonderful and meaningful day no matter what the fishing was like. Lu has an easy smile, brilliant mind, and kind heart. If I never caught a fish during my three days at Montauk, the trip was worth it for the company of David and Luyen and the conversations we were to share. Fishing is about so much more than catching fish—although catching fish almost always helps.

Whenever I find myself out at sea, I feel at home and at peace. There are no boundaries out here, only possibilities. I love the feel of the saltwater spray in my face, and the way the bow rises and falls with the moods of the ocean. I love the sounds of seagulls and terns as they ply their fish-catching trade with precision and grace. And I love the way the landscapes look from the viewpoint of the ocean's rolling surface. It's like discovering a new world that you somehow already know. Yes, whenever I find myself out at sea, I feel at home and at peace, and I think of my dad and how much he felt that way too.

We rounded the point and entered an area known as Colloden that is a good first stop when looking for albies. The day prior David had managed to catch a black sea bass on a fly in this little cove, and he told me of how they are becoming more prevalent with the rising sea temperature. Climate change is not only real, but also a real problem that is impacting fisheries, rookeries, and the future of every living thing from sea to shining sea. And as nice as it might seem that tasty fish like black sea bass and cobia are moving north, important prey fish such as sand lance are vanishing in waters that once held them in abundance. It's a domino effect, and now the last colonies of nesting Atlantic puffins off the coast of Maine are failing as the parents find only the larger butter-fish for their young, instead of their traditional bite-size prey. Hatchling puffins are starving to death among piles of oversized butterfish that the parents can eat, but the smaller chicks cannot swallow. Without prey species like sand lance, menhaden, anchovies, and herring, everything else collapses, from striped bass to bluefish and from pelicans to puf-fins. Eventually, this will include us, as so it should. Nature ultimately demands accountability.

We had set out from Montauk Harbor a little later than we would have wished. Out of concern about the strength and direction of the morning winds, we had chosen to delay leaving port by a few hours. But once we arrived at Colloden we found that a lot of boats had beat us to it, and after a quick look and a couple of blind casts, we didn't stay long.

There were a few dispersed slashes on the water from the occasional "snapper" bluefish, but no sign of false albacore anywhere. We moved on.

The air was crisp and clear, and the sun was shining across the water at such an angle as to create that diamond-like, broken glass sparkle that can be both mesmerizing and blinding. Sometimes, it reminded me of the light that comes through a bubble in the sunlight as it floats away from a child's plastic wand. There was a diaphanous blue roundness to the light. It glowed in a manner that suggested a perfect dream, and that is how it felt to me. Perfectly dreamlike. It was the kind of moment from which one doesn't wish to wake anytime soon.

I collect moments not things. As we motored across Napeague Bay toward Gardiners Island, I couldn't help but feel fortunate to be alive in that place and time. We each pulled our hoods up over our caps so that they would not blow off as we seemingly flew across the bay. The sound of David's powerful boat engines did nothing to drown out the peacefulness of the day, and I felt childlike as we skidded across the salted waters from one cove to another. Life was good, as it always is, no matter the circumstances.

When we arrived at Gardiners Island we found a fair amount of boats had already done so, and the activity was only slightly better than at Colloden. There were fish, but they were mostly small bluefish smashing into anchovies at the surface. Here and there we saw a flash of green below the shades of slashing blue, and so we tried a few casts into the mix hoping to dredge up an albie and avoid the razor-toothed bluefish. I avoided everything, but in a few minutes both David and Luyen connected with and lost two smallish blues. Earlier David had joked, "Anyone who loses a fly to a bluefish owes me five bucks!" It didn't take long for David to be ten dollars in the hole to himself. I suspect he forgave that debt.

The good news was that the anchovies that bring the false albacore in were everywhere. The less good news was, the albies didn't seem to know it yet, at least not in any numbers. We kept seeing the small bluefish, and for a while I wondered if we should switch out our leaders and add some forty-pound shock tippet so we could at least bring the bluefish in without losing the flies, but our captain was determined that we keep our eyes on the prize, and I knew he was right.

So, we continued to run-and-gun from one small pocket of splashing surface water to another, and while the fishing was fine, the catching was not. There were over a dozen of us out there seeking the same quarry along the island's shoreline, but in a metaphorical way, we were all in the same boat. Plenty of hopeful anglers searching for seemingly absent false albacore. That's when David devised a new plan and he revved the engines, setting us off toward a long, choppy rip where the albies sometime hunt anchovies, herring, or bunker that get bundled up in the currents.

We didn't see any albies hitting the surface in the rip, but we took a few blind casts as the boat bounced and swayed with the sea. I'd get a few good casts and retrieves in, and then end up stepping on my line as I maneuvered to stay upright in the chop. It didn't matter because we weren't finding any fish, only wearing out our casting arms for no return on investment. And that's when David noticed some albies smashing anchovies on the surface just beyond the rip, and it was run-and-gun time again.

By the time we arrived, the albies were back down, so the three of us stood on the deck poised for action at the slightest sign of surface activity. There were anchovies in the sea all around us, and the conditions seemed right with the moving water of the tide. But finding our quarry was proving difficult as they sparsely appeared and disappeared here and there— first appearing everywhere and then nowhere. We persisted but to no avail. Albies would pop up "over there," but once we got over there they were gone again. Then they'd pop up back where we were, but once we got there, they were nowhere to be found. Cheeky silver-green bastards!

Along the shores of Gardiners Island seemed to be our best bet, so David took us back to where all the other boats had been jockeying for position like seagulls fighting over french fries in a dumpster that was rolling downhill. "Snapper blues" were popping up and slashing the anchovies into oily slicks upon the water's surface, but false albacore appeared infrequently at best and even when they did, they weren't picking up what we were laying down. Still, they did rise now and again and there were fewer competing boats and anglers along the shoreline than there were earlier in the day. We did get some shots at boiling, leaping, feeding albies, but no takers. And then the tide went slack and the activity followed, and so we collectively decided that lunch time seemed to be in order. Pastrami on rye, sea salted chips, raspberry-flavored soda water, and good conversation on the ocean, beats almost anything we could be doing on land. Almost anything.

One of the best things about fly-fishing with good friends is that you get to share in each other's successes and cheer each other on. Another good thing is that you can share in each other's failures and cheer each other up. But in times like this when you are just drifting along waiting for the tide to turn metaphorically and in actuality—it is a gift to just sit together on the gunnel of a boat chatting about life, love, and how everything relates to fly fishing. And everything does.

A certain amount of good-natured ribbing is also a part of the joy of fishing with friends. David, who is Jewish but not kosher, began giving Luyen a bad time about his pastrami Reuben sandwich, saying once again, "It's just not done. No self-respecting Jew would put cheese on pastrami." Luyen, who is of Chinese descent but married to a wonderful Jewish woman, took the ribbing in stride, shaking his head and smiling. He and David both knew that he had nothing to hang his head about. And, as far as I can tell, he is doing his part to carry on the traditions of his wife's family faith. After all, Luyen Chou's boat is named *Chousen One*.

THE SECOND DAY

David's wife Cathy is a true force of nature. She is also my dear friend. Cathy is highly intelligent, full of life, and kind of heart. They are both a blast to be with, and I have to say that it can be quite amusing to watch these two strong-willed people as they playfully butt heads on everything from how to make the next cast to how to cook the best green beans. They remind me of two tiger kittens playing rough. It seems to keep them youthful and filled with light and energy—the push and pull of a love that includes great friendship and familiarity. I just love these two crazy kids, and I was so happy to hear that Cathy was joining us on our second day of albie fishing.

The first day with Luyen concluded with no fish being caught, good friendship being shared, and a nice dinner under the stars at Montauk's

"Clam Bar." The Clam Bar is an iconic little red and white roadside hut that serves awesome local seafood. The fish, shellfish, and rosé wine were wonderful and the mosquitoes were persistent, but that's all part of the adventure. I'm betting that my blood tasted salty.

In the morning we began the day back at Goldberg's for some delicious breakfast sandwiches and to pick up other sandwiches for our lunch. I bought a pastrami Reuben in honor of my friend Luyen, and just to give David a little razzing. The cheese, sauerkraut, and Russian dressing were all wonderful with pastrami. As it turns out, just like Lu, I'm not kosher either.

There's something about great morning coffee that is almost orgasmic for me. It gives me pleasure and comfort, like morning sunlight filtered through white cotton curtains. I'm in love with it and don't want to live without it. If this is a sin, then I am a sinner. I confess. And I love breakfast sandwiches where the egg and cheese are just oozing from whatever type of bread contains them; in this case, a bagel, of course. After all, it was from Goldberg's.

I love being outdoors in nature but I must admit that there are some human comforts that I love to take with me. I am not ashamed to say, I am not a "hardcore" angler. I have nothing to prove. For me, all of the experience is as important as any one part of the experience. It's not just about what's at the end of that persistent tug; sometimes it's also about what's inside that ice-cold mug. The company we keep matters too. The first day with David and Lu and this day with David and Cathy both had their charms. Either day, fish or no fish, I felt like a fortunate man.

Once we bounced out of Montauk Harbor our first stop was Colloden. It was sporting fewer sports and bobbing boats than the day before. Still, the action was slow to start, and this time not even the bluefish were popping. After a while David spotted some albies smashing anchovies on the surface and he positioned us between them and another boat so that Cathy could cast to them from the bow and I could backcast to them from the stern. We both had anchovy-like flies tied to our tippets and we both proceeded to cast toward the boils as they came. But they didn't last long, and after a bit of watchful waiting David decided to move us farther along the coast. That's when everything finally came together!

Albies began to strike the surface, attacking the hapless anchovies from every angle. Fish were boiling on both sides of the boat as Cathy and I began casting in opposite directions with equal chances of success. But chance is often fickle so while Cathy got a tug but no hookup, I got a tug and a solid connection to the first false albacore of my life! That fish had me into my backing in about ten to twenty seconds with my ten-weight rod tip bent over like a question mark—which it was. There was no way of knowing if I'd get this fish to the boat, but we battled with each other like Papa Hemingway's Santiago and the great fish. Had this been a handline, I would have lost for sure. But after several fast runs into the backing and several slow retrieves of both my line and my angler's dignity I was finally able to maneuver the fish close enough to the boat for David to seize him and place him ceremoniously into my aching, waiting arms. This was a magnificent fish on so many levels.

False albacore are incredible swimming and feeding biological machines. They are sleek, fast, and powerful swimmers. Lacking a swim bladder, albies are in constant motion. These are physically beautiful fish with bright silver under bodies, greenish-blue upper bodies, and a unique black, wavy pattern along their backs. Like other schooling predatory fish, false albacore will drive their prey species to the ocean's surface or against the shore in order to concentrate the food source into targetable bundles.

Whereas bluefish tend to chop and slash the prey into bits, more often than not, the albies seem to bite and swallow them whole. When they are actively feeding, a patch of the ocean's surface can turn into a froth of churning predators and prey, often leaping completely out of the water in the process. Another telltale sign of feeding albies is the presence of gulls and terns diving frantically into the sea in hope of picking up a stray wounded anchovy, herring, or menhaden. As always, one of the best things about fishing is that you have to learn to understand the fish and its relationship to the entire habitat, and false albacore are no exception.

I'm not one for grip-and-grin photos, but David took a quick one just before I released the fish, almost as quickly. False albacore are susceptible to shock if kept out of the water too long or improperly handled, and survivability will be greatly diminished in these instances. David taught me the proper way to release an albie—face-first, toward the water, from about gunnel height, and in one quick plunging drop so that its open mouth receives a quick gulp of life-giving, oxygen-filled water.

As an angler, I do everything I can to reduce the stress upon any fish I catch, and I release it in as healthy a condition as possible. With almost eight billion humans on Earth and an ever-growing population of anglers, we need to give these fish every break we can. And sometimes, we need to know when to refrain from fishing for them at all. If the only reason I was on the sea was to haul in as many fish as possible in the shortest amount of time, I might buy an old rust bucket of a trawler and drag my expansive half-rotten net across the ocean's bottom, destroying everything in my path for a quick profit. I'm not that guy. I just couldn't live with that—actually, eventually, none of us can.

It's a big ocean but we need to realize and remember that it still has a top and a bottom and only so much in between. If it were empty of life, would we still love the sea? If we really love the sea, how can we continue to mindlessly empty it of each element of life? From plankton to Pacific salmon, the impacts of Homo sapiens are many and most often harmful. Just food for thought—and you can put cheese on it if you like.

—◦—

The day prior with David and Luyen, the weather was bright and beautiful, but rather hot. This second day with David and Cathy, the weather was cooler and breezy but just as bright and beautiful. We could not have asked for anything more, other than the fact that the albie fishing was still proving to be tough.

We crossed back over to Gardiners Island, where this time there were slightly more fish and fewer anglers. Before long we were running and gunning from one splashy, frothy, leaping mass of feeding fish to another. Cathy got another tug but lost the fish in a few seconds. Once again, fortune went to the foolish and I found myself connected to my second albie. It gave me a blistering run into the backing faster than I could do anything other than remove my knuckles from the path of the spinning blur of my reel handle. When an albie runs, the first order of business is to move your fingers out of harm's way or prepare to be bloodied in battle.

I landed my second fish as quickly as I could and released it as efficiently as possible, quickly determining that I wanted to catch another. Fishing for false albacore is potentially addictive, and I'm not sure anyone is going to conduct an intervention once you fall victim to its mystical charms.

The hunt was back on and so we continued our frantic search for feeding fish and willing takes. The tide was still moving but soon would turn and momentarily stall, and we knew that the fishing would stall too. All three of us were spotting fish crashing on the surface. Sometimes they were the bluefish we were trying to avoid and other times it was the albies we were trying to catch. David decided not to fish today and instead generously used all of his considerable abilities to give Cathy and me as many good shots as possible at these torpedo-like targets.

At one point David noticed that the seagulls were standing on the beach in a phalanx along the water's edge. They were jockeying for position in the shallow surf—obviously attracted to that spot for some practical reason. (Seagulls rarely stare out to sea for philosophical reasons.) He moved the boat closer to shore and we noticed that something was bunching up the anchovies along the shore. He said, "Steve, send a cast toward shore. Maybe there's a few striped bass in there." I made a series of casts toward shore, stripping in the fly with as much speed as I could manage. After several attempts I noticed the slightest tug on my line and set the hook with more vigor than necessary. To my amazement I had caught the smallest bluefish that I've ever seen. Still, its toothy mouth was something to be handled with care. I set the tough little guy free, hoping to see him again in a year or two.

That tiny bluefish was the last catch of the day. When we got back to the docks we checked in with the local marine biologist who was taking down angler catch information for NOAA. We told him of our deuce of albies and asked how the other boats had fared. "Everyone was skunked except you and one other boat!" he said. The day was beautiful, the fishing was challenging, yet the catching was a shadow of time past. There's so much more to this story, but the conclusion is not yet forgone. We still have a little time remaining—to edit. As a writer I know that all stories of lasting consequence are meaningfully edited into greatness, not mindlessly and thoughtlessly written. Let's get out our red pencils, together.

THE THIRD DAY

There are people of significance who come into everyone's life if we're lucky. People who for no apparent reason other than your own good fortune, see something of value in you, and tell you so. These are the people who give us that push, just when we need it. Ted Williams is such a person in my life. He is perhaps best known for his decades of insightful and often brutally honest conservation journalism in publications such as *Audubon*, *Gray's Sporting Journal*, *Fly Rod & Reel*, and *American Angler*. But I also know Ted as a friend and as one of the toughest and most determined anglers I have ever known. If the fish are biting, Ted will not stop until the fish get tired. He is passionately relentless. It was so nice to see him again as he motored up to the docks at Montauk Harbor to meet us for a day on the water chasing albies. I love this guy.

I became friends with David Blinken because Ted chose to bring us together. And I have to say that this was yet another great kindness he showed me, as David has become one of my dearest friends, and someone who has added immensely to my life. I am forever grateful. And David introduced me to his wife Cathy, and his friend Luyen, and now we are all wonderful friends together.

Here in the final decades or days of my life's journey, it has been a shared love of nature that has brought me together with the best people I have ever known. I'd regret that it took me so long, but regret is a waste of time and something tells me that these autumn and early winter days of my life will be some of the best days of my life. It's just a feeling, but I feel it is coming true and my advice to you my dear reader is, don't wait. Stop putting authentic living off until some imaginary "someday." Follow your bliss and find your tribe. Accept nothing less.

In three days at Montauk, I was fortunate enough to fish with David and three other friends, Luyen, Cathy, and now Ted. The ocean had a bit of extra chop as we powered out of the harbor and rounded the point toward our obvious first stop at Colloden. This is a pretty little cove with an empty wooden frame of what once was a gill net operation at one end and a rocky point at the other. I cringe whenever I see gill nets set up anywhere. I was relieved to see that the net had been removed. They are weblike indiscriminate killers of everything that haplessly swims into their path, targeted fish or not. "Bycatch" is another way of saying apathy. Nothing is as deadly to nature or humanity than apathy.

David was planning to fish later in the day but for now he was focused on getting me and Ted into some albies. There were a few small spurts of action at Colloden, but like the other days we had visited it was sporadic and short lived. David maneuvered us within range of a few schools of feeding fish and Ted got a tug, brief hook-up and then a cut leader, most likely from a small and sharp-toothed bluefish. I got some casting practice in, but nothing more.

Back across the bay we bounced toward another shot at Gardiners Island. As we crossed I looked across the boat's center console and toward my two friends. David was at the wheel with Ted opposite me and beside him, each of us holding on as the boat skidded across the water at a breakneck speed. It occurred to me that both David and I are sixty years of age and Ted is in his seventies, but in that moment, all I saw were three kids having fun. The salt spray in our faces, the cool bracing sea air and the expanding wake we left behind us all conspired to make us each forget that we weren't six or seven years old, anymore. Or were we?

Our arrival at Gardiners Island felt hopeful. There were far fewer competing boats present and flocks of seagulls and common terns were smacking into the sea wherever a splashy surface gave away the plight of being an anchovy. David slid the boat in beside the feeding albies and Ted and I began firing off casts toward the melee as quickly as we could. Ted was on the bow and I was at the stern with David watching impatiently at the wheel. After Ted and I took half a dozen casts at the albies David grabbed a rod and dropped a cast between where our two casts had landed. Of course, he immediately connected with a big albie on his first cast and we cheered him on as he fought it eventually to the gunnel and onto the boat. The skunk was off us now since at least one of us had caught a fish!

I was relieved and happy for my friend, even if he was giving Ted and me quite a ribbing for a while. "I got that on my first cast!" he'd say, again and again as he gave us both a sly sideways smile. "That's how it's done guys . . . just like that." I'm not sure if Ted was rolling his eyes as we laughed and gave David as much comic grief as he was giving us. All I do know is that we were having too much fun—if that's possible.

Our hopes had risen with David's nice catch, and now we were back in the rhythm of running and gunning from one patch of frothy sea water to another. It's so much fun watching Ted and David kidding each other. At one point David asked, "Ted is that a wind knot in your leader?" Without missing a beat Ted said, "No, that only happens when you cast one of my rods." We all laughed. Apparently, there is something about successfully landing and releasing a false albacore that can turn any group of "golden guys" into a couple of giddy kids. I like that. Einstein was right; time is relative and entropy matters little when the fish are biting.

As we approached the next promising patch of salty water, a pair of white-winged scoters flew quickly away from us with rapid wingbeats, holding just barely over the surface of the sea. It seemed the wrong time of the year for them to be there, but there they were, nonetheless. The fairly large black-and-white ducks tend to winter in this area and breed in the high Arctic. But in the last number of years, it seems that everything is off its traditional schedule and out of its traditional range. The changes that are coming to our oceans might be adapted to by flora and fauna over the span of millennia, but when centuries become decades and decades become mere seasons, nothing in nature is prepared to adapt that quickly. While it's true that birds are mobile and can fly north with the changing climate, how far can these birds go when their nesting grounds are already at the seemingly barren ends of the Earth?

It was a perfectly beautiful day, but saying that the fishing had been slow is an understatement. David's catch gave us hope, but a lot of time had passed since that morning moment of triumph. Since then, we had moved across one edge of Gardiners Island across the rip and stopped to have lunch on a nice little cove where a large herring gull paddled around us hoping for handouts. I had corned beef that day, and I can tell you that herring gulls seem to like it, with or without cheese.

Ted sees eating lunch as a waste of valuable fishing time, but he was patient with us since the albies were proving to be few and far between. In fact, we had run into several boats with anglers from Rhode Island and Connecticut who had traveled all the way to Montauk in hopes of finding the false albacore that had failed to arrive in their home waters. And all of us were noticing something else of concern—where were the massive schools of striped bass that should have been there with the albies? It was the same story almost everywhere. We need to think about that.

⁓

If you've never seen the movie *Muppet Treasure Island*, you should. Tim Curry is brilliant as Long John Silver, Miss Piggy is bawdy as Benjamina Gunn, and the song-and-dance numbers are a lot of fun, especially when you watch it with your kid. (It's a shame we don't regularly break into song and dance in real life. The world might be a better place.) I was reminded of a particular scene in the movie where the pirate ship is stranded out at sea because there was no wind in the air to fill its sails. The boat just sat there in the heat under a relentlessly blue sky with not even a seagull to keep them company. That's how we felt as the tide turned and the movement of the water seemed to stall, turning the surrounding sea into a massive pond of silent uncertainty.

Once the tide began to move again we continued our dogged hunt for fish. The albies were few, the striped bass were once again remarkably absent. David even began to acquiesce to the idea that maybe we should consider changing leaders and trying to find a few smallish bluefish for tonight's dinner. But we couldn't even find the bluefish. David remained determined for a long time, and we kept casting to "likely spots" for bass and blues while waiting for any signs of albies. Eventually we found some activity in a cove that was filled to the brim with a mixture of bunker and anchovies, and Ted got a tug while I got in more casting practice. That's fishing.

Still, I couldn't help but hear the voice of my Alaskan fisheries biologist friend, Mark Hieronymus, when he said, "It's always your fault if you don't catch fish. Every cast is a question, asking the fish, what conditions do you need in order for it to choose to take the fly?" In a way, I think Mark's comment can be taken a bit further. What are the striped bass, bluefish, and false albacore trying to tell us when they don't show up at all? What do menhaden, anchovies, sardines, and squid teach us, when they vanish from a place where we know they "should be," this time of year?

I knew that things had gotten slow when I looked over at the most determined angler I've ever known and found him asleep in the bow of the boat. Prior to that while we were all watching the surface of the sea and conducting a 360-degree lookout for any movement of fish or fowl, I heard Ted say four little words I have never heard from him before. He said, "I think we're fucked." And we were, as far as catching any more fish was concerned. But for a day we three old friends had become three kids just having fun in the water—and that's magic enough for any day. And it was a good day as every day on the sea is when we're casting for connections and catching memories.

As we skidded across the sea with the salt spray in our faces, we laughed together at the vagaries of fishing and life. We were all feeling fortunate just to be alive. And besides, we hadn't been skunked! It had been another challenging day of fishing in a series of challenging days, but I had caught two albies the day prior and David landed another nice fish today, so while the fishing was tough we remained tough throughout the fishing. Life unfolds as it will, no matter what we plan. I do my best to roll with the tides and the times. Still, I feel good about how hard we worked and that each of those three fish in three days was hard earned and well appreciated. Did I already tell you that David caught that fish on his first cast? Well, he did. And if you don't believe me, just ask him.

CHAPTER FOUR

Striped Bass

Return to the Estuaries of Eastern Long Island, New York

What if revering and protecting nature became the unifying element in our splintered time, the shared center of our Venn Diagrams, no matter one's spiritual orientation?

~ MEGAN MAYHUM BERGMAN

I'M NOT AN URBAN MAN. CONCRETE CANYONS AND ASPHALT JUNGLES hold no amount of charm for me and yet during my many decades of traveling across America and the world, I have come to know quite a few cities. I've walked the streets of Rome, London, Munich, and Edinburgh. I've explored Abidjan, Nairobi, Windhoek, and Cape Town. I gasped for the thin air of Cuzco and slept under the stars on a rooftop in Arequipa. And in my own country, I've traveled from Miami to San Diego, and from the "City of Angels" to the "City of Brotherly Love." But even after six decades of meandering I had never been to New York City until the day I arrived to go fishing with my buddy David Blinken. I came to the Big Apple because I was searching for one of my favorite fish in the world—striped bass. I also came to spend time with my friend on the waters of Eastern Long Island—a place I've come to love.

The pandemic has changed everything from the way we travel to the way we treat each other. I wish I could say that either travel or courtesy has changed for the better . . . but it hasn't. In a way, the pandemic brought to light the worst and best of American society. The worst came in the form of selfishness, disrespect, and fear, while the best rose up in the selflessness, respectfulness, and courage of healthcare workers, teachers, and grocery store cashiers. I kept hoping we'd come together with good judgment rather than come apart judgmentally. We're not done yet, and Nature is not done with us. There is still hope that more and more of us will realize that from climate change to pandemic—we are all in this together. In the end, it will be either most of us or none of us. Nature will ultimately call the shots. Nature doesn't need us; we need Nature.

As for travel, it has become more difficult, with fewer options and at higher cost. What used to be an easy and reasonably priced flight between San Antonio and Islip, Long Island, has become a high-priced fiasco that resembles one of those television shows where the contestants are trying to get from the starting line to the finish without being crushed by a giant ball or whacked by a huge foam hammer. After much effort I managed to secure a one-way flight from San Antonio to Newark, New Jersey, and another one-way flight from New York to San Antonio. On the upside I had nice and respectful seatmates on all the flights, and my dear friend David was there to greet me. It was so nice to see him again. David is one of my favorite people.

While driving from New Jersey to New York we got to talking and talking and talking and this led to David making a wrong turn that turned out to be the right turn because now we were driving all the way through most of Manhattan which is something I've always wanted to do. Until now, my visions of New York City came from movies that either made it seem glitzy or gritty. As we traveled I began to see that both were true.

As we drove though Chinatown and the edges of Little Italy I saw some of the grit and texture—crowded streets with people walking, standing, and sitting in almost every available space. Graffiti-laden walls next to a McDonald's where the sign was in both English and Chinese. Delicate paper lanterns suspended above a street lined with restaurants and tea shops. Inviting outdoor cafés just around the corner from dumpster-filled alleyways. Texture is the sand in the paint—the thing that makes the painting come alive.

And then while crossing the city on an elevated freeway my gaze was drawn to a half-dozen well-dressed women standing on an immaculate balcony while drinking white wine and chatting. A table was set with the remnants of an elegant lunch. To their right was a view of the skyline with its geometric artistry and to their left was a train track, highway, and the tiniest sliver of "greenspace" in between with a few stunted foreign trees. I could almost hear Michael Bublé music playing in the distance. Their balcony seemed like an island of tranquility in a sea of chaos.

As we wound and wove in between high-rises and jumbled bits of cityscape, I found myself searching for water. I was trying to get a glimpse of the East River or the Hudson, and I was thinking of the urban anglers that I'd read about in David DiBenedetto's book titled, *On the Run: An Angler's Journey Down the Striper Coast*. In one chapter he chronicles his time fishing for striped bass all around Manhattan, and how he met three men fishing in the rain on the East River with traffic zooming by and the noise of the city filling their ears. It was a far-removed image from the tranquil and solitary rivers of my Texas hills, but I was intrigued by that image and kept my eyes wide as I searched for kindred spirits among the tangle of concrete and steel.

And then just as quickly as we had been surrounded by all the bustle and buildings, we came out the other side and onto the Long Island Expressway where cold grays gave way to warm greens. By the time we reached David's mother's home on Georgica salt pond, the world had transformed. I was breathing again. We got settled into our rooms, then met back up on the porch overlooking the salt pond and the ocean, the perfumed fragrance of wisteria in the breeze. We poured two glasses of refreshingly crisp white wine . . . and smiled. Life was good!

If not for the kindness and support of my friend Ted Williams, you'd most likely never be reading these words. It was years ago that I shared with Ted that I had written a book but had done nothing with it other than push "save" on my laptop. He offered to read it and afterward said, "It's good. Send it to Lyons Press." So I did.

That book was *Casting Forward: Fishing Tales from the Texas Hill Country*. Writing *Casting Forward* saved my life and allowed me to find feelings of hope. Having my words published changed my life and allowed me to share my feelings of hope. But that is not the only reason I have to be grateful to Ted Williams; in fact, the list is long. There was the time we shared fishing together off the coast of Cape Cod. We caught striped bass and bluefish until my arms and back ached. And then all the wonderful conversations we shared while sipping G&Ts on the back porch. And one of the greatest gifts Ted gave me was when he introduced me to David Blinken and in doing so, sowed the beginnings of a meaningful friendship. I am forever grateful for all of this but most of all for the friendship of Ted and his wife Donna, David and his wife Cathy, and for the many wonderful times we've shared. These are the gifts I have unwrapped in my later years of life. True friends and meaningful memories. The fish and the fishing are extra.

And it was with that sense of true friendship that we began our morning, towing David's skiff out to the dock while listening to the third of a trilogy of David's music genres. On my first trip it was all Grateful Dead and bluefish. Then came The Beatles and false albacore, and now it was jazz and the hope of connecting to striped bass. Of the three, I think I liked the jazz best. I'm a bit of a Parrothead but not really a Deadhead, and David's going to hate this but, I never really got into the Beatles. I know . . . blasphemy. Forgive me "Fathers of Rock," for I have sinned. On the last trip my penance was paid as I listened to various renditions of Rocky Raccoon which I could not get out of my head for a week. Damn . . . it's back in my head again. I'll try to think of jazz.

It felt good to be back on the waters of Eastern Long Island. For all the traveling and fishing I've done from Alaska to California to Florida to Cape Cod, Eastern Long Island is one of my favorite places. I want to see it get better, and it's possible. All it takes is a commitment to prove that we can coexist as part of nature so that diamondback terrapins and diamond-bedazzled troubadours can live and let live. Clean water and green trees make life better for everyone.

Our first stop was the mouth of a brackish creek that I call "Turtle Cove" because it is where I saw my first wild native diamondback terrapins, something I've wanted to see for a lifetime. It was a big deal because these once common yet unique turtles have become increasingly scarce, but here, not far from New York City, they are thriving. I also gave it that name because it is a wonderful place for striped bass in shallow water and I promised not to give its location away.

I always keep my promises. My dad taught me that. His word was his bond and I remember all that he did to make sure he kept his word when he told me we'd go fishing together—no matter what got in our way. Not rain or hail or gloom of night kept my dad from being true to his word. I learned how to be a good man from my dad.

The last time David and I tried to connect to striped bass in this cove was a year ago, and for whatever reason, everywhere we went we found lots of bluefish, but no bass. We had a great time catching hard-fighting blues, but this time we hoped to find what we were seeking, so we set up at the mouth of the creek and David began poling the skiff along the cordgrass edges as I cast a sinking line out to where the water depth dropped from extra shallow to less shallow. It didn't take but a few casts before I saw a flash and felt the pull of a striped bass and my rod bend and then the fish shook its mighty head and rolled right off the line. I had inadvertently "trout-set" the hook. I think I heard that fish laughing.

Of course, I knew better than to trout-set in salt water, but my reflexes were still remembering what they did in Texas two days earlier. It was time to deprogram and reset my muscle memory. I cast again, and after a few casts I connected with another striped bass and guess what? You guessed it ... I trout-set again and lost it. We moved on while I began thinking to myself the words "strip-set" over and over again in my mind. David was kind and although I knew the friendly ribbing would come later—in that moment, he let my angling missteps slide.

The morning was superlative. It was not too hot or too cool and just a bit overcast, which may have put the fish at ease in the shallow water.

We simply resorted to blind casting to likely spots until the sun came out.

A bald eagle screamed and soared overhead and a mixture of herons, egrets, terns, and cormorants kept us company, while the no-see-ums of our last visit were, for the most part, absent. I was grateful but kept my bug net at the ready. Sea robins struck minnows near the surface and then quickly returned to the muddy bottom, looking every bit like underwater aliens with jagged fins and wicked jaws. And my beloved diamondback terrapins popped their wonderful mosaic gray and white heads up on the water's surface . . . a little boy's dreams realized.

David noticed a striper feeding in the shallows at twelve o'clock off our bow and I began casting toward it—to no avail. Then we saw more pushes and V wakes along the submerged edges of the spartina grass and so I began shooting the line out to that nervous, moving water—again, without a take. I still felt hopeful. We were seeing striped bass everywhere and I had missed my chance with two but I could just feel that we were going to get into them, as if it had already played out in "real time" and now it was up to me to make it happen, in what an angler might call, "reel time." You know what I mean . . . when you finally have that fish of your dreams "on the reel" and in that moment—all other time ceases to exist.

We had the cove to ourselves save for a young man on a paddle board. He was making a lot of commotion with his splashy paddling technique and David said, "I hope he stays on the other side of the bay." Almost as soon as David made that wish, it was dashed into the water as our new paddle boarding friend decided to paddle our way. He wasn't trying to be a jerk; in fact, we had a nice conversation. He just didn't know any better. Still, he had most likely frightened every fish on that side of the bay, so we fired up the engine and headed for new water.

Just across the cove there was a duck blind and a nice shallow shoreline of spartina grass backed by a mixed pine and hardwood coastal forest. We could hear the ascending series of *zee, zee, zee* notes that make up the sweet song of a prairie warbler. Another diamondback terrapin peeked from the surface as if checking on my progress. He didn't seem in any way judgmental or condescending . . . although they always seem to be smiling. If he could talk I think he would have been helpful and supportive as he whispered, "Remember to strip-set the hook." And I was thinking about this and saying it to myself like a Hindu mantra just about the time I went to pick up and recast the line and a bass rose up from the gloom and swallowed the fly. I was so surprised that I missed the hookset. Mr. Turtle was nowhere to be seen.

This happened a couple more times except I did strip-set, and the fish was solidly hooked, and my rod was deeply bent with me actively fighting the fish when it opened its maw, shook its massive head, did a half barrel roll and threw the hook as if it was the easiest thing to do. I was gobsmacked!

I looked back at David and asked, "What am I doing wrong?" He said, "I can't see that you're doing anything wrong—it just happens." I knew that might be the kind of thing a professional guide tells a client or a friend to spare his feelings but, in this case, I knew I was setting the hook solidly—I think. Did I?

We tried a new area near the mouth of the creek without result and then decided to go back to the duck blind and give that spot another shot. I asked David if he wanted to fish and have me push him around (not that I know what I'm doing with a push pole), but he insisted that he fishes here almost every day and wanted me to land a bass. So, I did.

Whenever I am visiting a friend's home waters, and he or she is trying to connect me to a fish that is deeply special and personal to them, I desperately want to catch and return that fish—for them. I don't want to let them down. I want to share the joy of that moment with my friend, just as they envisioned it. Of course, we all know that life happens as we plan, but I do my best to put positive energy into the universe and manifest my daydreams into reality. And that is what I did this time as David and I stoically covered every inch of that shoreline until I saw the flash, felt the pull, solidly strip-setting the hook—again, and in short order brought a nice striped bass to the gunnel. We were both ecstatic and probably a little bit relieved. I was grateful. And that brings me to a couple of thoughts that I'd like to share with you, my faraway friends.

First, everything is created twice, first in our minds and then through our determined, enlightened, actions. If you are reading these words, you are experiencing the results of creating a vision and then taking the necessary risks and making the necessary effort to transform that vision into a reality. I learned a long time ago that every marathon is run one step at a time.

Second, no matter what life gives me or how it unfolds, I remain grateful. I count my blessings and not my burdens. If I go fishing and fail to catch fish, I still had a great day of fishing. Add a friend into the mix and the fishing is even better. Don't get me wrong, I'm glad I finally landed a striped bass to take the "skunk" smell off . . . but I was having a great time either way.

David moved us to another little cove that we'll call "Predator Alley." With a name like that you know it either means we found big voracious fish there or we came across a herd of flesh-eating dinosaurs. We found fish. I'm grateful for that too.

At first it was the same drill with David poling this wandering Texan along a likely shoreline and me doing my best to cast and retrieve in a way that might lead to me catching a few more fish, and I did. After getting a couple more nice bass to the boat, we both noticed the scythe-shaped tail fins of predatory bluefish slicing the waters. At last, a chance for us to fish together!

David powered us out into the deeper water and cut the engine allowing us to drift as we both switched to the ten-weight rods with forty-pound shock tippet and started casting to the marauding blue-fish. The air felt electric. The water seemed to swirl and tremble with anticipation.

When I see hunting bluefish, I see velociraptors chasing down slithering lawyers and screaming scientists. I see an apex predator that is a perfect pelagic killing and eating machine. And I see teeth that can take my finger off like a guillotine with gills. In case you can't tell . . . I love catching bluefish on the fly!

The water around us was alive with the smell of death. The forage fish here are many and varied. There are herring, anchovies, menhaden, silversides, and sand eels, just to name a few. But whatever was just beneath the surface, it was being hunted and devoured in a mélange of blood, guts, silvery scales, and sweet-smelling fish oils. We tossed our flies into the mix and David naturally got the first hook-up!

I stopped casting and watched the battle unfold with a big blue-fish taking David back and forth from bow to stern. In these shallower waters, bluefish will occasionally leap into the air shaking their metallic heads with ferocity, and this one was true to form. But after a tussle that was worth watching, David brought it boat side and carefully set it free without missing a beat or losing a finger. We celebrated and cast again. The bite was on!

David connected with another blue, and it fought just as valiantly but without the acrobatics. Then it was my turn so I stood on the bow as we scanned the surface looking for more knife-edged fins cutting the surface. The water erupted far off our starboard side and David repositioned the skiff so that we'd be in the path of these magnificent predators. Sure enough, I saw them coming dead ahead toward the bow. I cast just in front of them and began stripping the line as fast as I could but it wasn't fast enough. After a brief follow, they veered away and passed us by. No matter, more were coming and coming fast!

I couldn't see what they were chasing; most likely bunker, but whatever it was, I felt sorry for those little fish who were born to be eaten. This time after casting I tucked the rod under my arm and began stripping the line with both hands as fast as I could. That got their attention, and a big bluefish slashed at my fly. I felt his weight and set the hook, and in an instant we were connected like two warriors fighting hand-to-hand in the trenches. And it was a lot like that, because I had nothing against him, and he had nothing against me, but fate and fortune had brought us together in this moment and in this way. As always, I was grateful that I prevailed in this short battle, but even more grateful when I watched him return home. The mark upon his lip and the line-burn across my fingers were simply reminders of our meeting—two warriors from two worlds on one bright blue planet.

❧

That night, David, Cathy, David's cousin Robert, and I enjoyed a wonderful dinner with wine, forties jazz, and conversation that ran from silly to serious. I loved every moment of it including when Cathy and I shared a spirited discussion on the causes and potential cures for the various human-induced challenges of life on Earth. Differing perspectives are worth exploring when two people respect and value each other—as Cathy and I do.

It concerns me that our ongoing and ever growing national and global loss of empathy is causing us to forget that we learn and grow by inviting positive discourse and by challenging our own paradigms. Echo chambers teach us nothing. Opinions are worthless; understanding is priceless.

At our core, most of us want the same things . . . health, safety, security, joy, laughter, and love. We just get in our own way—on the way. It's kind of like stepping on your line when you cast. We have to pay attention and keep casting onward.

In the morning, David and I took to the sea and retraced our path of the previous day where fish were caught and released and memories were made and retained. Our first stop was the turtle cove. David wanted me to redeem myself for the two fish I lost in this spot the previous day. My muscle memory was reprogrammed now, and I had caught a few fish the day before to reinforce the lessons of the first morning.

We started working our way across the same spartina grass–covered shoreline with me blind casting into the deeper water with the sinking line and one of David's brown shrimpy-looking flies. After a few unfruitful casts, David pointed out that we were back in the same spot where I hooked and lost that first fish. That's about the time I saw a bass follow and swallow the fly and this time I strip-set the hook solidly and found myself battling a beautiful chunky striped bass! It didn't take too long to get it to the boat, but it took a while. It pulled left and I pulled right, and then we reversed the direction of the dance. Ultimately, I found myself holding that lovely bass by his lower lip and watching him pump refreshing oxygen-filled water though his flaring gills. Then, I felt the little nip of his mouth closing around my thumb and he turned and swam away as if nothing had ever happened—but it had. The fish was revived and I was redeemed.

I'm not sure if it was the same fish I had lost the day before, but I'd like to think it was, because, being a poet at heart, I love coming full circle with both fish and friends. And there are lessons to be learned in stories like this. We should always do our best to help each other revive after a battle well fought. And we must always leave each other with space and time for redemption.

Nature teaches me a great deal. Nature is ambivalent about "justice" or "fairness" or "rights." I suspect bluefish never feel bad for anchovies and brown bears never hear the salmon's plea for a little more time in the river. But we humans have the ability that seems almost alien, if not divine. We can choose to be kind. We can choose to save something or someone from destruction. This is who we are when we are at our best.

After catching that bass, we traveled a long way at full throttle across the wide-open bay. I love the bouncing, skidding, sliding movement of a sleek boat crossing water and the fresh feeling of the salty spray on my face. I love the smell of the ocean, and the sights of the seabirds overhead. I love seeing the coastline slipping behind us as the surface of the ocean slips beneath us. It all reminds me of my childhood. In many ways, I'm enjoying a second childhood now, in my later years. And in many ways, it's my first happy childhood.

David slid the skiff into a brackish creek with grand houses on either side and docks with expensive boats tied to their pylons. I couldn't help but notice that no matter how expensive the house or fancy the boat, most of the docks were covered in seagull shit. Here and there we saw pairs of osprey tending to their massive stick-made nests on the wooden docks of someone's vacation home, who had apparently not yet returned for their vacation. I doubt they will be pleased by the osprey nests or the seagulls' droppings, but I was pleased to see all the young osprey families thriving on pylons and pine trees.

We tried a bit of sight-fishing along a crescent-shaped flat but we saw only one striped bass, and I cast to it, saw it follow, saw it eat the fly, and was so mesmerized that I failed to set the hook before it spit the fly and turned away in disgust. So much for redemption. It's okay. Everything in life is practice. We live, learn, laugh, adapt, and move on.

This was about the time that my buddy came up with a wonderfully poetic idea for the last fishing spot of the day. On my first trip to the Hamptons, we visited a little cove that seemed simply perfect for striped bass, but we caught bluefish instead. So, we decided to end this day where that day had begun. The cove is like a little aquatic cul-de-sac of water flowing in and out of a single passageway, surrounded by a narrow, riparian saltmarsh shoreline. Along that shoreline are wooden docks and muti-million-dollar homes. This is a living community—human and otherwise.

If you look up the term "cul-de-sac" in the dictionary it reads: "dead end, passage closed at one end, route or course leading nowhere." I disagree. Perhaps these circular endings of linear passages are just what we need to slow us down and remind us that there isn't anywhere we need to go in order to live a meaningful, joyful life.

David pushed us along as I cast and with my mind still focused on producing a strong hook set I struck so hard on the first fish that I broke the tippet and lost the fly with the fish. David laughed and said, "You hit that one too hard." But casting and catching, reeling and releasing, are all fluid processes—just like breathing. So, I tied another shrimp-like thingamajig on my tippet and cast again, this time setting the hook well and bringing a few more bass to the boat.

It had already been a good day and for both of us, fish were caught. But we had arrived at the last bit of plausible bass habitat in the watercourse "leading nowhere." In short, we'd come full circle. I began casting and retrieving again and again until there was only one cast remaining. That was about the time David said, "Wouldn't it be something if you caught your biggest fish on your last cast?"

When I saw the fish strike, I could hardly believe my eyes. It looked massive. I set the hook and the fight was on. David called out, "Let it run if it wants to run!" And run she did, taking me into my backing twice. A homeowner had come out on his dock to watch the battle and his British accent was clear as he said, "That's amazing! I didn't know there were fish that big in here." In time, I managed to land the fish. She was beautiful and David pointed out that she didn't have any sea lice on her and might be a resident fish. All I know is that I loved her and held her gently in the water with my thumb on her lower lip as she pumped fresh reviving water through her gills like an athlete breathing deeply after a hard run. In time, I felt her bite down softly on my thumb. It was her way of telling me that she was ready for me to let her go . . . and so I did. I touched her tail as she swam powerfully away and I watched as she vanished back into the waters where I had found her. And I will never know what became of her after that moment, but I do know this . . . as long as I may live, I will never forget her.

The older I get the more I like being home. And as grateful as I am for all the adventures I have known from Africa to the Americas, these days, I'm just as happy to sit at my kitchen window, watching the birds at my feeders. I'm at peace standing in my little local stream casting a three-weight to sunfish and the occasional Guadalupe bass. It's always comforting to be home.

But there are other places where for a brief moment in time, I have felt at home. And there are people with whom I have felt at peace and deeply grateful for their company. I have been surprised at the places I've come to love. One is not too far north of Los Angeles and the other is not too far east of New York. And like the character Richard Blane of my favorite classic movie, *Casablanca*, I too came here, "for my health. I came for the waters." But also like that saloon-keeper-turned-reluctant-warrior, I came here to fight the good fight . . . to not surrender to the cynical voices that look the other way and whisper, "It doesn't really matter." It does matter, y'all. It really does.

CHAPTER FIVE

American and Hickory Shad

Potomac River: The Journey to Chesapeake Bay

This is how humans are: We question all our beliefs, except for the ones that we really believe in, and those we never think to question.
~ ORSON SCOTT CARD, *SPEAKER FOR THE DEAD*

I'VE BEEN PONDERING THE IDEA OF "HOME." I'VE LIVED IN SO MANY places during my six decades of breathing, and there have been times and places when and where I may have felt "at home," but it never lasted. Things change. Even those times and those places proved to be transitory, temporary, and transitional.

Humanity and its environs are consistent in their inconsistency. Your beloved home waters begin to dry, and warm, and empty. The fish you once caught in abundance become ever more scarce, and in time, you no longer recognize the river you once loved. So, you travel to new waters, landscapes, and communities that are far removed from the place you once called home. And if you're fortunate you find new waters that feel like home, not because it reminds you of from where you came, but rather, because it reflects you and how far you've traveled. Why is that, I wonder?

Change is the only constant in the universe. Like tides and currents, the places where we live are familiar—yet everchanging. Even my own battered body at times feels like home, until a new ache or pain reminds me of its fleeting impermanence. Sometimes that change is frightening. Other times I accept it with grace.

Stardust and seawater blowing in the wind—evaporating in the sunlight. That's me. That's you. That's us. We try to forget and look away, but again and again we are reminded, and the life we once lived seems like a dream you once dreamed.

Sometimes my life seems like a dream and I wonder about the reality of "reality." After this life, do we sleep forever or finally wake up? What is home for a traveler in the human construct we call time? Is it someplace we are, or something we choose to be? These are the questions that run through my mind at the water's edge. I seldom invest thought in choosing between a clinch knot and a Lefty's loop. I tend toward deeper waters and my attachments are few.

I have often felt like a lone astronaut hurtling away from the Earth—my temporary home planet. As I watch our beautiful blue orb in my rearview mirror, I can hear the voice of David Bowie singing my own special version of "Space Oddity": I hear ground control calling me—reminding me that it's time to leave. As my rocket ship moves farther from Earth, I send hopeful messages back to loved ones and strangers. Sometimes all I receive in return is the empty silence of open space, and other times I receive replies without meaning—just simple acknowledgments that my message was received. But receiving and acknowledgment of reception is not the same as having a conversation that reflects understanding, engagement, connection, and empathy. It does nothing to take away the aloneness of this journey we call a "lifetime"—each of us hurtling toward the sun. It's like listening to the conversations between strangers—empty, hollow, emotionless, and without meaning. A box made of wood and brick may be called a house, and yet never become a home.

So, I wonder, what is home? Is it a place and time? Is it a state of mind? Is it a choice? I suspect, it is all of the above, and yet none of the above. One thing I do sense is that when you find "Home," you know it. And I find that I always feel at home on the water.

For my friend Chris Wood, Fletcher's Cove is home. Fletcher's Cove, often called Fletcher's Boathouse, has been there in its current state since the 1850s. It has always been a natural indentation in the shoreline of the mighty Potomac River but it has suffered the indignities of human choices that were lacking in forethought while containing a desire for quick profit for a few, at any cost, for the many. *E Pluribus Unum?* Not much has changed in the way things are changed.

The Potomac River has been called "America's River," and for good reason. It reflects us then and now. It was once so clean and wild that it contained and sustained a multitude of wildlife. In earlier times anyone might hold its water in the cupped palm of their hand and drink it down without concern. But by the 1950s it became so polluted and diverted that fish and fowl began to vanish along with as many citizens who could afford to relocate away from its pungent brown stench. Now, there is good news—the Potomac is on the mend. We've made some better choices. Still, America's River has a long way to go to regain its rightful place as an example of what Americans can achieve when we choose to work together with determination and a deep desire for a healthier, more joyful world.

And for Chris, you can add to that definition and designation of "Home" the three-level row house in northeastern Washington, D.C., where he and his family have lived and loved for so many years. It's not just a house, it's a home. It's where he and his wonderful wife Betsy have raised three solid sons, Wylie, Casey, and Henry Trace. These are the kind of young men for which any parent would feel pride. And their home is alive with laughter and conversation on the inside, and with vibrant flowers and thriving vegetables in Betsy's garden on the outside. There is serenity on the top floor, unity on the ground floor, and hilarity in the basement where the whole family joins each night to play video games and watch movies. Between Fletcher's Cove and that three-story house on the city's edge—they have found or made a home. I'm so happy for my friend and his family.

The last time I visited Chris, he and I were chasing longnose gar fish in the cove. After two days of casting to bubbles, we caught nothing. It was still a wonderful time on the water. We were fishing; catching is just a bonus. But there were to be no bonuses of catching on that trip because the native garfish eluded us and not even an invasive snakehead gave us a second thought. I had a blast casting Chris's wet-mop-like rope flies into the muddy, murky waters of Fletcher's Cove. We were two friends fishing, and that's good enough for me.

This time I had flown up from Texas to join Chris in the annual shad run that happens each year in ascending sequence from the St. John's River in Florida to the Bay of Fundy in maritime Canada. In his 2002 book on the American shad, author John McPhee refers to these sleek and wide-eyed creatures as the "Founding Fish." This is in part due to the lore and history of these fish feeding the previously starving Continental Army on the banks of the Schuylkill River at Valley Forge. In the spring of 1778, the shad came and were caught in great numbers. They were eaten fresh or salted and stored in wooden barrels. To be clear, shad did not save the army, but they did feed them. History shows that the Continental Army was freezing and starving on the banks of the Schuylkill in February, and the shad run would not have occurred until April. But throughout human history, along these watersheds, shad have played an important role either as food or fertilizer. I wanted to experience firsthand the Atlantic Coast shad run, so that I could share it with you. It is an American success story in the making . . . an example of us collectively learning and turning a corner—for the better.

It was raining the night before Chris and I were slated to fish. I don't mean a dripping drizzle or soft shower; I mean a torrential downpour. It lulled me to sleep as it hit the rooftop of Chris's home and the window of the room he and Betsy had allowed me to make my own for a few days. As a child I was always lonely in the darkness of my room—the door closed, the nightlight giving little solace. But when it rained I would press my ear against the wall next to my bed or simply listen to it hitting the tin awning at my window, and I felt at peace. The raindrops kept me company and washed away my fears. That is how I felt the night before we fished. At peace. Both shad and I love rainy, overcast fishing days. The sight of raindrops on the water's surface seems to calm and comfort both fish and fisher. I love fishing in the rain.

The downpour had turned into a drizzle by morning, and then only a light mist by the time we arrived at Fletcher's Cove. Dan Ward was behind the counter wearing the same soft smile and welcoming gaze that he had the last time I saw him, two years prior. Dan has worked at Fletcher's for over fifty years, and his love for this place along the river is evident. Alex Binstead, who now runs Fletcher's, learned to walk his first steps as a toddler, while visiting at the cove with his family. Alex's father, Mark Binsted, has been fishing the Potomac River for almost six decades and has become the resident sage and source of knowledge when it comes to American shad and hickory shad on the Potomac. And now my buddy Chris Wood's son will be joining their ranks while working a summer job at Fletcher's. The circle remains unbroken. Such is the magic of home waters.

A pileated woodpecker had made its home in a dead tree behind the tackle hut and was busy tapping its rhythm of resonate drumming upon the hollow tree while intermittently calling out its rapid and boisterous "woika-woika-woika . . . kuk, kuk, kuk" notes into the damp morning air. Pileated woodpeckers seldom seem discreet, but I love watching their antics and must admit that I was more focused on the bird than I was the conversation about fishing that was going on all around me. If I love any creature more than fish, it is birds. They have captivated me and saved me since I was a child. In fact, I could never call any place home if it was devoid of wild, native birds.

Chris and I walked out on the docks, grabbed some oars, life jackets, and hopped into one of the signature-style wooden rowboats that are a fixture and artifact of fishing at Fletcher's. Each boat looks much the same, painted red with white letters that reads, "Fletcher." Our boat was number DC 1038E. It may have looked like all the others, but it was ours—complete with its "anchor," which consisted of a large, round rock wrapped and tied up with rope which itself was tied to the bow. Every boat at Fletcher's Cove has a rock and rope anchor. Each rock is different, but the ropes seem much the same. I like that.

Chris loves to row, and that's a good thing, because he's good at it, and I'm liable to have us zigzagging across the currents and drifting into God knows what. We worked our way down river to the very end of the cove and Chris had me drop the rock-anchor so we could get down to serious shad fishing. The shad move in and out of the cove in surges. The hickory shad were lying in mid-water while the Americans were holding to the deepest spots. If we wanted to catch American shad, we needed to get past the hickory shad so that the "shad dart" had time to descend to where those fish were holding. The shad dart is a small, almost cute fly with a bulbous head, pudgy body, sparse fiber tail, and oversized googly eyes. Mine was chartreuse. I named him "Bob."

Cormorants were moving across the river in great armadas of diving and dipping predatory commotion. Great blue herons angled the shore-line while osprey soared and screeched above us. One dove out of the sky on the far side of the river and came up with a fish in its two-by-two talons that act like a combination of vise grips and pitchforks. Each of the four toes is covered in tiny fishhook-like protrusions especially fitting for slippery prey. A mature bald eagle called out its approval or disdain as it passed over us—anglers one and all. But they were using beak and talon while we were sporting seven-weight rods with full sinking lines. I cast out from the bow, Chris cast from the stern, and we began the process of shad fishing.

The process is methodical and magical all at once. First you cast and then you count as you allow the dart to sink, let it swing with the current, and then begin the slow, rhythmic, strip-strip-strip of the line until with any luck you feel the bump, bump, bump, of an annoyed spawning shad showing its displeasure with your minnow imitation messing around their spawning space. Like salmon, shad aren't feeding as they spawn, but they can be induced to bump-strike the fly. I'm not sure that we really understand why shad strike, but I'm grateful that they do!

It only took a few tries before I received and missed my first bumps. It was exciting to feel them, and I was taken by the fact that the bump of a shad doesn't feel like anything else I've ever experienced. I missed a few before I connected with a smallish fish of about eleven to thirteen inches, but I was happy to see it as I slipped out the barbless hook and sent it home. Chris paused and said, "Is that a shad? I think it might be a herring." Then he looked at me with eyes that I knew were reliving our two days of being skunked last time I was here, and he said, "It might have been a shad." I wasn't convinced that he was convinced and since I'd never even seen a shad in real life before, I wasn't sure myself.

I cast again and felt another bump, made the hookup and watched as a good-sized hickory shad leapt into the misty air like a wanna-be tarpon. When I brought him to the boat there was no mistaking it for anything other than a hickory shad with its protruding lower lip and sleek silver-green sides. Once Chris saw that I had caught my first shad he fessed up . . . "I'm not gonna lie to you," he said. "Your first fish was a herring." I smiled.

Like shad, blueback herring are an anadromous fish which can live in both fresh and salt water. In their life cycle they spawn in fresh to brackish waters and then the fry migrate out of Chesapeake Bay and into the open ocean. Each herring has spawning marks on their scales recording the number of times each individual fish has spawned in its lifetime. Most shad also experience multiple spawning runs in a lifetime, the exception being those that migrate into the relatively warm waters of the St. Johns River of northern Florida. Like Pacific salmon, the southern shad experience complete mortality at the end of their one and only spawning run. I was fine with the idea of catching a herring on a shad dart. It seemed special.

Chris and I both caught a few more hickory shad before things slowed down and we pulled up anchor and drifted upstream a little ways until we came within talking distance of where local shad fishing legend Mark Binsted was anchored. We had been watching him as he hooked and landed one fish after another, most of them American shad. We asked what his secret was, and he said, "You've got to get deeper and go slower." After giving Mark enough space so we didn't intrude on his fishing, but could still enjoy his company, we dropped the rock-on-a-rope—I mean, "anchor"—just as the rain began to pick up, along with the fishing.

As I've mentioned before, I love fishing in the rain. I love the way the water looks and sounds as the raindrops join the river or the sea. I love the fresh smell of the air and the way the water drips off the edge of my oilskin hat. I love everything about it. It feels like adventure.

The rain came down and the three of us continued to cast, count, strip, strip-set, catch, and release one shad after another. I lost count of how many fish we caught, but I did notice that we were finally landing some American shad—about one American shad for every three or four hickory shad we caught. It was exactly the opposite for Mark.

In between casting and catching we chatted back and forth between our two boats, which brings me to another thing I love about Fletcher's Cove. It is a community of people, not just a place along a river. It feels like everyone who lives out their angling life here also has a feeling of belonging here. It feels as if it's their home. I was clearly a welcome visitor—but a visitor, nonetheless.

I don't want to live in Washington, D.C., but I do wish I had the same little notch in a river where "everyone knows your name" and there is a feeling of us all being in this together. Perhaps it's that feeling of community that at least partially defines and describes "Home." I love that feeling of being where I belong . . . like a cypress tree rooted on the riverbank. I support the river and the river supports me.

I'm not sure if home is something we find or something we create. I suspect it's a little of both. I do know this . . . when I was a younger man I sought out solitude and adventure. I wanted to travel away from the places I already thought I knew. Now, travel and looking outward hold far less charm or allure. I love the comfort of the familiar. And I enjoy companionship when it is with someone who adds to the experience, not detracts from it. My best fishing companions are always the ones who can be at peace in total silence, or in the kind of conversation that is calming, restful, and comforting—like a soft rain on a dreamy night.

───

The next morning, the rain had cleared. It was a bright, beautiful, sunny day. Chris was flying out to Montana that afternoon and I was flying back to Texas, but we still had a few hours to fish—so we did. On the way to

Fletcher's Cove, we stopped at "Black Coffee" coffee shop and picked up a couple of the most delicious breakfast sandwiches you can imagine. This is a good time to share that I am a "breakfast guy," and I find that most of my friends with whom I fish are not. They can take or leave coffee and breakfast and are used to doing the latter, so often I either have to say something so we can work it into our plans or go along and feel like half the man I could have been. Needless to say, I felt like a complete version of myself when we cast off for a few short hours of pre-flight fishing in the cove.

When we reached the spot in the river where we had so much success the day prior, we dropped our rock anchor and began casting. The rock in this boat was shaped like a potato and did not seem to hold the bottom quite as well as the round boulder of the previous day. But we managed to hold our place with a few minor adjustments from time to time, and we both happily cast our darts in the early morning sunshine. There were no other anglers on the water and even the cormorants were gone. An immature bald eagle swooped down from the tree line on the opposite bank of the river and scooped up a shad for breakfast. Chris and I watched as it took its catch to an overhanging tree limb, and I thought of how happy I was to see bald eagles again, after decades of their absence. We are the problem and the solution. I feel such joy when we take the higher road.

The sun was out and the bright sunlight shimmered on the water's surface. Shad eyes shy away from bright light, but we got a couple of bumps and hooked a couple of fish before calling the morning a wrap. Most were hickory shad but one or two were American or "white" shad. They were all beautiful. I loved how the hickories jumped into the air and how the Americans sounded as deeply as they could manage each time I connected with one. Shad are sensitive to handling, so I kept each fish in the water and did not feel truly at peace until it swam away under its own power. It's a curious thing to seek something but hold your breath until you've let it go and watched it become free again. Perhaps this is a metaphor for our own human existence—both civilized and feral but never truly wild.

The American shad is becoming a human success story. After two centuries of damming its spawning tributaries, polluting its waters, and overfishing with nets and traps, we are finally beginning to heal those wounds. All we had to do is get out of its way to allow it to thrive.

I guess that's kind of true for what we need to do in our own lives. We need to tear down the barriers and clean up the environment that surrounds us. We need to move together in great surges of benevolent joy and shake off the detritus of our former lives. And most of all, we need to realize that our home is not a house or a village or a nation as much as it is this beautiful blue orb we've been given—the only true home we will ever know. We have a long way to go before we arrive closer to where we began—but I remain hopeful.

CHAPTER SIX

Speckled Trout and Redfish

The Estuaries of the Low Country, South Carolina

War was always here. Before man was, war waited for him. The ultimate trade awaiting its ultimate practitioner.

~ CORMAC MCCARTHY, *BLOOD MERIDIAN*

SOMEHOW, I MANAGED TO COME "FULL CIRCLE." THE LAST TIME I FLEW into Charleston, South Carolina, was forty-two years ago as an impatient nineteen-year-old Marine recruit with something to prove—to myself. At the time I and other recruits from across the American southland were enroute to Parris Island and Marine boot camp. As long as I may live, I will never forget that day or the impact it had on the direction and dedication of my life. Then, February 3, 1981, the airport seemed small, dark, and foreboding. Marine Receiving Barracks Drill Instructors greeted us at the airport with loud and hostile voices. In short order we were locked at attention and bused through the coal-black night to the infamous Parris Island where our lives were changed forever. We were kept awake for the first forty-eight hours, harangued and hurried, and directed to write identification numbers in black ink across our forearms.

69

The process had begun, and my newly shaved head, uniform, and combat boots acted as constant reminders that I was a voluntary prisoner of Parris Island. I had turned myself in to the authorities and said, "Do with me what you must so that I might become a U.S. Marine." As we crossed the bridge onto the island, I knew . . . I was no longer "me"—I was "us."

Thus began a three-month-long crucible that stripped me of my impetuous immaturity and selfish ego and reconstructed me as a man who valued service and honor over any creature comfort. At Parris Island I was reborn—and from that moment on, my life was a new life—one that welcomed challenge and cultivated determination. This was just one of several homecomings that I would undertake in this journey. And it mattered as much as any.

And so here I was, with my plane descending, looking down on the same South Carolinian Low Country that like me, was much changed by both time and tide. The once youthful and idealistic recruit had returned as a sixty-one-year-old man with nothing to prove to anyone—including himself. And the place that back then seemed like a small town in the middle of a vast wetland now contained a network of roads and bridges, buildings and marinas. The new airport was large, open, bright, and cheerful. And I was greeted by the soft, welcoming voice of my friend Captain Greg Peralta.

Greg and I had spoken on the phone many times, but this was the first time we'd ever met in person. Still, it felt as if we were old friends having a reunion. That's how it is with people of our tribe. We may have traveled different paths but still had so many things in common. As we drove toward Greg's house, we shared our love of family and friends, nature and the best of human nature. And as we discussed our plans to seek redfish and speckled trout in these salt marsh waters, it became apparent to me that we both welcomed the challenge—while letting go of any expectations. We were going fishing, and that was enough. Our only goal had already been achieved.

Greg and his wife Amy live in a carriage house that seems almost mystical and is magically placed under live oak and magnolia trees at the edge of the salt marsh. The house is built upon concrete stilts to allow for the increasingly frequent hurricanes and its potential flooding. With the heart of an optimist, the ground-level garage had been converted into a recreation room filled with Greg's many fishing rods, lures, flies, and other gear, as well as a small guest apartment where I would be staying for the next few days. It was like heaven.

To the front of the house were the remnants of the original spring-house of the colonial community of Beresford Hall. The cool, fresh spring water that once provided an early form of refrigeration for the colonists still runs from its source near Greg's front yard to its terminus near Greg's back dock. Forage fish, redfish, and speckled trout congregate near the mouth of this spring, as do many other forms of wildlife. In the 1700s colonists kept perishable foods cold by placing them in ceramic containers in or near the cooling waters of the spring, an example of early human innovation and natural adaptation that was useful yet minimally disruptive or extractive. We can do things like that when there aren't eight billion of us around.

Greg had a few business calls to make, so I made myself at home in the little apartment and then walked out the back door to explore the grounds and waters. The docks in the Low Country are large wooden structures with boardwalks that cross wonderfully large expanses of spartina saltwater marshland. If water is the "lifegiving blood" of this ecosystem then spartina grass—*Spartina alterniflora*—is its "heart." Spartina, also known as cord grass, marsh grass, and sea grass, is actually a freshwater grass that has adapted to tolerate brackish conditions. It has evolved with the ability to absorb the water through the roots and separate the salt from the water that it needs for the photosynthetic process. Almost all life on Earth is dependent upon this process of transferring energy from sunlight with the use of clean water and oxygenated air. The salt in the water is ultimately expelled by the grass through small pores along its leaves, which can be felt whenever you run your hand along the length of each blade.

Spartina grass and its system of roots are an essential filter that absorbs and breaks down pollutants in the water. It is also an essential element for building landmass along barrier and sea islands. Its connecting roots and abundant leaves gather sediment to create soil and reduce coastal erosion. And it acts as the engine for the food chain by providing base nutrients for other species to feed upon. Saltgrass marshes provide shelter and act as a nursery for everything from fish to crabs, shrimp, and mollusks. The largest things in nature all rest upon the metaphorical shoulders of the smallest things. Without spartina grass, there is no marsh, and without the marsh, there is no fishery. As an angler and naturalist, I pay attention to these things. I hope with each passing day, more of us will pay attention and act to protect each part of the whole.

This was our third try to make this trip come into fruition. The first try was postponed due to weather conditions and the second due to the COVID-19 pandemic. This time we were facing issues of stormy, windy weather and the advent of the "peeler crab" season, but we decided to move forward anyway. So, as clouds gathered overhead, we loaded up Greg's dad's boat and cruised out into the marsh hoping for a quick catch or two before the evening storms rolled in. We could hear the rumble of thunder in the distance and a soft misting rain fell as we motored to a place I will call the "River Bend Docks." Greg looked up at the sky and said, "I hope you don't mind if we get a little wet." I smiled and replied, "I'm a Marine. I'm amphibious." Greg smiled too. There was no way for Greg to know that I love fishing in the rain.

I was using Greg's favorite fly rod—a nine-foot-long Shimano Asquith using an eight-weight RIO fly line that was designed specifically for redfish. He was using a Shimano Poison Ultima 6'10" light spinning outfit paired with a Shimano Stella 1000 frame reel. I should mention here that Greg's son Elliot works for Shimano. I will also mention that the Asquith was so amazing that it made me seem like an expert fly caster—which I am not. I asked Greg what that rod cost and when he begrudgingly told me, I realized that this was most likely my one and only chance to use one. So, like a lucky high school boy who somehow landed a date with the head cheerleader, I savored every moment with that rod. Damn, she was amazing!

We began casting tight under and around the docks, allowing my fly and his lure to sink and drift with the tidal current, and then retrieving back toward the boat. After a couple of casts Greg got a massive strike from under the docks and his featherweight spinning rig was doubled over as if it were begging for release. The trolling motor was set to hold us in place and I held my cast as I watched Greg fight what was likely a big redfish. He grunted and laughed and shouted out, "This fish is kicking my ass!" And even with the trolling motor wigging and wagging to hold us at "anchor," the bow of the boat began to wander toward the pulling fish. That was just about the time I began wondering how tough that little spinning rod could be and discovered that it didn't matter because, the redfish was tougher. We both moaned as the fish came off the hook and then we laughed and relived the epic battle like two kids with cane poles and a bucket of worms. And I think this is one of the charms of fishing with friends . . . we are free to be childlike again. Growing up and growing old are both scams that I'm not buying.

I figured it was my turn, and Greg said this was a "sure place" for reds, so I kept casting, drifting, and stripping in that chartreuse streamer with hopeful resolve and mindful focus. There was an area of spartina salt marsh behind the dock and a likely looking strip of deeper water between there and the next dock, so I cast up-current, counted down to "six-Carolina" to allow the fly to sink and began stripping it in ever so slowly and haltingly—like a dying minnow might act. I was methodical and melodic in my presentation and did not allow myself to become discouraged when again and again my cast led to . . . strip, strip, strip, zip. "Patience," I told myself. "You are not trying to get anywhere." And that's when I went to pick up my cast and saw a silvery flash come up from the murky bottom and felt that beautiful rod bowing like a monk in a monastery. It was my first speckled trout of my lifetime and I was thrilled!

We worked that entire riverbend along the wetland edges and each little freshwater creek mouth as we searched for my first redfish. The wind freshened and the grasses began to bend as big raindrops struck the water's surface and ran off the brim of my hood. It felt refreshing and reaffirming as I watched the replenishment of the Low Country unfold all around me. The wading birds paid the rain no mind and neither did we until the first rumble of thunder and flash of lighting when we decided that discretion was the better part of wisdom. I had just flown into town from my Texas Hill Country home during the early afternoon of this first day, and already I had caught my first fish from the Carolina wetlands. I felt blessed, fortunate, and at peace as we landed at Greg's dock. It was time to clean up, have dinner, and drink wine as the rain fell upon the carriage house roof and across the marsh and off the broad, green leaves of magnolia trees. That night, the tide would roll in and flood the spartina marsh. Raccoons would search for crabs, and otters would hunt for killifish, and I would hope for dreams of adventure and happiness. And all of those dreams did come true.

~ ~

In the morning we went out for breakfast as we waited for the tide to turn. The omelet tasted cheesy, the bacon of satisfying salt and fat, the toast of real butter, and the coffee—well, the coffee was simply heaven. Everywhere we went people seemed to know and like Greg. I began to suspect my friend is a bit of a local fishing legend, even if he would never admit to such a thing. The other thing I noticed is that like me he actually cares about people, including people he barely knows. Greg is kind, thoughtful, modest, and so obviously doing his best to give back to a world that he feels has been quite good to him. Like me, he loves his family in a way that gives hope to the world and joy to all involved. And like me, he seems to feel that the act of fishing is only part of the act of living. Lunch and laughter has as much to do with the success of a fishing trip as lures and leaders. We were already successful at breakfast.

The evening before, we sat in the living room of Greg and Amy's house on stilts that looks through the treetops and over the salt marsh to the tidal creek. We talked about life and love and getting older and the legacy we are leaving our children. We talked about my wife Alice and daughter Megan, and his daughter Maddie and son Elliot, both of whom live on James Island. And I was told all about Brodie "the amazing fish finding and stock trading dog" who Greg said is doing about as well as the financial experts at choosing stocks to trade, by the seemingly random push of a paw. And then we spoke of our fathers.

I began speaking of my father, Stephen J. Ramirez, who raised me as a single parent. I shared that I was named after him but given the middle name "Michael" because he didn't want me to be called "junior." Then I told of his courage and kindness and how he served as an Air Force medic during the Korean War because he wanted to serve his country but not hurt anyone. And finally, I shared that this book was dedicated to my father, and that I submitted the outline on his birthday—December 26. Greg got quiet for a moment and then said, "I just got goose bumps! My father, also named Greg, fought the Japanese as part of the Philippine resistance and he was also born on December 26. The boat we are fishing off was his boat."

I'm not sure if things happen for a reason or not, and I'm not sure if there is or isn't something we call "God," and I'm not sure of much except that human certainty is laughable. But I get the feeling that there are currents and eddies in the universe that bring people together and that nature reflects the existence of something much bigger than humanity. And in that moment, I was so grateful that Greg and I decided to brave the weather and fish together—like two long-lost brothers of the same universe. Life is magical in its mystery.

The first thing we did as we walked along the long boardwalk to the docks was to do so with stealth and awareness—and it paid off. In the early morning light, we could see some good-sized redfish cruising in and out of the tidal edges of the spartina. I set up a limp little cast off the dock which landed too close to the fish and spooked them. So, we waited for the next few reds to come noodling in and I cast again, getting a quick follow and quicker rejection. I blew it. We loaded up the skiff and pushed off.

As we rounded the riverbend we saw some dolphins following us as they hunted for finger mullet that were leaping all around us. Greg said that the dolphins had learned that fishing skiffs meant fish and that it wasn't unusual for them to follow along hoping to pick off something as it was caught or released. He cut the engine and began splashing the water with his hand and sure enough the pod of dolphins began to turn toward us until they figured out that it was a ruse and went back to the hunt. Soon we saw them in the shallows rounding up a school of mullet, life and death unfolding as they do each day. As my friend J. Drew Lanham once wrote, "In nature the only absolute truths are life and death, eat or die, pass your genes on to the next generation or disappear from the evolutionary landscape. Sex and hunger drive survival. It's that simple. There is no evil in nature." I never try to anthropomorphize nature into some sort of Disney cartoon. I prefer nature's honesty over human deception.

We began working the length of the docks at the bend in the river. It was the same place where Greg had hooked and lost what we took to be a big redfish, and where I managed to land my first speckled trout the day prior. We had an outgoing tide with good movement of water, but after a while with no takers, we decided to motor down the river toward new water. Passing Greg's docks, we turned upriver while keeping a weather eye on the clouds overhead. There wasn't any lightning or rumble of thunder so all was well as we passed through intermittent rain and drizzle. The water was dark and the sky was gray, but we saw signs of parting clouds and sunshine, here and there.

The tidal creek grew wider, too wide to be considered a creek, and we came to a place with some substantial oyster bars and inlets where fresh water mingled with brackish. Greg used the trolling motor to put us in position, and we both began casting to likely spots. Every now and then we'd get a glimpse of a redfish moving off along the bank, but there were no takers, so we crossed the river to another oyster bed that was known for having a steady supply of smallish reds. Greg gave me the best shots but before long he had a nice sized trout on the line, and then another, while I got a bump but no hookup. We made another pass through, because he was still amazed that neither of us had connected with a redfish and was sure this was a good place. After a couple of casts, I felt the tug, tugged back and brought another trout to the gunnel. It wasn't as big as the first one or either of the fish Greg caught but the colors along its side were stunning. I was happy to watch it swim off with a strong kick of its tail and an indignant sideways glance toward me. I might enjoy the releasing more than the catching. I guess that's how it is with things we love, and I love native fish in their natural waters.

When we rounded the bend to Old Kiln Creek a freshwater-leaning alligator slid into the same water that the saltwater-leaning dolphins had been swimming in earlier that morning. This is part of the magic of the marsh—the meeting and mingling of habitats and inhabitants. Just beyond the spartina grass was a wall of oak trees, each one dripping in Spanish moss. Periwinkles dotted the muddy banks like diamonds in the dirt. Mullet swirled in the shallows as a bald eagle soared overhead, calling out its displeasure at our intrusion into its home waters. Carolina diamondback terrapins popped their whitish-gray, mosaic heads from the creek's surface, and marsh hens clapped out their ridiculous call across the spartina grass. This is only the second time in my life that I have seen wild diamondback terrapins. The Carolina race is even found on the island of Bermuda far off at sea where the Gulf Stream warms what would otherwise be waters too cold for the bonefish that can be found there in summer. To my knowledge, no one knows for sure how they got out there—natural migration or human intervention.

As we puttered down the ever-narrowing tidal creek, I took notice of the boat we were traveling in—Greg's father's boat. It was a circa 1980 Kenner Pro Skiff, which was the same year I joined the Marines. It had a seventeen-foot tunnel hull designed to run in shallow water and powered by a Yamaha seventy-horsepower four-stroke engine that moved us briskly from place to place as we crossed more open water at speed. There was something special about being in Greg's father's skiff.

His dad, like mine, passed away some time ago. He, like me, still thought of him every day. Sometimes I talk to my dad. His phone number is still on my phone. I will never disconnect it. I can't bear to look at his photos. The flag that draped his coffin along with each empty shell casing from his military rifle salute at his burial are in a box in my writing den—but I still can't look at them. It's just too painful. His last remaining sibling died a few weeks ago and before he passed I told him, "Uncle Tony . . . I chose to walk in Mystic Canyon instead of going to dad's burial not because I didn't care, but rather because I cared so deeply. It was the last place Dad and I walked together, and he always told me to remember him through our mutual love of nature." I was thinking of my dad when I turned to Greg and told him, "This is perfect, my friend. I'm so pleased and honored to be here with you in your father's boat on the same waters you shared with him and your son." I guess we pass on more than our genes to the next generation. We pass on our passions and our soul's greatest yearnings.

I asked Greg what the boat meant to him and after a brief pause he shared, "It is not the ideal platform for how I fish, but I get great satisfaction from fishing with it. My father purchased the boat in 1994 to encourage family time together. My brother Dave, my son Elliott, and I spent countless hours with my dad fishing and shrimping on this boat. I have been meaning to restore the inside of the boat ... but I probably never will. Each blemish and imperfection has a memory or funny story associated with it. They always make me think of my dad. He passed away many years ago, but I feel him every time I step onto the boat. Elliott was very close to his grandfather. Sometimes when we fish on the Kenner, I see him touch one of the imperfections and quietly smile." I smiled too.

Greg cut the engine and started up the trolling motor as the water became skinny, narrow, clear, and crisscrossed with oyster bars. The eagle had been joined by another. I thought of my dad as they both flew off into the distance over a grove of southern pine trees. I began to see places along the embankment where piles of old bricks lay just beneath the moss-covered oaks. And there were many more bricks under the water including in some deep oxbows that Greg told me to cast into because they often held small- to medium-sized redfish. I was surprised not to get any tugs in those nice deep pools or around the rock piles, and as we rounded yet another bend Greg said, "This is the place where I got a slam of redfish, trout, and flounder not long ago." I cast into the mouth of an outflow and felt the light pulling of something, set the hook, and soon landed another speckled trout, this one quite small but pretty nonetheless. We moved on.

All along the tidal creek were the signs of engineering and ingenuity, both human and nonhuman. Piles of broken oysters along the banks showed the ingenuity of otters who pried them loose and ate them one after another in a place chosen for its comfort and relative safety. And the bricks that were piled on the shoreline and under the surface of the creek were a testament to the engineering of early colonial settlers after the Great Charleston Fire of 1740. After that destructive fire the building codes were changed to encourage bricks instead of lumber, and the riverside kilns of Beresford Hall went into overdrive to meet that demand. Every landscape on Earth is a historical landscape—touched by human choices. Even the icefields of Antarctica are melting because of the efficiency of the oil fields of Texas, coal mines of West Virginia, clear cuts of Brazil, and thawing permafrost in Siberia. In nature, what happens to one, eventually impacts all.

━━━

We both managed to catch and release a few more speckled trout before the tide went slack—just in time for us to dock the boat and consider the important question of lunch. Greg asked, "Do you like barbeque?" I answered, "I'm from Texas." Down the road we went.

The Swig and Swine barbeque pit was located along a set of docks in a wide spot along a main river. The image on the front of the building was of a silhouette of a pig, with the words, "Swig & Swine, Horrifying Vegetarians Since 2013." We sat down and were immediately greeted by a smiling and friendly server without a name tag who instantly got the name, "Big Gert" in my head and even after I asked her what her real name was—that stuck. I ordered a local red ale and Greg got a local dark porter that made me a bit envious, even if the ale was magnificent. The music was blues, the atmosphere authentically Low Country open and inviting, and the barbeque was so good that I'm getting hungry just writing about it.

Greg was sharing about his past life in the software business, and I was almost reluctantly sharing about my many past lives in the military, policing, and Homeland Security worlds. I'm proud of the good I did, serving my country and community, but I'm also happy to have left that life behind me—I'd rather talk about trout than terrorists. Not wanting to taint a good fishing trip with bad memories I asked more questions about my friend's professional life path, and that's when he told me the story that had me laughing so hard that I was afraid Big Gert might try to resuscitate me!

He asked me if I had ever golfed and I said that as close as I've been to golfing was being chased off a golf course as a kid where I routinely trespassed in an attempt to fish for bass in the ponds. Greg admitted that it wasn't his game either, but that having been part of the business world, first as a computer software developer and then as a business owner, he felt the need to try. As the story goes, one day he took a group of high-powered clients golfing. It was his turn to tee up and when he smacked the ball he ended up executing a "worm burner" that skidded across the grass at high speed and impacted one of the many geese that had congregated by a nearby water hazard. Well, the goose squawked, flapped, and fluttered in circles for an inordinate amount of time while everyone watched in shocked silence. Although I did feel a bit sorry for the goose, the vision of Greg and his stunned audience caused me to laugh so hard that I almost choked on a hushpuppy. After a moment of silence and a sip of my beer I looked at Greg and asked, "Well . . . did you ask for a Mulligan?"

After lunch we relaxed at the house while waiting for the outgoing tide to begin. Like so much of saltwater fishing, tides are crucial. Incoming tides give fish access to new feeding areas, and outgoing tides draw prey animals out toward waiting fish. To catch a gamefish, we must think like a predator and act like a forage fish. We were determined to connect with redfish since we'd had so much good fortune catching speckled trout both days and we had cast toward a good number of reds, but thus far, without result.

When the tide was turning and water started moving again we loaded up the skiff and headed out toward a distant shoreline across one of the main rivers of the area—the Wando. A local saying is that the confluence of the Wando and Copper River is the place where the Atlantic Ocean is born. This is hyperbole of course, but the Wando is interesting in that it is a tidewater river with no true inflow source other than tidal waters from the sea.

The river was wide and choppy where we crossed, and I held on tightly to the bowline as we bounced along from one shoreline to the other. As we crossed the river my mind wandered back to memories of my father and how much he loved to ride the waves of a rough or rolling sea. Waters that I once found frightening only caused him to laugh hysterically as the salt-laden spray rushed over the bow, soaking us from head to foot. Now as I thought of the man we all called "The Captain," I quietly whispered, "I love you, Dad . . . and I miss you." I still do.

We began working some more promising outflows and cord grass–lined tidal creeks and in the process we both caught a few more nice trout, but no redfish. We were blind casting to likely spots, but as likely as they seemed the results were the same. One of the challenges we faced was the ever-changing weather and the cold front that had moved in and hung around longer than expected. But the other challenge that we discussed was that it was "peeler crab" season and we suspected the redfish had been gorging on crabs. I guess when you can't explain why they're not biting, you search for any plausible reason. We were pondering this deep question about the time we saw a massive bank of blackened sky moving toward us along with a few flashes of lightning, a quickening of the wind, and something that looked a lot like a funnel cloud forming not too far away. Back across the bouncy water we went as quickly as we could in hope of finding a way to keep fishing but stay out of the path of that storm. We did.

Of all the tidal creeks we fished, the most scenically beautiful were the ones I named Old Kiln Creek and Angler Creek. The plentitude of bald eagles, osprey, and herons at Angler Creek indicated that it was the kind of place that attracts anglers, of all kinds. And there were redfish. In fact, there were a lot of redfish. There were redfish along the shallow spartina covered shorelines, and around the many jagged oyster beds, and in the deeper pools near docks that were the terminus of boardwalks which no doubt cost a fortune to construct, and that crossed salt marshes that were priceless. The hunt was on for the eagles, osprey, herons, Greg, and me—anglers one and all.

The redfish were in water that was often no deeper than knee-high and even more often about mid-calf level if you could stand in the creek without sinking into the mud—which was most likely impossible. Sometimes we'd see their backs out of the water or even a tipped-up tail which indicated that they were feeding on something and negated our peeler crab excuse. We began casting toward moving fish, me with that heavenly fly rod and he with the magnificent spinning rig that seemed like it could cast a mile. But for all our divine gear and determined effort we could not elicit a strike and there were no trout around to bail us out. We worked it hard from oyster bed to freshwater inflow and we cast to so many nice-sized redfish that I never even bothered to count, but "tide and time wait for no man" and the water was getting increasingly shallow and the oyster bars and muddy bottoms were getting steadily closer to the hull of Greg's dad's boat. So we reeled in and headed for home, just as the sky opened up and the rain came down in sheets of oversized drops that drenched my raingear and refreshed my soul. Did I mention that I absolutely love fishing in the rain? As we traveled at top speed through the downpour I pulled my hood as far over my cap's bill as possible and turned my head so that I could watch the shoreline slip behind us and the river sparkle in a dance of light and shadow. It was a sight I will never forget.

On our final morning together, Greg had arranged for us to spend some time with a guide friend of his named Peter Brown. We fished a new area behind the barrier islands of Capers and Dewees. This was Peter's stomping grounds and Greg wanted me to see them as well as hear Peter's point of view of the various ecological challenges this magnificent area and its wildlife are facing.

More than anything, Peter spoke of the issues of poaching, overfishing, and the threats that practices like virtually unregulated "deep hole shrimping" may be causing to the fishery and the estuaries as a whole. These concerns were accompanied by the usual suspects of reduced freshwater inflow quality and quantity, climate change, and pollution from sources like agriculture, aquaculture, and urbiculture—in other words, stormwater runoff. As he and Greg spoke of these diverse threats to the South Carolina Low Country and its wildlife, I was casting for redfish, catching nothing, and marveling at how beautiful the wetlands that surrounded me truly were. I watched as bonnethead sharks thrashed in circles, chasing down their prey. Terns, gulls, and cormorants angled beside me, no doubt more successful in their quest than I. A sea turtle drifted past the boat; its massive shell damaged by prop scars—yet it swam on anyway, reminding me that no matter the wound, healing is possible.

Still, I couldn't help but wonder how magnificent these waters once were, even as I envisioned how magical they could be—once more. What if we choose to turn the tide and act to restore, revive, and revere these national treasures—our coastal estuaries and shorelines? I'd love to live long enough to see that day, but even if I don't, I want to see it in my mind's eye.

The wind picked up and made fly-casting more than merely challenging. Peter asked, "Would you consider trying a spinning rig? Sometimes they just don't want to eat feathers and I know a place where I feel you'll get a good shot at a redfish with a spinning rig." I thought of the gear that Greg had been using during the previous two days with its simple rubber lure and single barbless hook. "Sure," I said. "If you think it will help."

We skidded across the water until we came to a small cove that was somewhat protected by the wind while simultaneously affected by the way the wind pushed forage fish around the point and toward the shoreline. That's when I saw Peter reach down and grab a mud minnow from a baitwell that I hadn't noticed. He quickly pulled out a spinning rig with a massive bobber attached and ran a circular hook through the minnow's lower and upper jaw. Then he lifted the rod and swung the whole contraption of bobber, hook, and hapless minnow into the water while instructing me to cast it toward shore.

I was stunned. It was too late for the minnow, and I watched it struggling against the hook as I cast it out in a high arch, as instructed. He said, "When the bobber goes down, just reel it in." "I didn't know you intended to use live bait!" I replied. Just then the bobber submerged, I reeled the line in and found a small redfish attached. I unhooked it and set it free. There was no sense of effort or skill on my part, only mechanical compliance. I knew Peter was trying to be a good host and I appreciated the effort, but I felt no joy in catching that fish. Please, allow me to explain.

As a hunter and angler, I have killed wildlife and eaten its meat. This is part of being a participant in nature; it is akin to harvesting fruit from trees, berries from vines, and vegetables from a garden. Something dies, so something can live. That's nature. That's natural.

As a U.S. Marine, Peace Officer, and Homeland Security professional I have witnessed a lot of violent death and human suffering. I have seen cruelty and have experienced it firsthand. I simply cannot cause suffering for any living thing—for my entertainment.

Yes, I clearly understand the hypocrisy I may be guilty of as I gleefully hook and then release fish as recreation. And no, I am not suggesting that anyone else feel as I felt. It's just that when I read Ernest Hemingway's Nick Adams story of Nick going fishing after coming back from the war, and how he used a salamander for bait and was haunted by what he had done . . . that's how I felt about the mud minnow. You might think I was being silly, but I felt guilty.

When we got back to the docks, I thanked Peter for his kindness and for sharing his knowledge of these waters. Greg asked me, "What would you like to do after lunch?" I said, "I want to go out in your dad's boat one last time and cast a fly line for redfish." We did. We caught nothing. And I loved every silent, thoughtful, redeeming moment of it. It felt right to end my time here in this beautiful waterscape, fishing with my friend Greg, and the memories of our fathers. You might think I was being sentimental but . . . I felt grateful.

Somehow, I managed to come full circle. I was no longer the impatient nineteen-year-old Marine recruit with something to prove—looking to be tough. I was now the man of six decades of living and learning that heroes don't need medals, and courage doesn't need a battle. Now I knew what I then suspected. True heroism and courage are expressed in every act of kindness and every feeling of empathy, and every effort toward seeking greater understanding so that we might act—not react, with agency and wisdom. Just as I did as a wide-eyed child, I choose to be the ocean . . . not the fish.

Part II
The Pacific Ocean

BobWhite

CHAPTER SEVEN

At Sea in Search of Pacific Salmon

Tongass National Forest, Southeast Alaska

*Humans aren't as good as we should be in our capacity to empathize
with feelings and thoughts of others, be they humans or other animals
on Earth. So maybe part of our formal education should be training
in empathy. Imagine how different the world would be if, in fact, that
were "reading, writing, arithmetic, empathy."*

~ NEIL DEGRASSE TYSON

THE TONGASS RISES UP FROM THE SEA IN THE FORM OF MONOCHROME
mountains, towering trees, and tumbling tributaries that briefly become
rivers of hope. Cold, clean, life-giving water rolls over multicolored
stones, each one slick with biota and thick with the memories of millions
of salmon over millions of years. And the salmon, pushing ever forward
against the falling water as their ancestors did . . . away from the ocean
that gave them strength, toward the place of their birth, and their death.
They will end their days giving their last full measure for the survival of
their kind. And in the end, they will drift lifeless against the same wet
stones that sheltered them as young fry.

Here, in the largest contiguous temperate rainforest on Earth, the rain falls in almost constant dribs and drabs, and the occasional downpour. It falls onto the branches of spruce, hemlock, and alder, and over the devil's club, ferns, and fungi. It falls deep into the mosses, the leaf litter, and the ever-moist soil. And it travels along the bedrock to form the tributaries, streams, and rivers that eventually, inevitably, inextricably, join the sea. Gravity is the one great truth I know; it exists no matter if we believe in it or not. But as I looked out across the mist-covered fjord, I realized that even gravity gets defied by water.

If you envision the rivers as the water that creates them, then like life itself, they have no beginning or end. H_2O becomes the DNA of the Earth. Without it, we are a lifeless rock, rotating in the sunbaked void. But the rivers are so much more than their water. Rivers are geology in motion, watersheds and weathermakers—the truest bloodstreams of this planet. It is water and sunlight that animate this living, breathing planet . . . this beautiful blue orb that we all call Home. Whenever they meet the sun's energetic light—tributaries, rivers, estuaries, bays, and oceans are the planet's original sources of life. Our earliest ancestors were microbes. Even if it seems impossible to see any family resemblance, it is there, nonetheless.

The Tongass forms a large portion of the lungs of the Earth. These forests and waters are temperate twins of those of the Amazon. Here, bald eagles adorn the trees and orcas decorate the sea. It breathes out oxygen and inhales carbon dioxide. It absorbs our poisons and gives us clean air. It turns the sun's energy into fuel for a myriad of living beings, including us. It shelters black-tailed deer, black and brown bears, moose, and salmon. And at this moment, as we boarded the *Narwhal* and powered up its motors, the Tongass took my breath away, while giving me reason to breathe. I felt so fortunate just to be alive in this moment, in this magnificent place.

The *Narwhal* is the sleek, silver vessel of one of my newest friends, Captain Alan Corbet. We were introduced by one of my other newest friends, Mark Hieronymus, who serves as the Community Science Coordinator for Trout Unlimited's Alaska Program. It was my first morning in Alaska, and together we were beginning the first leg of an epic journey, following Pacific salmon and their kin, from the sea, up-river, and into the tiniest tributaries that act as rearing waters for what can arguably be called North America's greatest fish.

The Tongass National Forest has been referred to as "America's Salmon Forest," because it supports all five species of Pacific Salmon plus steelhead, Dolly Varden char, coastal cutthroat, and anadromous rainbow trout. Sockeye, chum, pink, chinook, and coho salmon depend upon this land and seascape, from the high mountain tributaries with depths measured in inches, to the deep, dark, ocean, with depths of several thousand feet. Over the next few days, I was destined to discover how much these fish cannot live without these forests, and how unlikely these forests are to survive without these fish.

If I were to describe Southeast Alaska in three words, they would be Wet, Wild, and Wounded. The first two words became apparent as the *Narwhal*'s powerful engines pushed twin wakes of silver-gray sea behind us, thus causing the snowcapped and mist-covered mountains to drift slowly out of sight. I sat just barely inside the cabin, stretching my sight as far across the water as I could see . . . out toward the mountains that had wispy gray-white clouds wrapped around them, like condensed seawater scarves. And I looked out across the slate-blue-black waters, hoping for a glimpse of a whale or dolphin. I did my best to embed the power of the moment into my memories, and as always, I wished I could pass these images on to another, when my time comes, to cross the river. In a way, I guess that is what I am trying to do now.

Alan and Mark sat up in the front of the cabin, speaking in a language that only longtime friends and residents can comprehend. They spoke of places where the fishing had been good and places where it was nonexistent. They spoke of people that they knew and times that they had shared on the water and in the forest. And although they were both speaking English, it might as well have been Tlingit. Because these were the places they called home, where I had never been. And those were the faces that they called friends, whom I had never met. But it gave me great comfort, listening to these good friends as they spoke and laughed over the roar of the engines. It was like the sound of the ocean when seas are calm and the tide is high. It was the sound of friendship, understanding, and a shared love of this place. It was reassuring and I smiled.

Alan is a tall, fit Irishman with an easy smile, kind heart, and a mischievous twinkle in his eye. He has a great sense of humor and a strong sense of humility. He also knows these waters as well as anyone, and was supremely generous with that knowledge on my behalf. I am forever grateful.

The *Narwhal* is a custom-made craft that felt like it was made for these waters, and it was. We cut through the black-glass sea along the inland passage, surrounded by steep snow- and mist-covered mountains, where the dark forest tumbled down each slope like a green avalanche, all the way to the water's edge.

The electronics of the craft displayed clear images of the contours of what laid and lived below us. The bottom of the marine passage reflected what is above it, with steep-sided sea mounts and canyons that plunge below the surface in hundreds or even thousands of feet. The ocean has its own magnificent topography and being able to see below it and better understand the lives and lifestyles of its inhabitants are what Mark refers to as "Piercing the Mirror."

And that was what I was here to do . . . "pierce the mirror" and look into the lives of salmon and the other Pacific anadromous fish. I didn't just want to catch and release these fish; I wanted them to capture my imagination, heart, and soul, and not let go. I wanted to enter their world at least slightly and come to realize more intimately what it means when we are connected to each other from two ends of a fishing line, or by the circles and cycles of life on Earth. I wanted to follow them from the sea to their natal rivers and up into the tributaries where most anglers never venture. And I did.

This kind of fishing relies on a good bit of technology, and even more human ingenuity and innate intelligence. The technology included sonar that reaches down into the depths and bounces back an image of the seascape, as well as schools of forage fish like menhaden, sardines, anchovies, or in this case, herring. Using this imagery, it is also possible to locate the salmon that are working the contours of the sea bottom as any predator would on land. The salmon make choices, based on currents, seascapes, and other conditions so that they can find and successfully feed on the herring.

Alan uses both the technology aboard the *Narwhal* and his vast knowledge of how to read the conditions of air, land, and sea to locate the salmon, and with the use of downriggers, he gets the lures down to where the fish are feeding. It is both science and art for both the fish and the fisher. After all, the natural senses of both fish and fisherman are their own biological technology.

I asked Alan about the way he was rigging the lines as it seemed elaborate and indicated an in-depth understanding of salmon behavior at sea. He hand-ties his own flies which are attached at the end of a line that includes a paddle-like "flasher" several feet ahead of the fly. The flasher is intended to imitate a salmon as it is rolling and hitting a school of baitfish. As the flasher gets pulled through the water it rotates in a four-foot circle and gives motion to the fly. A salmon at sea generally doesn't target an individual fish when it feeds. Instead, it swims through a school of prey fish, striking them with its tail and then doubling back to collect the wounded fish. The fly is imitating a stunned herring falling behind the "salmon." In addition, Alan puts a little piece of herring on the fly to generate "scent." Ingenious and effective!

There are only degrees of difference between a dry fly presented to the surface of a stream with a delicate cast to a six-inch brook trout, and a wet fly presented with indelicate downriggers to a six-pound coho. The bottom line is that we must understand the fish's world and behavior enough to present a suggestion of something natural and "bite worthy" at the end of the line. In essence, we are connecting to the fish by getting to know the fishes of its kind, and then we use that understanding to gather food . . . just as the salmon does with herring.

Perhaps to progress as beings all we need to do is see each fish not as a "thing" but as a living creature worthy of respect, no matter if we choose to release it or not. Perhaps the one separation we should seek as humans is having the sole ability to feel respect and empathy for our living food, both flora and fauna, and still be able to do what comes naturally, and eat it. I treat each fish I catch with a sense of individual value. But I am not being sentimental. In fact, on the day after I went salmon fishing with

Alan and Mark, I ate salmon tacos at "Deckhand Dave's" in Juneau, while drinking an Alaskan Amber and listening to blues music. It was heaven in a corn tortilla.

It wasn't long before the first downrigger popped and we had a fish on the line. I grabbed hold and began to reel in what turned out to be a nice, shiny coho. Alan worked the net and brought it on board and asked, "Do you want a photo?" I said, "No . . . let's just take care of the fish today and get them back in the water as quickly as we can." Both Mark and Alan seemed pleased with that answer, but it was nice of them to offer me the opportunity for a grip-and-grin photo. In general, I never take them. I gather memories instead.

We were trolling these flies down along the depths where the technology indicated the herring and salmon were mixing things up. In some areas we were pulling the fly at about sixty feet and in others the fish were feeding at only thirty feet or so. With an impressive bit of precision Alan drifted the flies along the edges of underwater canyons and around a seamount that caused the herring to gather and the salmon to follow. After that one coho I caught, Mark and I began reeling in a number of nice king salmon; each one was sleek, silvery, and fishy looking in their ocean-going bodies. We released them all quickly, and usually without even taking them out of the water.

This kind of fishing took great skill on the part of the boat's captain and virtually no skill on my part. And yet I still managed to screw it up a few times, popping the salmon off as I tried to pull them in when I should have let them run. I didn't seem to mind and we laughed when they ended up as long-distance releases and smiled as we released them carefully, quickly, and purposefully at boat side. It was turning out to be a perfect first day and just what I hoped for save one element . . . I really wanted to see a pod of orcas. Alan shared that while fishing with some clients the previous day he did come across some orca, but that seeing them was hit and miss and said it would most likely end up being one of those, "You should have been here yesterday!" stories. Still, I kept my eyes on the water searching for a dorsal fin or telltale spout of exhaled Alaskan air.

The fishing was good, but even if it hadn't been we were having a great day. We were trolling the salt-laden waters between Admiralty and

Douglas Islands. The people of the Tlingit First Nation refer to Admiralty Island as "Kootznoowoo," which means, "Fortress of Bears." And it is, because that one island is said to contain and support more brown bears than exist in the entire lower forty-eight states combined. Knowing this caused me to see the island with a sense of wonder, awe, and foreboding. Its mist and cloud-covered forest felt dark and primordial, even from the deck of the *Narwhal*.

I couldn't imagine walking through and fishing in a place with so many massive apex predators, but part of me desperately wanted to do so and come out the other end as something better than a pile of bear scat. I love that bears exist in the wild, and I have always felt privileged when I see them. But deep down inside my caveman DNA is a memory of trying to fight off a cave bear with a pointed stick and losing. When they look at me, I think they remember too. I think they remember, somewhere deep down in their cave-bear DNA how ineffectual my pointed stick was and how a naked ape like me might taste. I've got about as much faith in my can of bear spray as I would a sharpened stick . . . that is to say, almost none.

As the *Narwhal* rounded a corner of Douglas Island, I noticed an area along its steep-sided mountains where the constant dark blue-green of Sitka spruce was interrupted by a band of light-yellow green alders and a treeless slide of mud and stone above the alders. It was a scar upon an otherwise pristine landscape, and it showed no signs of healing. Years ago, a lumber company purchased "rights" to clear cut that stretch of precious temperate rainforest, turning spruce into boards and forests into mudslides and tributaries into trickles between the tangled alder branches. The raindrops that once fed the forest now pick at the scab in the Earth, and it is unlikely to heal any time soon.

Leaving the wounded mountainside behind us, Alan brought us to a seamount that rose to within sixty feet of the surface. It was a place he knew where the herring would gather and the salmon might follow. He set the downriggers and began to troll the edges of the submerged mountain, and a short time later the lines popped and I found myself reeling in another fish, this time it was not a salmon but rather a black cod which is normally a fish of the deep benthic zone of these salty waters, and I am told they are quite tasty! This one was undersized, so we returned him to the cold waters of the passage, and continued to troll around the seamount, and along the underwater canyons below.

The fishing continued while the catching slowed, and Alan kept busy as he reeled in one line after another, changing out the rigging now and then on a hunch or a hope that this new fly or flasher might be just the ticket to lure in yet another king or coho. And in time, it did. And that was nice, but not necessary. We had already caught and released enough salmon to satisfy my itch, and I was just as happy to simply sit on the deck of the *Narwhal*, taking in the magnificence of the Tongass.

Toward our bow was the seawater cut between Douglas and Admiralty Islands. If we turned starboard just beyond that cut, we'd follow Stephens Passage to the southeast. If we turned port, we'd enter the Taku Inlet which leads to the Taku River, Tahlequah River Watershed, and Taku Glacier. With the rapid and ever-increasing advance of climate change and global warming, all of the glaciers in the Juneau Icefield are melting and retreating except the Taku. The Taku Glacier is the deepest, thickest, alpine and tidewater glacier in the world. At about thirty-six miles long and 4,845 feet deep, it continues to advance . . . so far.

This is the land and water of the Taku Tribe of Tlingit people, also known as the Taku River Tlingit First Nation. Salmon, the Tongass, and pure, cold, running water have been integral parts of their noble heritage through the ages, and there is much we can learn from the Native American understanding of our human relationship to the Earth, water, and sky. European Americans traditionally envisioned Homo sapiens at the pinnacle of a hierarchy with other living creatures, but the Tlingit and many other native peoples never forgot that we are simply another part of Nature, not apart from Nature. In ignorance there is fear; in understanding there is balance.

The Tlingit are indigenous peoples of North America's Pacific Northwest. It seems fitting that they have self-identified as "People of the Tides" because with the exception of the few inland bands, they are a tidewater people. And even those Tlingit who reside in Canada's Yukon or British Columbia do so along the rivers that like the salmon, eventually, inevitably, become one with the sea. The salmon is an integral part of the Tlingit diet, culture, and spirituality.

Traditionally the Tlingit were animists with a belief that all things of the Earth, living and non-living, contain a spiritual essence or living soul. And since I see spirituality in everything from songbirds to streams . . . I guess I'm an animist too. For me, the Earth is a living being that we humans are killing with ever-increasing rapidity. We are committing matricide of sorts, although Nature may be ambivalent to our existence, we cannot be ambivalent to that which sustains us. I can almost feel the Earth crying.

Alan had an afternoon charter with some people who wanted to fish for halibut, so our time was running short. He reeled in the rods and prepared the *Narwhal* for our journey back to the docks in Juneau. I sat on the deck absorbing every living moment. A loon performed its fluttering display just off our port while a small flock of pigeon guillemots and common murres crisscrossed the bay from every angle. Just beyond the murres a lone pair of marbled murrelets flew with rapid wingbeats and a palpable sense of purpose.

Although common murres are currently abundant, they have taken a beating in the past due to their susceptibility to oil spills. As I watched them skid across the sea I imagined these same seemingly fragile birds as they boldly dove up to five hundred feet below the ocean's surface in search of sand eels, anchovies, and herring. They nest in massive colonies on rocky cliffs that rim the sea, each stone whitewashed with the memories of their ancestors. But it is the tiny murrelets that exhibit the most surprising habits as they fly well inland from their saltwater homes to nest high in the branches of a deep-woods conifer. The Tongass is full of miracles.

The low-slung Alaskan sky had darkened as we came into port, and the rain fell in more or less steady rhythm upon the water, the *Narwhal*, and us. And I loved every moment of it. I loved the feel of it and how no one here seems to ever make the slightest effort to "get out of the rain." As Mark pointed out before I arrived, "It's a rainforest. Expect rain."

There were bald eagles on many of the trees and light poles along the docks. I came to notice how so many resident Alaskans have grown so used to them as to pay them no mind at all. I've heard them say, "If you want to attract eagles, just open a dumpster." But I think that is more of a reflection upon us than them. We are the ones who inserted dumpsters into the mix. Had we not, the eagles would be content with the carcasses of post-spawning salmon.

I still feel that same way I did when I saw my first bald eagle launch from a Colorado treetop, when I caught my breath in midair and held it, as if the great bird had carried it away beneath its wings. I don't ever want to reach a point in life where eagles no longer catch my breath and carry it with them.

The older I get, the younger my soul yearns to remain. And this is how I feel, whenever I watch an eagle take flight. It's how I feel watching the mist and clouds embracing the mountains. And it is how I felt holding my first silvery coho salmon, and watching him swim away, back toward his destiny.

—◆—

I felt a twinge of sorrow as I said goodbye to Alan. He has that easy smile and good nature of an Irishman and contains layer upon layer of intelligence and depth that told me we would become true friends. I felt fortunate. Alan, Mark, and I all have life stories that include walking away from outside expectations and capitalistic values . . . and walking toward a more meaningful and joyful life.

Alan grew up in Ireland, on a small sheep farm. His "mum" was a lawyer, and he followed in her footsteps. After completing his law degree and while in the process of taking the necessary exams to qualify as a solicitor, he worked in a law firm as an assistant to one of the partners. By his own account, the money was good, and his career path was stellar, but spending his life sitting behind a desk practicing law just wasn't his cup of tea. So, he quit his job, sold everything, and moved to Malaysia to become a diving instructor. After investing a couple of years in Southeast Asia, he met and married his current wife and moved to her home state of Alaska, where he became a boat captain, running both whale-watching operations and fishing charters. He's never looked back. We have much in common.

Mark grew up in the Pacific Northwest, and first came to Alaska in 1988 as a seasonal worker, participating in many of Alaska's commercial fisheries including salmon, shrimp, halibut, and blackcod. Even after a few stormy winters spent covered in fish guts and rarely standing on land, he knew that Alaska would figure heavily in his future plans. In time, he learned the business from the deck of a boat to the boardrooms of potential customers, and in 1993, he and three partners created Northern Keta Caviar, Inc. in Juneau, Alaska, a seafood processor focused on preparing salted salmon roe, a business that was wildly successful in earning profits and less so in developing peace of mind and heart. And this eventually led to him selling his part of the business, earning a degree in Fisheries Science and Aquaculture, and joining the team of Trout Unlimited, where his lifestyle was far less lucrative, but much more joyful. There is a pattern here.

With Alan and the *Narwhal* heading back out to sea, Mark and I drove to a rain-soaked parking lot next to a food truck that was adorned with the image of a sweet, pony-tailed girl leaning over to kiss an unsuspecting curly-tailed pig on the lips. Behind her back she held a butcher knife. Pork does make an appearance on the menu of "Pucker Wilson's" food truck, but Mark and I opted for the all-beef "Husky Dawson Burger" which dripped in juicy goodness and crunched with the flavor of crispy fried onion rings. It was decadent extravagance, and we ate it in the front seat of Mark's truck as the rain fell and some of the best bluegrass music I've ever heard played from his speakers.

Among his many surprises, Mark is a bluegrass musician who seems to experience both music and nature with a poet's soul. He plays guitar, banjo, mandolin, and "never quite learned the fiddle because it made my dog howl when I played." I think if there is anything that makes humanity the least bit noble, it is our occasional ability to create art and feel empathy. Both seem to be evermore rarified, and it is as tragically sorrowful as the dwindling steelhead runs, the melting of glaciers, the dying of forests, and the seemingly ever-expanding chasms between people. Why can't we all just sing along, naturally?

I must admit that I was ravenous after a morning of fishing at sea, and no refined meal ever tasted better than that hand-pressed food-truck burger, and no music ever felt as joyful as those hard-won Appalachian melodies of resilience and redemption. As we listened, Mark said,

"Bluegrass has the drive of rock and the authenticity of classic country music. It is a music of the folks, by the folks, and for the folks." I had to agree. The trick of course is, how do we keep the folks resilient, and how do we find redemption in an unforgiving world?

The rain continued to fall upon the roof of the truck, the pavement, the surrounding forests, the lapping sea, and "Pucker Wilson's." The music continued to play over the sound of the falling rain and the aroma of melted cheese. And I continued to relive the feeling of being on the *Narwhal*, reeling in king salmon and setting them free. I will never forget this morning, and now, I am forever connected to these noble fish . . . just like the eagles, bears, and Tlingit. After all, we are all of the same Earthly Tribe. We are One.

Chapter Eight

Upriver in Search of Pacific Salmon, Char, and Coastal Cutthroat Trout

Tongass National Forest, Southeast Alaska

Cease being intimidated by the argument that a right action is impossible because it does not yield maximum profits, or that a wrong action is to be condoned because it pays.
        ~ Aldo Leopold, *A Sand County Almanac*

With our day at sea behind us we were ready to follow the salmon upriver. It was a new day in Southeast Alaska, where the sun never rose as much as its light shone through the weeping gray skies. Water fell out of the luminescent heavens, and onto the brim of my oilskin hat, and off the brim; just in front of my sleep-filled eyes, and then onto the Earth, seeping deep into the soil and along the bedrock where it eventually formed a river, an estuary, an ocean, and ultimately another raincloud. I guess we were following the life cycle of water as much as we were that of salmon. It just came naturally. After all, so much of what makes up the sea also makes up me.

The coffee tasted luxurious as we drove through the Tongass along the Glacier Highway toward our destination of Cowee Creek. The "creek" is more of a river which tumbles out of the Tongass and into the salty waters of Berners Bay, spawning habitat for pink and coho salmon, as well as the char and coastal cutthroat trout that follow them. Toward the sea the bears tend to be big, brown, and formidable, and farther inland they mix with black bears that probably look over their shoulders as often as we do, because brown bears sometimes kill black bears. But anywhere you look here you must remember: this is bear country. Mark armed me with a bright red can of bear spray, but I must admit, I'd have more faith in my twelve-gauge Benelli slung jauntily over my shoulder. Still, even without my trusty blunderbuss I had faith in Mark; after all, he has guided, fished, and hunted in these coastal mountains for decades. I am just a "cheechako," a newcomer. I put my faith in one who knows.

He chose the second week of August for our little expedition because he said, "The bears are full of salmon and berries by then, and so, they are less grumpy." I was fine with avoiding grumpy bears even as the adventurer in me wanted to encounter one, from a safe distance. Flashbacks of past-life cave bears still haunt me and in my dreams I feel their hot breath on my caveman neck and hear the sickening sound of my vertebrae cracking. I am fully alert and alive in bear country. It feels primal.

The day I arrived in Juneau was the first day I had ever seen a wild salmon. Mark picked me up and we drove together up the Mendenhall Valley toward the glacier and Steep Creek. We kept a wary eye out for the many black bears that come to Steep Creek to feed on the salmon that arrive here each year to spawn. The salmon are drawn here, and so are the bears, eagles, and Tlingit. Everything in the Tongass connects to salmon. Even the trees are fed by the nutrients of their spawned-out carcasses. The circle of life always passes through death on its way toward rebirth. It is the way of things.

We walked along the creek on that first day, and before long I saw the thrashing, swirling, churning goings-on of the sockeye salmon spawning. Red-sided, green-headed, and hook-jawed with needle sharp teeth displayed in crocodile fashion, they seemed more frightening than handsome. But then again, I'm not a female sockeye salmon, and maybe they just go for that sort of horror-show look.

Not long ago, these same fish were sleek and silver-sided ocean predators that became the fear of every anchovy and the food of a few fortunate orcas, seals, and sea lions. These sockeyes spawning beneath the willows had traveled from the Gulf of Alaska, through the Icy Strait, into Auke Bay, up the Mendenhall River and into the lake almost to the Mendenhall Glacier itself, before returning to spawn and die in their slender ribbon of natal water that we call Steep Creek. Within sight of the salmon were the sadly retreating Mendenhall Glacier and the thundering waters of Nugget Falls. The falls that once spilled into a sea of glacier ice now mingle directly with the open waters of the lake. And for now, the sockeye salmon return and renew their lease on life in a final effort for the continued existence of their species.

All life on Earth is reflected in their journey. As far as nature is concerned, we all exist so that we might move our species forward in time. Reproduction is our only natural form of self-actualization. The rest is an anthropic invention.

We didn't see any bears along the first section of Steep Creek, but farther down along the roadside we came across three black bears that meandered across the little stream and into the blueberry-choked underbrush. One bear began to climb a tree for reasons that remained a mystery to me, but he thought better of it halfway up and decided to join the others in the tangled greenery below. It was nice to see the bears and they seemed to pay us no mind, but I knew that these were more like "town bears" that had become habituated to humans. They were not the potentially aggressive bruins we might encounter while fishing deeper into the Tongass.

Just beyond the creek we entered a muskeg, and we were careful to keep on its narrow "board walk" that consisted of single planks laying end to end. This is delicate habitat full of carnivorous sundew plants and primordial-looking ferns, fungi, and skunk cabbage. Everywhere we looked there were berries of every kind: wild blueberries, crowberries, and salmonberries. I gathered them in my hands and ate them as we walked and their sweetness reminded me that their store-bought doppelgängers are nothing more than artificial and tasteless imposters. With water, salmon, and berries all around us, this was a black bear's heaven.

That same day we made a stop at Montana Creek searching for char that might be following behind the pink salmon which appeared to be spawning in the gravel of every likely bit of river bottom. Mark made a few prospecting casts into the creek but only caught a small sea run rainbow trout. He seemed surprised that there were no Dolly Varden and I was a little disappointed because it was a beautiful piece of water and I would have liked to fish it for a few hours rather than a few minutes. But that was on our first day together, and now on our third day, it was finally time for us to follow these fish up-river.

I was like a six-year-old boy on his first real camping trip, but this was much grander than catching bluegill in a pond. This was true adventure complete with dripping rainforest, raging rivers, and potentially life-threatening bears. I couldn't wait another moment. I just wanted to arrive and cast my line toward a wild fish, at last. It's not even that I came all this way to catch these fish, but rather, I came all this way to have these fish capture me.

———

When we reached Cowee Creek the rain had slowed to a mist, and this gave us time to set up our five weights, pull on our waders, and set off down the trail, which was more of a bear trail than a human trail. I can attest that bears do in fact shit in the woods because bear scat was everywhere along with the disemboweled carcasses of pink and coho salmon. We walked downstream through the tangle of devil's club, salmonberries, ferns, and moss-encrusted deadfall. Spruce and hemlock trees formed the overstory, everything else that was green and wet formed the understory, and we formed a waterlogged line with about twenty feet of muddy pathway between us. Mark whistled as we walked. He said that he found whistling easier on his throat than trying to talk to the bears all day. Sometimes in the thickest stuff, I'd sing. I'm not a very good whistler.

Mark started down a steep, muddy, embankment, his long legs easily clearing the deadfall and stepping across a back eddy into the river. I followed but managed to lose my footing and tumbled face-first into the swirling swill and immediately felt the fresh cold water of Cowee Creek as it plunged into my waders and dripped off the rim of my oilskin hat. Mark looked back through the brush and said, "Are you alright?" Draining the stream water from the sleeve of my rain jacket, I smiled the smile of an embarrassed clodhopper and said, "I just wanted to experience the river up close." It was an icy baptism of sorts, and the only thing to do was stand up, shake it off, and get back into the river . . . just like we must all do, every time we fall.

The "fly" of choice here is not really a fly, but rather a pinkish bead that is intended to imitate the eggs of the spawning pink salmon in the river. The bead is positioned about an inch above a smallish hook and a foot or two above a strike indicator that looks suspiciously like a tiny bobber, but being fly fishermen, we don't use bobbers, we use "strike indicators." I'm not sure if I am supposed to keep my pinky finger extended when applying a strike indicator, but I rarely do.

Spawning pink salmon were everywhere, the hook-jawed males biting and fighting each other for the chance to spawn with any one of the larger hens who occupied every bit of water where the gravel substrate was of the proper size and texture. But while the salmon were obvious as they rolled and rollicked from bank to bank, the fish we were after were not. I don't think I ever saw a Dolly Varden char in the stream until I hooked it, but they were there, trailing just behind the spawning salmon and eating as many wayward eggs as they could manage. So, the goal of the angler is to drift that artificial salmon egg just behind the spawners, without snagging or otherwise attracting the attention of the salmon. Then, we'd watch the indicator as the egg-fly drifted along the stream bed, hopefully into the waiting fish lips of a Dolly Varden. That was the plan, but like all plans they can tend to fall apart once contact is made with your adversary. In this case, the angler must detect the take and set the hook in the micro-moment that exists before the char realizes it's a fake and spits it out. Easy peasy, right?

Cowee Creek does feel more like a river. It has wide, sweeping, spaces of numbingly cold water that forms plunge pools, back eddies, shallow riffles, and roaring rapids. I love the feel of wild water pushing and pulling upon my legs, and the sense of edginess I get as I try to wade across fast water on slick stones. In places, it felt like I could have walked across the backs of salmon and I did my best to avoid disturbing their deeply personal moment of continued life and inevitable death.

Looking at them I felt a mixture of awe and empathy. I felt a deep and poetic pathos as I watched their struggle, not to survive, but rather, for the survival of their species. I recognized that for all our imaginary constructs that seek to separate humanity from nature, their story, and our story, are the same story. We are inextricably connected, and the impact of our choices will reflect not only on the destiny of wild waters and wild fish, but also, the destiny of Homo sapiens as a minor species with outsized influence. Either by choice or by force, humanity will have to face the reversal of fortunes and Nature will take charge again. It is inevitable, like death. Everything dies; even the sun itself. It's all a matter of entropy.

Mark and I began drifting our flies along creases of current just past and behind the spawning salmon. It took no time at all for Mark to connect and bring up a beautiful char which he showed me, and quickly released. At first, I was missing the takes, the indicator would bob or simply stop moving for a moment, but I was too slow on the hookset. Mark caught a few more before I finally got the hang of it but with a little coaching from the expert, I managed to connect with my first Dolly Varden and she was beautiful.

Every time I catch a fish I feel grateful and every time I catch a new variety of fish for the first time, I feel an almost ecstatic sense of joy. I guess with both fish and lovers, we always remember the first and last. I will never forget her brightly colored skin, shining in the Alaskan sunlight, but I'm quite sure she has forgotten me. I hope so. It was nice to set her free. Love lets go.

I had begun to relax and fall into the rhythm of casting and catching, instead of falling into the river. But from time to time my imagination would take hold, and I'd see the ghostly image of a massive brown bear standing at the river's edge with a look of hunger and mayhem being projected from his blackened marble eyes. It was just my imagination, of course, but it didn't seem all that unlikely as I stepped over the freshly gutted carcasses of shoreside salmon. I noticed that with the exception of the sounds of the river, the forest was unbearably silent. No birds. None. Just the sound of silence and the questions it brings.

Once the fishing began to slow, Mark mentioned that he used to be able to reach an upstream gravel bar from this side of the river, and that the fishing was often good along that shoreline. Since the last time he was here a couple of spruce trees had fallen into the river, causing a deep pool to form, and blocking any safe crossing. We discussed the possibility of hiking back up to the road and finding our way down the other side to the gravel bar. While we discussed it Mark and I caught a few more char and he inadvertently caught a couple of hefty pink salmon. We were trying to avoid the spawners, but as I watched Mark release a couple of big humpbacked salmon the sinner in me quietly wished I could hold just one. I'm a conservationist, not a saint.

We made our way back up the river until we reached the road, and then Mark began the descent into what looked to me like an impenetrable wall of brambles and devil's club, but that he loosely referred to as a "trail." In between stalks of spiny devil's club, I noticed the rain-soaked scat of bears, so in that sense at least, this was a trail. When I was a boy imagining the adventures of grown-up me hacking my way through some exotic wilderness, I never envisioned that everything in the forest would stick me, sting me, stab me, or bite me, but that is the reality I've often found from Africa to Alaska. Nature does its best to defend itself.

When we arrived at the opposite side of the stream, I watched as Mark lowered himself down yet another steep and muddy embankment, over moss-covered and rotting logs, twisted, ever-slick roots, and then onto a deadfall log that crossed a deepish pool. He looked back and up at me and said, "Be careful on this log . . . it's slippery." I made it, but with none of the grace that my companion demonstrated. At least this time, I didn't fall in.

It was a beautiful, long, gravel bar with river rounded stones of blue, black, gray, and white and the fallen spruce trees and the deep pool were now on the opposite side of the river. There were humpies everywhere, sparring and spawning, reeling, and rolling. Their massive heads rose up out of the water and their battered bodies slid porpoise-like back into the depth. To my knowledge, no one has ever been able to say why they do that, with any sense of knowledgeable authority. I suspect they do it because they can, and that's reason enough. All I know is, just like seeing an eagle fly, I never want to lose my sense of awe and wonder at the sight of a salmon rolling. And I feel sorry for anyone who is immune to these miracles. We should all do our best to keep our eyes and imaginations childlike.

I was fully aware that Mark was consistently giving me the best water, even if he understandably caught many more fish than me. But I was getting into the swing of things and although I never keep count, if I had wanted to count the number of char we caught, I couldn't have done so with all my finger and toes. Mark accidentally caught another pink salmon, and the sinner in me reared his ugly head again. I knew that we were trying to avoid the spawning salmon but deep down inside, I confessed. "Bless me Great Spirit for I have sinned . . . I have lusted after a forbidden fish." I wanted to confess and tell the Earth that I would never do it again, but I learned a long time ago in Catholic school that it was a bigger sin to lie in the confessional than to simply admit to your humanity, without shame.

Once when my entire class was compelled to go to confession I found myself at an impasse when I couldn't think of anything to confess. I wasn't sure what to say, so I made up a few minor sins that I actually had not committed just so the priest wouldn't think I was lying about not sinning. Then when he asked if I knew how to say the Rosary, I was afraid to admit that I didn't and I lied about that too. Leaving the confessional, I knelt down next to another kid and began trying to figure out how to say my penance—I confessed to him what I had done. I was seriously worried about this compounding quagmire of deception. After all, I was a good kid, and that was the problem in the first place! When I told him what I had done, he laughed and said, "Just say a few 'Our Fathers' and a 'Hail Mary' and move on." I did. He was a wise little sinner.

Since then, I have given up confession, penitence, and guilt and I only kneel when I'm trying to send a stealthy cast into a small stream, pet a dog, or listen to a child's words, eye to eye. Instead, I just go fishing and do my best each day to be kind, grateful, and empathetic. It's worked out just fine so far. When you are good for goodness' sake, you don't have to memorize anything. You just live it.

This stretch of stream had a deep pool above and below us, and another on the opposite bank where the trees had fallen. The current picked up along the gravel bar and there we could see the salmon lined up, end to end and side by side, performing their last act. Mark and I took turns on the upstream and downstream stretches and although we were catching char in both places, I grew partial to the downstream spot where the currents converged and tumbled over a riffle into a pool. I managed to land a nice-sized char or two in that spot, and Mark did too. We fished it until we decided we had fished it completely, and then it came time to fight our way back up the embankment, through the tangled wet forest, and up through the brambles to the road. The walking was not fun, but the fishing surely was.

———

For a moment, we stood on the bridge overlooking the river, and I could see the salmon spawning below, sometimes so densely that it seemed as if there was no part of the river that didn't contain at least a few salmon. The river was alive with life, and death. Lifeless, spawned-out bodies drifted toward the sea. Still-living spawners writhed together, their flesh already falling off their misshapen bodies.

Beneath them, I knew fertilized eggs dropped into the gravel with the hope of another generation contained within. Some would be eaten by trout and char, and some would hatch into alevins, complete with yolk sacs that sustain them, for a while. Once the nutrients provided to them at birth had been absorbed, each tiny fry will leave the shelter of the gravel and rise up into the water column. Depending on the species, the fry will either find refuge in the back eddies and undercuts or turn almost immediately toward the brackish estuaries where they will struggle to survive and thrive. Once sufficiently grown, the smolts swim out to sea where they live, feed, and grow to their adult size, unless they fall prey to whale, seal, sea lion, or commercial fisherman's net. Those that survive will know the appointed time, and they will return from the sea as the salmon below the bridge had done, to spawn and die, and provide nutrients to the forest, river, and even to the tiny organisms that will one day feed their fry. Life is a circle, not a line. Everything is connected to everything. We are no exception.

I felt so much hope as I watched the wild salmon spawning in the clear cold waters of Cowee Creek. And then my mind wandered back into the construct we call "time," to that first day when Alan, Mark, and I fished in the salt water. After, Mark took me to see another side of the modern-day story of these magnificent fish. When I looked down upon the salmon of Sheep Creek, all I felt was sadness. It was tragic. It was poignant. It seemed so hopeless. I could almost hear Camus whispering into my ear, "Do you see? Life is absurd."

There were no sheep at Sheep Creek, but there might as well have been. Instead, there were hundreds of salmon jammed together, humpbacked and shoulder to shoulder, slashing canine teeth and thrashing tails with white fungus eating at their flesh even as they struggled to live . . . a few more hours. Sheep Creek is a shallow water dead-end ally where nothing much awaits them but failure. It is a hallway with no doors that contains about fifty feet of spawning water before a natural barrier stops the struggling fish, cold. It seemed like a cruel and unnatural joke, and it was.

This is a tidal zone and the tide was receding. Everywhere I looked there were dead and stranded salmon strewn across the shoreline. Bonaparte's and herring gulls took turns picking at the guts of the deceased. Just a few feet away, the pulsating masses of spawners pushed and prodded for position, as if in a trance.

"It seems as if I could reach down into the water and touch them." I said.

"I think perhaps you can," Mark replied. "The only thing driving them now is the desire to spawn."

I bent down at the water's edge, reached out and stroked my fingers across the backs of several salmon. They paid me no mind. Zombies on their way to oblivion or immortality, depending on perspective.

"I feel sad for them," I said.

Mark said nothing.

He knew what I knew . . . nature is neither cruel nor kind. Nature is apathetic to our existence. We serve a purpose, until we don't. Nature doesn't give a damn about our souls.

These fish were confused strays from the tens of thousands that were returning to the nearby hatchery. Released from the hatchery as smolts, they were now doing all of the work of delivering themselves back to the building where they were "born" and where they would die. And that building was our last stop of that first day.

For those fish, the circle of life led them to a concrete and metal fish ladder that was a poor substitute for a natal stream. I watched as they fought their way up the ladder . . . pink and chum with the occasional king salmon. It looked exactly like an aquatic stockyard and slaughterhouse because that is exactly what it was.

The salmon swam and leapt their way up the ladder, through the cold metal gates and into the sorting runways where they met their intended fate of an electric shock, being sorted by species, and stripped of their eggs and milt. Then each fish's body is sent on conveyor belts, lifeless and ready for processing into food for something within the human food chain. Some will become human food; some will become part of the food for farm animals and plants. Either way, their nutrients will be missing in the Tongass.

It was raining, a soft steady rain as we stood outside the hatchery discussing all that it means. And we're not sure what it means. All we have are questions that human society must answer, and we must collectively come to this answer soon before it's too late.

"Is a wild and native fish more valuable than a hatchery fish?"

"Is it justifiable to artificially increase the number of salmon in the water in order to keep the fishing industry viable and the insatiable hunger for salmon satisfied?"

"How do you ascertain the true health of a natural and wild fish population if you are artificially augmenting it with hatchery fish?"

"With all of the time and money being dedicated to augmenting the salmon population, why are their numbers still falling? Is it warmer waters and climate change, impacting both salmon and their prey species? Ocean acidification? Excessive competition for food and space with hatchery fish? Overharvesting of salmon or their prey species? All of the above?"

I think Mark nailed it when he said, "Salmon don't need us." I would add, salmon only need us to learn the lessons they are offering to teach us and then act to undo the damage we have done ... and let nature be nature. At some point, we need to be able to say, "We can't have everything just because we want it. We need to know when enough, is enough." I believe we are at that point, now.

The trail upstream was even thicker in vegetation and fallen timber than the one we'd taken going downstream. And it seemed to go on forever, over deadfall, between noxious devil's club, under rain-soaked spruce and hemlock trees, up and down the muddy, slick, fern and moss-covered Earth. After a while, I got into the rhythm of the walking, even though I found my asthmatic lungs once again tightening every time we entered a dense devil's club thicket. I later discovered the reason for my tightening lungs and labored breathing ... it was the ginseng-scented and noxious molecules that were being released into the air by this important understory plant known across the Pacific Northwest as "Devil's Club," *Oplopanax horridus.*

With its large palmate leaves, blood-red seeds, strange-looking green flowers, and erect, woody stalks which are covered in irritating spines, this is the dominating understory plant of much of these forests. It grows its massive colonies from rhizomes in the ground, and was an important source of tattoo ink charcoal, traditional medicine, and religious ceremonial materials for the native Tlingit, Haida, and Tsimshian peoples of the Tongass. It is also an important browse for elk and deer, and bears eat the fruits. Add to this the fact that the roots and rhizomes help to stabilize the soil of riparian habitats along the tributaries, streams, and river, and provide shade and shelter to salmon fry, and this becomes a vital part of this beautiful place, no matter how much their aroma irritates my lungs and spines irritate my skin. It's their forest, not mine. Still, it felt good whenever we came into an opening along the river where the air was fresh and I could breathe freely.

I must admit, had I not been following Mark and trusting in his knowledge, I would never have continued on this trail alone. It wasn't just the seemingly impenetrable wall of rainforest green that held legions of clever bears in the eyes of my mind . . . it was also the many times the trail seemed to vanish or teeter along a narrow and undercut embankment, with a twenty-foot fall waiting below, if the mud bridge might fail us. None of them did, and I trusted in Mark's woodcraft so we walked on and on, upriver, whistling as we went so that the bears might hear us coming and hopefully choose to move away and not toward us. Thus far, we'd been lucky.

Since I seem to be in the mood for confessions, I will unburden myself of one more truth that you might not suspect. I loved the nearly constant rain, drizzle, and otherwise dripping of the sky and forest. I loved it as I walked in the rain through Juneau along with all the people who call it home, and like them I simply dressed in my rain pants, coat, and hat, and went about my life as if nothing was falling from the sky. I loved defying the norms of the lower forty-eight and embracing the clouds, waters, and winds of this wonderful, wild place. And at this moment, with my oilcloth hat upon my head and the rain dripping from its brim, I was loving every soggy moment. In this moment, the sixty-year-old man was a six-year-old boy . . . once again but with one big difference. I wasn't imagining this; I was living it.

When we reached the river's edge, there was another steep embankment to negotiate, covered in ferns, fungi, and devil's club in between the spiny needles of Sitka spruce. There was blown-down timber and then a waist-deep pool before we began to cross the swift currents of Cowee Creek to reach the long, beautiful, gravel bar on the far side. Slowly we crossed, me doing my best to follow Mark's lead as there were times when sight of the bottom eluded me. When we reached the gravel bar the first thing I noticed was the scattered corpses of salmon, half eaten, some dried in the sun and others so fresh that if they weren't missing their guts, you'd swear they could still be revived and set free. We kept our heads on a swivel.

Everything we had done to get to this place on the river was supremely worthwhile. The gravel bar stretched in a long arc around a graceful bend in the river, and pink salmon were spawning everywhere we looked. It felt dreamlike, but it was real. For a moment, I just did what I always do, taking in the sights, sounds, aromas, and feel of this river and the surrounding forest. The sky above us was bright and clear . . . and I could breathe again. The water was cold and alive against my legs. It seemed to pull me closer, as if to say, "This is it, Steve . . . the place and time you've traveled so far to experience." I couldn't stop smiling. And so, we began to fish.

Mark pointed to a nice crease of current just below a shallow pool that contained a mass of swirling salmon. I knew he was being generous and giving me the best spot, but there were no bad casts along this entire expanse of shoreline. Fishing for char in this way is a game of concentration, but if you do the work the fruits of your labors come to you not infrequently. I had already caught quite a few char downstream, but the fish here were bigger, and soon both Mark and I had one on, my five-weight rod bending in the current and both of us taking turns landing Dolly Varden.

Occasionally we'd swap positions and Mark would pull one out of an area I had already fished but rested, and I would do the same farther upstream. We had a bit of surprise when Mark caught a beautifully marked coastal cutthroat trout. We admired him before quickly setting him free. And just when I thought it could not get any better, it did, because I accidentally caught a hefty spawner of a pink salmon. The conservationist in me did not want that to happen again, but the little boy in me was glad that it had happened once. Gaia forgive me, it was a thrill to hold and release that big fat salmon. She seemed no worse for wear, I hope.

Anadromous fish, like salmon, migrate from their birthplace in fresh water, to the sea to mature and grow, and then from the sea to fresh water to spawn. Catadromous fish, like eels, migrate from fresh water to salt to spawn. The coastal cutthroat that Mark caught and released is semi-anadromous because it spends some time in saltwater estuaries before returning to its freshwater spawning streams. Pacific salmon have a single reproductive cycle, returning to spawn once and then dying in the same waters in which they were born. Atlantic salmon, steelhead, and anadromous rainbow trout have multiple reproductive cycles and therefore do not necessarily die once they complete their first spawn. Why does this matter? Because it's all about habitat. And it's about all of the habitat, from ocean to tributary. Lose one and you lose them all.

After a while, we had caught enough char, and Mark asked me if I wanted to raise the level of difficulty. I said sure and asked what he had in mind. He said, "We're gonna do some 'dry balling.'" I listened for the sounds of banjo music, but none was forthcoming. I was intrigued. As it turned out, "dry balling" is like dry fly fishing but instead of a fly it's a floating pink bead that simulates a salmon egg floating on the surface, as if salmon eggs floated on the surface, which they don't. The challenge is to trick the char into taking the "egg" even though it would not normally expect an egg on the surface. I was all in!

Mark doesn't speak often on the river. Like me, I think he prefers the sounds of nature. But when he does speak, it has purpose and meaning. As he was rigging the lines for my first attempt at dry balling he said, "Every cast is a question. Every interaction with a fish is a conversation. You are asking, 'What do I need to do to entice you to take this fly?' In order to answer the questions and enter the conversation, you have to understand the fish and its relationship to the habitat. If you don't catch fish, it's always your fault." Riverside wisdom.

I moved downstream and Mark went upstream, still keeping in visual distance of each other because, well, anything might happen. I learned a long time ago how easy it is to get separated and turned around in deep woods or rainforests. I always keep basic survival gear in my pack that includes a knife, some paracord, a first-aid kit, emergency blanket and poncho/tarp, waterproof matches and kindling, water purifier and energy bar, and the all-important whistle and mirror. In Alaska, I added bear spray. Better to be prepared than end up as a statistic.

Dry balling was a lot of fun and made the entire process of catching a char more challenging. I was happy to catch on pretty quick and before long both Mark and I were catching a few fish on floating imitation eggs that should not have been floating. It was all about eliciting that predator response. Mark increased the level of difficulty by skittering the egg across the water and he picked up another Dolly Varden that way, but I did not. As Clint Eastwood used to say, "A man has to know his limitations." My egg-fly skittering technique obviously needed work, but given more time, I'd get there.

There comes a time in every angler's day when he or she must learn to say, "I've caught enough." It's important that we always keep in mind the impact we are having on a stretch of water, a bit of habitat, a population of wild fish. Mark and I share the ability to know when enough is enough. Neither of us is sentimental about fish, but we do love them, and if we had to choose between catching one more fish and seeing a future of abundant healthy fish, it's an easy choice. Someday, I'm going to snip off the hooks and just fish for the feeling of the tug. Today was not that day.

Crossing the river and walking back through the rainforest toward the truck felt easier on the return trip. The trail was just as muddy, the devil's club just as noxious, and the moss-covered deadfall just as frequent to climb over but somehow, the afternoon on the river had placed a renewed spring in my step. I was moving more fluidly behind Mark and doing a better job of keeping up with him. And this might have been because of the healing powers of nature or it might have something to do with all the angry bear stories Mark was telling me as we walked through the wet, green, almost impenetrable wall of the rainforest. I'm not sure.

All I am sure about is, I felt hopeful. The specter of Sheep Creek was replaced by a healthy river in a sublimely wild forest where salmon are born and die, just as nature intended. The miracle of wild, native, salmon is still alive—for now. If we fail to come together and act so that these fish and forests are saved from the impact of humanity, then we are the worst of sinners and deserve everything that's coming our way. And if we do not turn the wheel and go in a new and more enlightened direction, nothing good is coming our way. This, I also know. We can't allow this, my friends. We just can't.

CHAPTER NINE

Exploring the Tributaries in Search of Pacific Salmon, Char, and Coastal Cutthroat Trout

Tongass National Forest, Southeast Alaska

The opposite of love is not hate, it's indifference. The opposite of art is not ugliness, it's indifference. The opposite of faith is not heresy, it's indifference. And the opposite of life is not death, it's indifference.
~ELIE WIESEL, *NIGHT*, HOLOCAUST SURVIVOR

IT WAS RAINING WHEN WE ARRIVED AT MARK'S HOUSE ON DOUGLAS Island . . . not much, but just enough to feel authentic. We stripped off our muddy boots at the door, and Mark's wife Chris greeted us and offered me a cup of coffee which I gratefully accepted. Mark had a video call to make for Trout Unlimited before we struck out into the wilds, and Chris had one shortly after he did. They are both biologists, both brilliant, and both in love with Southeast Alaska, outdoor adventure, and each other. It was beautiful to see and for a moment, made me feel a little homesick.

While Mark went to another room to make his call, Chris and I sat at the table sipping coffee and watching pine siskins and chestnut-backed chickadees at a feeder that was suspended at mid-tree canopy level, on the end of their second-story deck. We talked of hunting and fishing and living the outdoor lifestyle. We spoke of eagles, salmon, and songbirds, and the way the mist looked as it crossed the coastal mountains. We spoke of the vegetables and herbs she was growing in the kitchen, and I told her how much I admired the magnificent Christmas cactus she was nurturing in the stairwell window. Most of all, we talked about the things in any lifetime that truly matter, and never once mentioned the things that don't. Why waste precious moments on absurdity and illusions?

When we parted ways Chris gave me a heartfelt hug, looked into the weary eyes on my battered old face, and smiled. She may never know how much her kindness meant to me in that moment, but I knew then that every wonderful thing Mark had told me about Chris was true. I told him as much as we drove away toward the trailhead and the toughest and most meaningful day I was yet to have.

Our plan was to follow the river from the sea, deep into the wet woodlands of the Tongass, and then up a tiny tributary in search of this year's coho fry. We had fly rods in the truck but today the brunt of our fishing was going to be done with dip nets. The goal was to put these little tributaries on the map as critical rearing waters habitat for several species of fish including salmon and coastal cutthroat trout. The hope is that once it has been verified that these tiny tributaries are critical habitat, perhaps they may be afforded some level of protection.

As anglers, hunters, hikers, or any kind of outdoor enthusiasts, it is easy for us to forget that this place needs these fish, and these fish need this place—all of it. If any part of the salmon's required habitat from tributary, stream, river, estuary, and ocean collapses, then the entire population collapses with it. You can't start building a skyscraper from the fourth floor up. It needs a foundation. Tributaries are the foundation of the salmon's life journey. Without these pocket-water cradles, the deep-water lives of sleek, silver-sided salmon never comes to pass. As Mark always says, "It's all about the habitat." As I always add, "It's all about ALL of the habitat."

Driving to the river was the softest, kindest, most gentle part of this day. The rain slowed to a mist, and, knowing this would be my last day in Alaska, I was soaking it up. I was soaking up the memories of floss-textured clouds that hung over steep-sided mountains that seemed to tumble helplessly into the sea. I was soaking up the flavor of Alaskan Heritage Roast Coffee and the warmth it gave me on a cool, moist, maritime morning. And I was soaking up the sounds of the artful, soulful, meaningful bluegrass music that Mark was playing from the speakers in his truck.

Music, like all true art, tells the most poignant stories of any human culture and its many moods. I was mesmerized by each element of this day, and even now, I try to recapture the rapture I felt as we pulled up to the river's edge, enjoyed our morning coffee, and watched as the river's fresh waters became one with the sea.

I will not tell you the name of this river because it needs to be respected and protected, and I cannot be any part of the reason it might be harmed by either well-meaning or ill-intentioned humans. I will tell you this . . . that this one little stream of water is the natal origin of every variety of anadromous and semi-anadromous fish in the Pacific Northwest with the exception of the sockeye salmon. The stream and the estuaries it spills into support the reproduction and rearing of chum, pink, chinook, and coho salmon, as well as coastal cutthroat and anadromous rainbow trout, and the quickly vanishing steelhead trout. I promised Mark, myself, and the river, that I would never tell of its location, and my father taught me to always keep my promises. What I will do is take you there, here and now. Together we will travel from the sea to the furthest reaches of the stream where the fish's entire universe is two feet deep and two feet wide. For a coho fry, existence may rest upon a mere trickle beneath the ferns.

When I looked over my shoulder as we began walking the trail along the stream, I could easily see the saltwater passage that led out to sea. Orcas could have fed upon the spawners entering this stream, but there were no orcas that I could see as I looked one last time. The trail was puddled, muddy, and slick, with the occasional obstacles of blown-down trees and blackened bear scat—in other words, it was a trail in Southeast Alaska.

Once again I could feel my lungs tighten as we entered vast groves of ginseng-exuding devil's club. All around us was a seemingly impenetrable wall of primordial-looking ferns, broad-leaved skunk cabbage, and emerald-colored mosses, covering everything. I took it all in from beneath the rim of my hat. Cool moist air beneath the dripping skies. Mushrooms of every shape, size, and color, changing death into life. The plaintive call of an eagle in the spruce trees above us. The aroma of damp-greenness, and the constant sound of water, rushing toward the sea. Everything about this place is alive and so far, that included me.

As we walked, I noticed the increasing profusion of wild blueberries and occasional salmonberries, and I could not help feeling childlike as I plucked them from the trailside and ate them by the handful. At one point Mark took note of a place in the trail where a bumper crop was growing. Foraging is a valued pastime in Alaska. If I lived here, I'd be picking berries at least as often as I was casting a fly line. It was a blueberry paradise.

We crossed the river several times in shallow places, the water cold, swift, and full of pink salmon. There were so many salmon that in some places we needed to be exceedingly careful not to step on one as we crossed. We made a joke of it in one instance by speaking to the fish in polite and apologetic terms. "Excuse me, ma'am." "Pardon me, gentlemen." "If I could just slip by you then you can go back to whatever it is you're doing."

But we knew what they were doing. They were spawning, everywhere we looked. The gravel beds were packed full of new life, just as the logjams were stacked with the corpses of dead spawners. And everywhere we looked there was evidence that the bears were feeding on more than berries. This was yet another bruin happy place. We whistled, sang, and talked to the unseen bears, and we kept a wary eye, even if we could not see much farther than the bright green thicket on either side of the trail.

Had we not chosen to leave the rods in the truck, we would have surely lost focus and stopped along the way to cast a line in search of char that were no doubt present, eating every wayward egg they could find.

But we were men on a mission, and that mission took us to a crossing that was just below a deep pool and directly at a juncture of a tiny tributary creek that tumbled steeply into the river. After a careful crossing Mark looked at me and pointed straight up into a steep, muddy, mossy hillock, and said, "Well, here's where we go in and up the trib!" I looked at the first part of the climb and said, "See Mark, here is where your experience and knowledge makes all the difference. If I were here on my own I would look at that and think . . . 'that's impossible.'" He laughed and started up through the abruptly inclined forest. I followed, but I wasn't laughing. I was just hoping I could keep up.

I will not hide the fact that the climb up this unnamed tributary of an unnamed river was arduous for me. I did my best to not lose the moments that were encapsulated inside every upward step. This place was mystical, mesmerizing, and primal. Everything dripped in the waters of life. The broad green leaves of skunk cabbage and arching feathered ferns all carried with them a million tiny diamond-like raindrops. The forest floor, stones, decaying timber, and living trees were carpeted in mosses, soft, damp, and vibrantly emerald in color. The tiny stream tumbled, spun, and tumbled once again, forever following the forces of gravity and destiny toward the river, sea, and sky. Water, water, everywhere . . . and life following with it.

Every childhood fantasy of struggling through a rainforest in search of mystery and adventure came true. But in fantasy you tend to omit the gasping for breath in wet, heavy air, the aching of back muscles as you clamber over deadfall, and the feeling of stinging needles whenever you inadvertently reach for the ridged stalk of a devil's club plant. Still, I kept my head up and continued climbing from tiny plunge pool to modest riffle, and Mark was patient as I did my level best to keep pace with his seeming ease and economy in movement and progress. It's okay that I had once again placed myself on the edges of comfort and ability. It's a good thing. After all, it is along these razor-sharp ridges that all growth, learning, and adventure are born. If it were easy, everyone would do it.

After a solid and strenuous stretch of working our way up the tributary, Mark stopped and pointed to a pretty little plunge pool, perhaps three feet deep and three feet wide. He said, "Let's try here and see what we find." And then he took out his dip net and went fishing for coho fry. I kept my net sheathed in my backpack, first because the pool was too delicate for both of us to wade without causing harm, and secondly because I was fully aware that Mark knew what he was doing, and I did not.

I watched his dip net fishing technique, hoping to learn a thing or two, and I did. First he did what any good angler does: he observed the flow of the water and its interaction with land, substrate, and structure. He coupled those observations with his knowledge of the fish and their habitat requirements at any particular stage in its life cycle. In most cases, an angler is searching for mature fish, but we were searching for juveniles. Still, the principles remain the same in that fish need clean, aerated water that remains within tolerable temperature ranges, shelter or cover from predators, and access to food sources.

In this case, coho, chinook, and sockeye salmon as well as the semi-anadromous coastal cutthroat trout require small, protected tributary waters for fry to mature in for up to eighteen months—while pink and chum salmon fry begin moving toward estuaries almost as soon as they swim up from the gravel bottom. For the species that depend upon the tributaries to rear their young, the habitat needs to include water with less than a 25 percent grade, and the existence of back eddies and undercuts that protect and shade the fry while bringing an aerated "conveyer belt" of fresh water and food to them in a consistent manner. Knowing this, Mark first tried to "sight cast" for fry by observing the pool, hoping to spot one. If this didn't work, he would drop tiny bits of grass or other vegetation that float, hoping to induce "a rise." Finally, he fished in the blind by sweeping the net through the undercuts and eddies, hoping to pick up any unseen fish. In this pool he was blind prospecting, but it paid off, sort of. He caught a tiny coastal cutthroat, then dropped it into a hand-sized aquarium that he keeps in his pack so that we could identify the fish and take note of its development and markings. It wasn't what we were looking for, but it was nice to see that cutthroats were spawning in this tributary.

The climbing and clambering continued, and, as we fought our way over the myriad of rotting logs, moss-covered stones, and through alder, hemlock, spruce, and devil's club, Mark told me the story of what directed his interest to this particular tributary. It was a friend of his who was a hunter. As it turns out, his friend was still-hunting Sitka black-tailed deer in the forest up above the river. As he stepped ever so slowly through the forest he watched and listened for sounds of life. What he heard did not lead him to a deer but rather to a mass of spawning coho salmon, thrashing in this tiny tributary. Now Mark and I would be looking for the fry from that year, thereby establishing this minor water as an important rearing tributary for salmon, thus hopefully providing some level of protection for it as the U.S. Forest Service updates its management plans.

It's amazing how exciting this became, and I never got the hang of it. Mark caught all the fish. But up until that moment, all we were finding was coastal cutthroat trout. In time, the little trickle of water began to level off across a geologic bench along the mountainside. I was relieved to have a break from the climbing, but the clambering over deadfall and through thick vegetation did not let up. Still, it was a beautiful spot on the tributary with long, sweeping runs of clear water over what looked like perfect gravel beds. We sat there for a while just absorbing the mystical nature of this place and time, and we watched the trickle of water for any signs of fishiness.

I gave up hiking a long time ago and replaced it with walking. It just felt like hiking always included a mandate to get "there" from "here" in a certain amount of "time." I'm in no rush to get where I'm going . . . and we are all going there, no matter if we want to or not. Instead, I walk mindfully with my eyes open, and all my senses engaged. I pay attention. I get out of my mind and into the moment. I notice the little things, which are really quite big. Every rotting log is a biome. Every submerged stone is a community of flora and micro-fauna. Every forest canopy is a highway for birds, insects, reptiles, amphibians, and the ubiquitous chattering squirrels. All we have to do to see is to simply be present and open, in the moment.

Sitting there in the rare silence of my mind I allowed myself to absorb and be absorbed by the forest. The sound of water as it made its way over and through the landscape. The slightest of breezes moving the treetops, an invisible force that is real, nonetheless. The aroma of moss, rootless sponges of water and givers of oxygen. The way the rain fell through the trees, ferns, cabbage leaves, and over the brim of my hat. In moments like these I realize how much living is going on across this magnificent planet that most of us will never witness. It seems a shame, but then again, what good would a world without mystery be? Knowing everything is not for me. I hope there is always just one more turn in the river to explore.

Mark approached the water and so did I and with great care we moved our nets through likely places along the little creek. Another coastal cutthroat! And then another! But still no sign of the coho salmon fry we were hoping to find. As it was getting late we began our descent, dip net fishing as we went. And then it happened. Seeing a tiny coho fry appear from under the cutbank was as exciting to me as watching a bonefish slipping under a mangrove tree. We froze like herons, and then Mark made his move, the dip net dipping and swinging with expert grace. "Let the equipment do the work" I heard in my head. "Economy of motion is key." And as soon as I thought this I witnessed it in action as my friend raised the little net in victory, a salmon fry had been landed!

We watched him swimming in the miniature aquarium and took note of his health and markings. Then, we released him unharmed and smiled as he swam directly back to his hiding place beneath the ferns. I wished him well and tried to imagine his travels if all went well. And if all goes well, this tiny salmon will return to this tiny tributary to spawn and die in the same peaceful little pool where he was born. It takes a miracle to make a salmon, but it's a miracle that has been happening for thousands of years, until now. Only now in the Anthropocene Age of humans has this magnificent creature begun to vanish. I don't want to live in a world without wild, free roaming salmon. I really don't.

On our way back down the mountain side Mark managed to catch another baby coho and a few more cutthroats, and I managed to catch some waterlogged twigs and a hunk of floating moss. I've got a lot to learn about this kind of fishing. It wasn't easy. I've caught bonefish on my eight-weight, but I couldn't catch a coho with a dip net. I guess everything takes practice and patience in order to gain mastery. I wondered if working part-time at a pet shop bagging guppies might improve my skills—but I'm still working on my double-haul, so maybe next year.

When we reached the river, we found a few pink salmon spawning at the base of the tributary. We were hoping to find them farther up but found no evidence that they were. Before crossing back toward the trail Mark waded with me upstream toward a waterfall that formed a large plunge pool full of salmon, each in perpetual motion within the constant current. Most were the hook jawed and humpbacked pink salmon but we also saw a few chum and one king salmon in the mix. It was one of the most stunningly beautiful and magical scenes I've ever witnessed. It was a moment I hope to relive in my mind's eyes just before I too am spawned out.

Walking back down the trail, I looked outward as my mind turned inward. I knew that I may never see this magical place again in this lifetime. And I knew that being here had changed me somehow. It was an epiphany that filled my metaphorical luggage in such a way, that it was going to take a while for me to unpack. How could all this natural perfection happen, by chance? And what went wrong that one species, Homo sapiens, ended up having such an oversized impact on everything?

Even as a child I wondered if we humans belonged on Earth. We seem alien. We seem like foreigners. We just don't fit. Perhaps the missing link is missing for a reason. Are there other planets where we've been dropped off by "gods"? Are we like locusts that consume everything until there is nothing left? But then, what about all that is beautiful within us? What about our imaginations, empathy, and ability to love and care for other species? What about our music, art, and stories? There is hope in humanity, if only a glimmer perhaps. And that is why I write. I write hopefully. I write to invite that glimmer to shine more brightly.

At one point on the trail, just about the time I was overindulging on wild blueberries as we walked, Mark stopped dead in his tracks and raised his hand in the universal sign of "halt." He was about twenty feet in front of me on the trail when he looked over his shoulder and said, "We need to pick our heads up and make some noise . . . there's a bear around here and he's really close." He got my attention. "Can you see him?" I asked. "No, I can smell him." He replied. I stepped forward and was immediately hit with the musky aroma of bear. It was like being sprayed full in the face by a skunk with a butt load of pent-up hostility. And it lingered for quite a while as we talked and whistled our way past the spot on the river that was covered in fresh, bear-eaten salmon carcasses, and out of the invisible wall of musk that screamed, "Bear!" It's interesting to see how moments like that can focus one's attention and perk one right up, toward the end of a long day.

When we reached the place where the river met the sea, we crossed a bog where Mark said there were hundreds of toads last year, but we found none. I watched the salmon entering the river and making their way up toward their collective destiny and personal doom. Even with the true-to-life mix of tragedy and triumph, I found the entire spectacle to be immensely beautiful. We both wondered aloud why the toads had vanished. I watched in wonder as several bald eagles flew overhead with another couple perched in the spruce trees. I remembered a time before Rachel Carson's *Silent Spring* when these eagles were vanishing. It was good to have them back. All it took was humans collectively choosing to behave differently. Every problem from war to crime and the destruction of the Earth's habitat is a human behavior problem. We are the cause and the cure and in that truth lies hope. I wondered, will we continue as we are, or will we turn the wheel in a new direction? Will these salmon still be here in ten or twenty years? Perhaps not. Perhaps that is why the sky is crying.

As we drove away from the river and across the vast wilderness that is the Tongass, I imagined wolves, bears, and deer, moving naturally through this landscape, as they once did in the lower forty-eight. The sounds of masterfully played bluegrass music filled the air, and it added to the moment almost as much as the mountains, mist, and memories. I tried my best to take it all in, like photographs and petroglyphs in my mind.

There are memories I don't want to lose in this lifetime. Like the first date in Rome, Italy, that led to a lifetime of love and togetherness. And the day I held my daughter for the first time, and her dark eyes looked into mine, and her tiny hand grabbed hold of my finger. I was a lost man, both times. Then there was the time my father took me fishing against all odds, simply because he had promised me that he would. And there are losses I do not want to lose sight off. The early death of my Marine brothers Dave and Monty. And the passing of my hero—my father.

Love is the most brave, beautiful, and yet binding thing I know. It gives joy and sorrow, courage and fear. It always ends in partings. But I would not forsake love for comfort, and as I parted from America's Salmon Forest, I knew I'd carry it with me always, until my own time to cross over. And yet I wondered, will it be here like this, for very long?

Just beyond the river is a glacier. It is melting at an unnatural rate, and as it does it exposes a landscape filled with the possibilities of short-term profit for a rare few. Gold, silver, and copper are waiting, and the mining companies are staking claims as fast as the ice can melt. There is big money and power to be gained in the destruction of the Earth. "Profit is progress!" they claim in their claims. They are lying. It is all a lie. We need to live in Truth.

Driving down the road through the Tongass, Mark and I absorbed the music of the moment. It had been a long day, but a miraculous day. In our efforts I found hope. I looked out the window at the coastal mountains as they met the sea. I listened to the evocative, emotive, wistful sounds of the bluegrass music, and felt the organic mingling of creation and adaptation—just like nature. My mind wandered with the music toward Appalachia and then onward across the ocean to the lush green glens of Scotland. Snow fell in my memories as I climbed the Cairngorm mountains of the Scottish Highlands, with my daughter Megan by my side. I see her lovely face smiling as we reach the summit, huddled together in the icy, wet cold. The music transports me back to another time and place, a fond memory that brings both joy and longing. And then the song ends and the silence brings me back to the here and now, already a part of my history as soon as it arrives. All is well. I have done what I intended to do. I had followed the salmon from the sea to the smallest tributaries of their birth, and in doing so, the salmon captured me. I am forever changed, and for this, I am grateful.

I slept peacefully and well each night in Alaska including my last, although this is not my norm. PTSD often rules my nights. Perhaps it was the fresh air and outdoor exercise, but I think there was more to it than mere physiology. I think it was a feeling of knowing that this place and this time was ordained by the universe. It was as inevitable as the falling rain. It was meant to be and I was meant to be here in this "Now."

In the morning I had a half-waking dream, perhaps even a vision, of life. I saw myself lying on the ground, eyes half open or closed, but seeing nothing . . . everything I had ever loved was slipping into oblivion. And then I saw my reflected self, bent down over what was left of me, hands upon my "other's" chest, pushing down and rising up, giving breath to lifelessness, in a last-ditch effort to resuscitate my own life and reasons for living—hoping the damage could be repaired. Hoping for redemption and rebirth.

Everything in life is a delaying action; nothing lasts forever. As I woke more fully, I realized that this dreamlike image was not solely of me trying to delay my own mortal passing into eternal darkness or eternal light, depending upon your chosen theological mythology, or the implacable rules of physics and physiology. What I imaged was also "me" trying to do what I could do to save this beautiful planet from an early demise. It's just way too young to die.

I mean, no matter what I do . . . no matter what we do . . . all of this will burn up in the swelling sun in a few billion years. To be more exact, the sun will begin to swell and will consume the Earth as fuel in about four billion years, and will sputter out completely another three to four billion years after that, but who cares? Everything we are fighting over, every scrap of air, land, and sea, every imaginary gain, will have long since vanished in the solar backdraft.

Still, our planet is only slightly past middle-aged—just like me. There's so much potential life and beauty remaining to live if we can resuscitate it now. I'm leaning into that task as best I can, although I am an almost insignificant raindrop that is hurtling toward a vast entropic ocean. Isn't it ironic how none of us are in any rush to go home? Still, gravity and entropy are the few truths I know.

These are the thoughts and images that the universe gave me as I woke once again, in the darkness of pre-dawn. It was raining outside, I suspected. And I suspected this to be true not because I could see it, but rather, I could feel it. In these times we need all of our senses to be awake, alive, and aware. We need to soak in all that is coming to pass and act accordingly out of a sense of understanding, empathy, compassion, selflessness, and wisdom.

We need to taste the coffee and feel grateful for the coffee farmer. We need to feel the Earth beneath our feet and understand that for now, it is alive. The Earth is a living being of sorts. Every handful of soil is a community of flora and fauna. Every drop of water in every river is teeming with tiny beings, all wanting to live. A new civilization calls the bottom of any stone its homeland. We are not alone; we are many. Everything is connected to everything and when one form of life vanishes we are all diminished. Extinction is a communal event. It's the death of a cousin.

I love the Earth. I am its child as much as I am of the heavens and perhaps even more so . . . after all, I was not born on Neptune. The stardust that became me mixed with sea water on this big blue marble. The Earth gave me the conditions for my life and I think I owe it the respect of any good child toward a life-giving parent . . . in a perfect world.

In truth, there is not much I can do. I will recycle, refuse, repurpose, and reuse the plastics we never knew in olden days, but now are convinced we cannot live without. I will endeavor to eat more fruits and vegetables and less farm-raised meat. I will smash down the barbs on my hooks and try not to catch too many fish. And I will write about love and respect for the Earth and every living thing including but not limited to those of my own species. It's not much, but it is something I can do. We all must remember that every tug-of-war needs someone to grab the "end of the line." And make no mistake; this is the end of the line. It's now or never. The Earth is dying. It's up to us to save it, from us.

Chapter Ten

In Search of Native Surf Perch
and Naturalized Striped Bass

Monterey Bay, Carmel Beach, Big Sur, California

It has always seemed strange to me. . . . The things we admire in men, kindness and generosity, openness, honesty, understanding and feeling, are the concomitants of failure in our system. And those traits we detest, sharpness, greed, acquisitiveness, meanness, egotism, and self-interest, are the traits of success. And while men admire the quality of the first they love the produce of the second.

~ John Steinbeck, quote from *Cannery Row*

It's hard to believe that Alice and I have been together for 39,000 years and married under the civil laws of the Ivory Coast and the common laws of the United States for 36,000 years—but it's as true as the existence of gravity. Some people date . . . we carbon date. And as this was the anniversary of that fateful day in Western Africa when a young girl from Scotland said, "Oui!" and she and I became us, we decided to commemorate our tandem life journey by traveling to the Bay of Monterey and the purple sand beaches of Big Sur. Of course, I was planning on doing a little fishing too; it was after all a celebration of life.

One of the most striking things I noticed as we drove along Highway One from Santa Cruz to Monterey was the juxtaposition between the legions of Mexican American migrant workers, bent over in the baking sun under broad-brimmed straw hats, picking the food we all eat, and the obvious opulence of many of the buildings and builders of the lovely towns of Monterey and Carmel-by-the-Sea. The vegetable fields came directly up to the sand dunes bordering the beach that bordered the ocean, and the workers could no doubt smell both the fragrance of sea water along with the stench of pesticides and port-o-potties. I guess not much has changed along Cannery Row.

People are people; nature is nature. And ever since those long-ago days when Steinbeck walked these seaside paths, human nature still seems to travel a sliding scale between wanton sinner and willful saint. Within the pages of that compact novel, he describes the humanity of Cannery Row, as either "whores, pimps, gamblers, and sons of bitches," or "saints and angels and martyrs and holy men" depending upon the "peephole" from which one chooses to view humanity and life. Perspective is everything. We can choose to see what's missing or we can choose to see what's there. None of us can save the world, but perhaps in saving ourselves from our own darkness, we manage to give a little light to the night sky. It takes a lot of stars to make a big bright universe, and from what I've heard, darkness got here first.

As we passed by the fields and along the beaches and through the remnants of the Elkhorn estuary, Alice began telling me of her childhood in Scotland where she and her parents worked as seasonal field workers picking strawberries and potatoes to earn a little extra money. I had never heard this story before, even though we'd been together longer than most of those migrant workers have been alive, but I had heard of how hard her father worked as a machinist for the coal mines of Fife, and of her mother holding multiple jobs so that together, they could provide food, clothing, and shelter for their children. I had previously listened intently to her father's stories of fighting the communist insurgency in Malaysia as a member of the Gordon Highlanders, and how they employed "head-hunters" to help track enemy soldiers through the jungle. How her mother had endured the bombing raids of the German Air Corps. I marveled at the stories of how they warmed their small house with a coal fire and collected the horse manure left behind by the passing of the dairy delivery wagon as fertilizer for the family garden.

I thought of the humble beginnings of my own parents and grand-parents, each one an immigrant or first-generation American. My father's mother spoke Italian and Spanish, my mother's grandmother spoke Irish. My father was raised by a single mother, his father having been deported. My grandmother was illiterate because the time and place of her upbringing precluded the education of girls. But she still managed to raise five children, each of whom became good Americans. My uncles fought and my father served as a medic during the Korean War. And as I thought of these things, I felt hope for us all, including these good people who now labored over the food I will someday eat. If only we'd learn from our many past lives and choose to treat each other with a little more empathy, dignity, and gratitude. More than our DNA passes forward in time. The consequences of our ideas and choices seem to live on forever. Still, ideas and choices can be changed.

When we checked into our hotel we walked out to the Fisherman's Wharf and took in the bawdiness of the wharf and the beauty of the bay. Mixed in with middle-class travelers and well-to-do tourists were the homeless and the hapless. I began reading the cardboard signs of the various homeless men that lined the sidewalks. In black Sharpie marker they said things like, "My Mother Told Me to Wait Here." And "Why Lie, I want to Buy a Beer." There was one young man who was wearing a top hat and dressed like the seventies shock rock star, Alice Cooper. Another was dancing in circles and then walking up to people and pro-claiming, "Just get crazy with the cheese whiz!" There was a banjo player, a tone-deaf singer and guitarist, a middle-aged trumpet player telling "dad jokes," a juggler with a little wagon filled with French bulldogs, a "magic show," and a pretty young girl singing into a portable microphone over the cacophony of the entire human circus and the distant barking of sea lions. The air was cool, misty, and smelled of salt and the rancid oil of a fish-n-chips stand. It reminded me of Key West's Mallory Square, without the bagpiper or the sunset.

Being who I am, I saw hope in all of this, even with all the comedic insanity and commercial hubbub. We found a nice little Italian restaurant on the wharf where the hostess was a sweet college kid who was studying marine ecology and the waitress was a young woman who seemed a bit jaded by life, but then began to smile and find joy in the evening as we shared simple acts of kindness. Seagulls called overhead, and sea lions barked from the water below. And during our walk along the bay, we saw harbor seals and sea otters and starfish in the water, and there were cormorants, guillemots, and brown pelicans in the air. And then there were the families of migrant workers, walking together along the same seaside path, each of them full of smiles, laughter, and love. In the evening, they were as wealthy as anyone walking along the sea.

The sky grew increasingly indigo as the lapping bay waters glistened in the moonlight. And with all the grifters and grad students off to wherever they go at night and all the tourists and travelers ensconced in their rooms, the bay belonged to wild nature, once more. Life does . . . find a way. The ocean waves lapped gently against the shore. The distant sound of sea lions echoed in the starlight. It was a peaceful night to sleep and dream of the ocean.

⌒

When my buddy Geoff Malloway, his American foxhound pup Daisy, and I arrived at Carmel Beach, the waves seemed impressive and dangerous to me, but Geoff said they were "only moderate." Daisy howled out her approval of our destination and demanded to be set free of the truck, perhaps catching a whiff of some resident fox meandering the streets of Carmel. More likely she was just excited to go fishing with her dad. I know I always was, although I hardly ever howled whenever my dad would take me fishing. Still, I would have wagged my tail if I had one, and I understood how she felt.

Daisy was a rescue dog that was brought into Geoff's shop one day by clients who had found her and temporarily brought her into their home. Geoff told me that she was undernourished, dehydrated, and in need of surgery and that he had no inclination that he "needed a dog" at that time in his life. But Daisy knew better. She walked over to him and sat on his foot. She decided that they needed each other; both of them dealing with life's hardships, challenges, and vagaries. Geoff told me, "I saved her and she saved me. She is the only one who really understands me."

Geoff had our eight-weight rods strung up with a Scientific Angler's Sonar Surf fly line that boasted a fast-sinking tip, shooting head, and a Mardi Gras fly attached with a tarpon knot to the end of five feet of thirty-pound, hard monofilament. Our targets were native surf perch and naturalized striped bass that may or may not be lurking just beyond the breakers. I was using Geoff's gear with the exception of my waders, boots, and belt, and when I pulled out my brand-new Orvis waders for their inaugural dunking in the sea, I realized that they still had the tags on them, so I quickly ripped them off, hoping that Geoff didn't notice. If he did, he was being too nice to say so. I had tried them on one time at home and then quickly stuffed them into my wader bag without ever thinking of removing the tags. And now, I've confessed to my transgression, and I feel a bit better about it as I laugh at myself, which is something I do often.

We walked down to the beach with Daisy running ahead of us and occasionally looking back and letting out a hound-like howl as if to say, "Come on! Get the lead out!" The objective is to cast out and across the waves just as one breaks and another rolls in so that the line is retrieved across the flat, open space between each wave ... for the brief period of time that such conditions may exist. You retrieve the fly at a moderate to slow rate while hoping to feel a tug before everything comes unraveled on the shoreline next to you. After all, while you are retrieving the fly line the ocean is trying to toss it back up on shore at the same time it is trying to suck you out to sea.

Stripping buckets are a must, as is paying attention to the powerful waves, currents, rips, and occasional white sharks that might eat you. It's important to not go in any deeper than knee deep on any beach along Big Sur and the Monterey Bay Coast. As Geoff put it, "Nature wants to kill you, and eventually it will succeed, but it's your job to delay that inevitable outcome for as long as you can. That is also why you're wearing a personal flotation vest and should never, ever, turn your back on these waves." Geoff was a good teacher; I was a good listener.

The action of the waves constantly excavates sand from around your feet, so you must be ready to step carefully backward toward temporarily firmer ground, while stripping line in and remaining prepared to strip-set the hook at the slightest bump, stop, or tug of the fly. Then there is the fact that the waves seem to come in progression, four or five moderate waves and then a single monster of a breaker that can knock you off your feet and make you a more permanent part of the scenery. Add to this the many beachgoers who seem to think it is a good idea to congregate directly behind you where your back cast is meant to go, and well . . . you can see this is a dynamic environment where anything can and will happen. I love that.

This was my first try at surf casting and so Geoff was in teaching mode in the beginning. I liked how he described the problem that needed to be solved. "You're a door-to-door salesman," he said. "You don't even know if anyone's home. And you don't know that what you're offering is a product they might want. So, your job is to find out if anyone's home and then present your product in such a way that it is irresistible and you make the sale." It's a big ocean and these fish are on the move. My goal was to read the beach and try to figure out where the fish might be, and exactly which fish might be "home."

Geoff bent down and dug his hand into the sand, eventually pulling up a sand crab or mole crab . . . same crustation by any name. He plopped it into my hand and it laid there on its back like a stranded turtle while its many legs frantically flailed in the air. I could clearly see the orangish-pinkish egg sac that so many surf loving fish will home in on, and as I tossed it back into the foam I watched as it quickly burrowed beneath the surface of the wet sand. I had seen these many times before growing up as a boy in South Florida, but I was surprised when Geoff showed a three-inch gap between his thumb and forefinger and said, "They can get about this big."

I started casting into the waves as Geoff looked on giving helpful and humorous commentary like saying, "Any time now!" whenever I'd hesitate . . . and that is when it happened. I was struck with MRS also known as Mrs. Rosenberger Syndrome. Mrs. Rosenberger was my fourth grade math teacher who terrorized me with times tables and flogged me with fractions. "How are you ever going to know what size pizza to order!" she would scream when I would become flustered. Ironically, I've been ordering and eating pizza all my life and I only memorized a mere fraction of my times tables. Perhaps one third of them . . . I'm not sure.

Geometry . . . now that was a subject I could understand as I cast my fly line across the water at approximately a forty-five-degree angle while Geoff stood there kindly watching my performance with his prized rod. He was patient and supportive with me but in my subconscious I saw him whipping out a flash card and screaming, "14 times 21!" I rushed my cast and it tumbled into a spaghetti-like mess across the surging sea and that is when I heard Geoff say, "Well that cast really sucked, Steve." I laughed. The curse was broken, and my fourth grade teacher finally lost her grip on me for now. It only took about fifty years or nine tenths of my life . . . I think.

Geoff walked a bit farther down the beach, and I relaxed and began getting a little more into the zone. We only had a few hours to fish. I wished we had more because I was loving the challenge of working out the puzzle between that dynamic moving ocean, moving fish, moving sea breeze, and moving fly line. If we'd had more time, I think I could have really gotten into the groove of it all, but we had what we had so I kept casting until I saw Geoff walking back up the beach while checking his watch. I knew it was almost time to reluctantly reel in.

Just as Geoff got back up beside me, I felt a hesitation in the line and quickly strip set the hook, feeling some slight resistance as I continued to reel in whatever was on the other end. This had happed a few times before and each time it turned out to be "lettuce," which is local terminology for bits of free-floating kelp. This time it was a three-inch-long mole crab! Geoff said, "Well at least it got the 'skunk' smell off of you . . . you caught bait!" Not being a bait angler at heart, I released my catch back into the sea. Daisy seemed disappointed that we had to go and was giving us both the "sad puppy" look. But the beach was beginning to experience a tourist hatch that was making our back casts hazardous, and our forward casts fruitless. Everything is impermanent, always changing, always rearranging . . . just like the sea.

I couldn't help but give everything one last parting look. I do this often with places that I quickly come to love but wonder if I will ever see again. I scanned the crescent shaped shoreline from the wealth of Pebble Beach to the north to the remnant wilderness of Point Lobos to the south. Behind me was most of America and in front of me was the rest of the world. And I thought about the ocean with its fish and fowl and whales and walruses . . . and I wondered, "What will become of this beautiful blue marble that we call Earth?"

❦

Point Lobos is a California State Natural Area that begins the arch of land and sea that forms the northernmost edge of Big Sur. The area derives its name from the point of massive half-submerged rocks that stand just offshore which was long ago given the name "Punta de los Lobos Marinos," or in English, "Point of the Sea Wolves." The sound of the namesake sea lions drifts inland with the ocean breeze, often heard, less often seen. Harbor seals lounge on the edges of turbulent coves, and kelp forests sway and swirl in perfect time with the currents.

At its northern end it overlooks the beach I had fished just a day prior, and to the south the long, turbulent, rocky shoreline of Big Sur stretches out until it seemingly evaporates in the mist coming off the ocean or the clouds tumbling down from the mountains. The open chaparral that covers the bluffs was blanketed in a profusion of wildflowers and poison oak. The wildflowers came in colors of yellow, white, pink, red, blue, and violet. The poison oak grew in shades of light and dark green, rusty red, and even a copper-like brown.

The wildlife here includes seals, sea lions, sea otters, and seasonally migrating gray whales that are escorting their babies. Orcas appear just in time to hunt the young gray whales, separating them from their mothers in perfectly timed and synchronized operations that are as terribly tragic for the gray whales as they are fortunate and hopeful for the killer whales. Nature is not gentle; it is practical. Every living thing must capture the energy of the sun—if it is to continue living. We are all made of carbon and water, destined to be transformed into the life of another being. Mere sentimentality has no place in the struggle for survival.

Just a few days prior, Alice and I were riding in a fifty-foot-long catamaran on choppy seas, searching for some of the thirty-six species of marine mammals that rely on these waters that make up the 6,094 square mile Monterey Bay National Marine Sanctuary. Closer to shore, the sanctuary is a mixture of rocky shores, sandy beaches, kelp forests, teeming tidal pools and tranquil estuaries. But miles out to sea we watched as humpback whales and dolphins swam, spouted, dove, and even breached along the bay's almost two-mile-deep sea canyon. Few people realize that this place supports 525 known species of fish and thousands of seabirds. And so much of this depends upon healthy populations of anchovies, sardines, and squid.

Every part of the Earth is a historical landscape or seascape, touched, modified, and forever impacted by the choices and actions of humans. I was struck by this as I walked along the seashore on Cannery Row, past the converted factories where not all that long ago millions of fish were converted into protein and profit. Consumption is an act of nature. Over-consumption is predominantly an act of humanity.

During the 1920s, 1930s, and 1940s, the sardine fishing and canning industry in Monterey Bay boomed. At its peak, the canneries along this coast processed more than 250,000 tons of sardines per year, until the population of these silvery fish collapsed and the businesses that relied upon them vanished with them. Overfishing was a big part of the problem, but not all of it. Scientists discovered that sardines and anchovies increase and decrease in the bay as water temperatures change. When sardine populations naturally decrease in Monterey Bay, anchovies begin to appear in large numbers to take their place. Sardines prevail whenever the water is warmer, and anchovies increase during those times when the water grows colder. These two species alternate approximately every twenty-five years. But what these fish were not adapted to withstand is a massive fishing fleet with nets that caught and killed almost everything in their path. The bay naturally evolved to be able to feed all the wildlife of the area . . . it simply wasn't able to feed all humans of the world.

With our large brains, opposable thumbs, and the ability to create socially accepted mythology, we have managed to override nature's checks and balances and overpopulate the Earth. At almost eight billion humans we have pushed way beyond the Earth's carrying capacity for upright primates who take more than they give. We've even managed to fill our deceased bodies with toxic chemicals and seal them inside ornate airtight metal boxes in our attempt to deny nature the benefit of our matter and energy. Every other creature from microbe to mastodon has recycled back to the Earth. But we have managed to cheat nature, even if we cannot cheat our natural mortality.

We can choose a new paradigm and give ourselves back to the Earth. We can learn to become part of nature once more, and see the Earth not as a resource, but rather, as our home. Resources are extracted and used; homes are respected, restored, lived in, loved, and returned to, again and again.

I was thinking about this as I walked along the shore watching sea otters playing in the kelp forests. I was thinking of how the smallest things in nature are holding up the biggest things. Without plankton, the menhaden, anchovies, and sardines vanish. Without these small silver fish, the dolphins, seals, sea lions, and even whales, disappear. The sea bass, lingcod, halibut, and swordfish become memories. And by the way, without phytoplankton in the sea, about 80 percent of the oxygen we humans breathe vanishes, just like the anchovies. We owe our lives to microbes and phytoplankton. As an avid angler, outdoors person, and naturalist, I think it's important that I am aware of these connections and consequences and use that knowledge to protect what I love. How about you?

Standing on the shore, looking out toward the sea, onward past the seals and sea lions and out toward the breaching whales, I found myself thinking back to Geoff and me standing in the surf, casting our lines hopefully toward surf perch and whomever else might be "home." I enjoyed the casting, even when from time to time, I miscalculated my timing and made a mess of it all. Between the waves, wind, and wandering tourists, there was a lot to consider with every cast. I was beginning to get the hang of it just as we had to call it a day. Geoff, being who he is, offered a few words of support. He said, "You have to remember that all those tourists watching you fish think that what you're doing is graceful and poetic. It takes someone like me to know when you screwed it all up." I laughed. "A little more time and I was going to be in the zone!" I replied. Geoff smiled and said, "You were pretty close to getting there, anyway."

We didn't catch any fish but after all . . . that's fishing. If it were a sure thing, it would be boring. In truth, I did hope to catch my first surf perch or my first transplanted West Coast striper, but I was okay that I hadn't. Instead, I had invested a morning with a friend on a beautiful beach, casting into the ocean and hoping for good fortune, and I found it. I felt fortunate, indeed.

As we reeled in Geoff looked at me and said, "People look out here and think because it's a big ocean that the supplies of fish are inexhaustible, but they're not. I've been fishing these waters since I was a kid and I can tell you, there are a lot fewer fish here now than there were back then. It's kind of sad." Everywhere I go I find the same story of extraction, consumption, pollution, and exhaustion. But being a storyteller myself, I know that we all have the power to edit. Together, I hope my fellow anglers, hunters, hikers, paddlers, and other outdoors persons will join me in that editing process. Let's rewrite this story and refill the surf and sea with life.

After our few brief uneventful hours of fishing the surf, Geoff was kind enough to offer to take Alice and me out to dinner, but I demurred because it was our anniversary trip, and besides, I explained, "Alice is quiet, shy, and private." Without missing a beat Geoff replied, "Well I'd be happy to completely ignore her if that would make her more comfortable." I laughed, and Alice laughed when I told her what he said. Geoff's a good guy with a great sense of humor.

I guess that's how people like us survive while remaining more or less intact as life beats the hell out of us. It's not because we're heartless that we laugh at gallows humor; it's because we're a bit heartbroken by much of what we've experienced. It's the "things we carry" that cause us to seek humor at every turn and give laughter at every opportunity. To my mind if Geoff and I can see and feel all we have seen and felt and still find a way to live a life of loving kindness and laughter, we have prevailed. When you've felt deep sorrow, all you want to give is joy.

The evening before we left Monterey I received a call from the hotel front desk that a man had left a package for me. I walked down to find a small white cardboard box with the words, "For Steve . . . Good Luck!" written upon its lid. I opened it to find a handful of perfectly tied and wonderfully buggy-looking saltwater flies. They were chock full of sparkle, flash, and color, with staring eyes and wiggling legs. And that's when I heard a voice say, "Hey Steve!" Geoff was sitting in the lobby, texting me that he'd left the farewell gift for me.

I smiled, walked over, and sat down, and said, "You don't have to text me now." He said, "I know you're going corbina fishing in a week, so I tied up a few nice patterns for you to try." Did I mention that Geoff is a good guy? (Now, if only I can get him to believe me when I tell him that he's a good guy and valued friend.) Then again, it doesn't really matter what I think. What matters is . . . Daisy thinks he's the best person on Earth. And I think she's a pretty smart puppy.

CHAPTER ELEVEN

Corbina—The Beaches of Ventura County, California

The First Days of the Quest

To love. To be loved. To never forget your own insignificance. To never get used to the unspeakable violence and the vulgar disparity of life around you. To seek joy in the saddest places. To pursue beauty to its lair. To never simplify what is complicated or complicate what is simple. To respect strength, never power. Above all, to watch. To try and understand. To never look away. And never, never to forget.
~ ARUNDHATI ROY, *THE COST OF LIVING*

YOU NEVER KNOW WHEN IT'S GOING TO HAPPEN TO YOU; IT ALWAYS comes, right out of the blue. You think it will be just another day, and then all at once, it's not. You are forever changed. You are captivated, transformed, metamorphized, reborn ... however you might wish to describe it, you have been touched by someone or something or some-place, and you know in that instant that this will not be "just another day." You never know when the day will come when you fall in love once again and you think of the object of your affections, infatuations, and obsessions both day and night. Sometimes you keep such longing locked deep down inside you, like your own eternal secret. Other times, you feel compelled to tell the world. This time, I am of the latter persuasion. And I have a confession to make. I have fallen in love with a bottom-feeding fish named "corbina." Please allow me to explain.

The first time I saw corbina was on a beach just north of Los Angeles that I gave the name of "Ugly Beach." I was walking Ugly Beach with my friend Kesley Gallagher as we both tried to spot corbina in the surf. Kesley was carrying her seven-weight rod just in case we saw corbina and I was carrying my flip-flops because I had just gotten off the plane from Texas and my California fishing license wasn't valid until the next day. We drove to Ugly Beach directly from the Burbank Airport. Kesley is all business.

I named this Ugly Beach because it felt ugly, unkempt, unappreciated, and unloved. It was at the end of the road in a town that felt dark, angry, selfish, slightly dangerous, and wholly without empathy. Older but certainly valuable homes lined the beach, each displaying an American flag and various political memorabilia that felt, to me, uninviting and un-American. Residents of these homes sat on front porches as if they were on guard. In the streets wandered seemingly aimless people of every race and socioeconomic class. Some appeared harmless enough, but others had that feel that I've know many times, of "sharks circling, looking for an unaware seal." Kesley and I remained aware as we walked onto and away from Ugly Beach, but our focus shifted from self-preservation to the art and science of corbina location. I was entranced.

There was a short jetty at the beginning of the beach where massive, blackish, slick, salt-soaked rocks extended for about a hundred yards out to sea. Kesley said that she sometimes caught halibut along those rocks. Just beyond the rock jetty we came to a stretch of beach that contained good holding water for corbina with a gentle to moderate surf, clearly discernable troughs, an occasional pool or depression in the sand, a few rips where currents collide, and areas of gradually descending beach where sand crabs burrowed just beneath the foam. When I saw my first corbina I caught my breath like a kid on Christmas morning. It wasn't doing anything spectacular, just cruising through a trough that ran parallel to the breakers. But then I saw another and another and the excitement grew, and I found myself wishing I had purchased my license for one day earlier.

Kesley and I worked in tandem, spotting corbina in the surf, sometimes leading to a cast and sometimes leading to nothing more than the thrill of seeing one of these fascinating fish in action. That in and of itself was worth the trip for me. When the setup wasn't right Kesley held back, but when there was a shot, she took it with a short, accurate cast just a few feet in front of the target. Most of the time, the "beans" ignored her offering. She had one take and went to set the hook but missed it. I was to learn this is not unusual with corbina. These are tough fish to catch, which is part of their allure. To paraphrase Kesley, who has much more fly-fishing experience than me and multiple world records to her name, permit are challenging; corbina are more challenging.

While talking with Kesley's partner Scott, a former Navy SEAL and editor of *Fly-Fish in Saltwater* magazine, he gave me a good overview of the obstacles that need to be overcome in the hunt for this elusive phantom fish of the California surf line. "Finding and seeing the corbina is 90 percent of the battle. This is a sight casting game, and simply casting blindly into the surf is more often than not a waste of time and energy." Once you see the fish, you need to present the fly in such a manner that it is perfectly timed to sink to the bottom before the fish arrives, while ensuring that the fly is within its line of sight when it does arrive. And you're doing all of this in a dynamic environment where the waves, currents, tides, sands, sand crabs, corbina, corbina predators, surfers, swimmers, shell collectors, you, your rod, line, leader, and fly . . . are all in motion. "And even if you do everything right, more often than not the fish will ignore your fly . . . you just never know." This is corbina fishing. And before I even tell the story of my adventures with these iridescent, ghost-like fish, I will confess to you that I am a lost man, forever deeply in love with the challenge and mystery of corbina.

Our stop at Ugly Beach was not a long one because Kesley still needed to drop me off at my hotel, so I had time to get cleaned up before meeting our mutual friend Aileen Lane for a dinner of pizza, wine, and fishing stories. It was all planned out. Kesley was going back home to have dinner with Scott and get the gear set up for our first day of corbina fishing together, and I was going to debrief Aileen about the fish and conditions I'd experienced at Ugly Beach. I couldn't wait to tell her what I suspected was in store for us, even if I really didn't want to stop looking for beans.

Of all the outdoor activities I have undertaken, none have been as meditatively focused as fly fishing. In the Marines I practiced martial arts. I'm not a competitive person, except with myself, but I did compete in both fighting and forms as a way to improve my skills and focus. In truth, although sparring gets all the attention, I found it to be a detraction from what I saw as a meditative art. I loved "forms" which are also known as kata in Japanese and hyeong in Korean. By any name, these are highly choreographed patterns of martial arts movements used to perfect the abilities of the practitioner, and also to focus the mind.

Fly fishing focuses the mind and causes the movement to be without thought, manifesting as free-flowing reactions to subtle changes in the environment. In martial arts, this state of being is referred to as "Mushin" which can be translated to "no mind." Athletes call it being "in the zone" but as anglers we can think of it as being "in the flow" like a current in a stream or ocean that adapts to every obstacle and fills every space. At its best it is the perfect melding of mind, body, spirit, and nature. At its worst, it is a tangled leader in a tree or an angry surfer protesting that "You hooked me in the ass, dude!" But I can say without equivocation that the most Buddha-like I have ever been was searching for corbina in the surf. Everything in motion. Everything in stillness. Everything timeless.

And so it was for me as Kesley and I worked our way back down the beach, toward the black rock jetty. The world had vanished except for the waves and the corbina and the synchronized partnership of me pointing and she casting toward the mere suggestion of a fish. Both of us remained hopeful with every effort. It was spellbinding, but the spell was broken when I heard a loud, frightened, angry bark that resonated directly in my ear and caused me to jump out of my skin! I had nearly stepped on a sleeping sea lion! She stood up next to me and we both jumped out of each other's way as she raced toward the water, dove into the sea, and then repeatedly popped her head up to scold me for waking her so rudely. We all laughed. It was a beautiful ending to my brief time on Ugly Beach. And although Kesley did not catch a corbina, we saw many, and she cast toward quite a few fish, and that was the point of the whole visit. All that was left of this day in L.A. was for me to share some pizza, wine, and stories of spotting mythical fish. Life was good . . . as always.

———

I've always been enamored with transitions. Even death seems interesting, although I am in no rush to explore that inevitable journey. But transitions are the *thump, thump, thump* of the Earth's beating heart. They are the inhale and exhale of the Universe, and yes, I treat Earth and Universe as living beings . . . because they are. Spring, summer, autumn, and winter. Forest, meadow, valley, and mountain. Deep sea, seashore, tidal pool, wrack line, dunes. High and low tides and everything in between. All are indications of vivid life.

Why are we humans so often yearning for "sameness"? It is our differences that give us texture and meaning. It is our rough spots and jagged edges that give life its flavor, aroma, and feeling. We need both joy and longing, one to hold us in the moment, the other to give us a reason for growth.

I love the seashore because it is forever shifting, changing, and evolving. There is something primal to that love. Perhaps we are all looking back to whence we came, so long ago, hoisting our amphibious beings from water to land. We continued well past the dunes; the ancestors of whales turned back for the freedom of the sea. Since then, like foolish hitchhikers our thumbs have gotten us in a lot of trouble. Working in tandem with our oversized but immature brains, we've built despotic empires, unjust courtrooms, and nuclear weapons. Sometimes I wish we just stuck to singing and swimming, like the whales.

We arrived at the beach before dawn and felt the cold and bracing jolt of the seawater against our feet. Kesley instructed us as to what to look for in the poor light of early morning. We would not be able to see into the water, so we had to watch for other signs of fish actively feeding.

Tails waving in the shallows. V-shaped "pushes" or wakes, where a fish might be moving in. A puff of sand just below the surface that was not caused by the action of the waves but rather, the actions of a feeding corbina. A change of water color or other hint of submerged life. And we actively searched for the dark half-light images of fish almost out of the water as they rode the waves over crab beds while searching for breakfast. In time, my eyes adjusted, and I began to see these things and take my first casts into the wash.

Corbina, *Menticirrhus undulates,* are a demersal fish, which means they are bottom feeders. As members of the croaker family, they most likely have quite a vocabulary. Sound travels well underwater, and research has shown that fish can be talkative creatures, communicating with various grunts, thumps, whistles, whines, clicks, and clacks, so much so that shallow bays filled with fish telling tales can sound like a real ruckus. Fish communicate in various ways. They strive to survive sometimes by hunting and sometimes by avoiding the hunter. Nature is in motion and commotion almost all the time.

These are amazing fish that come to the surf zones of the Sea of Cortez, and up along the coast of Baja California and Southern California up to Point Conception, in Santa Barbara County. They arrive as the water warms in late spring and early summer, and they vanish as the water cools in late summer and early autumn. And to my knowledge, nobody knows where they go. As hard as I searched, I could find no species-specific studies about the size, health, or yearlong travels of the corbina population. All we seem to anecdotally suspect is there are fewer of them than there once were, and they arrive near shore each summer—so far.

Corbina are uniformly iridescent and silvery gray in color, with pronounced black pectoral fins on the more mature fish. When the water is warm, they live in the surf zone of breaking waves, swash, and backwash where they hunt their primary food animal, the sand crab. With downturned mouths and a single barbel on the lower jaw, they seek out crustaceans, and the occasional bivalve or small fish by scooping up the sand around them, and then expelling water, sand, and other non-food items both through the gills and by spitting it out, just as they spit out your fly if you're not quick enough to set the hook.

We began walking southward along the beach, and I tried my best to focus on the surf and swash, looking for corbina and not the area just beyond it where harbor seals and dolphins were on patrol . . . also looking for corbina. Think about it. These fish are risking their lives by surfing the waves and swash up onto the beach in order to hunt and eat sand crabs, while seals, dolphins, sea lions, and sharks hunt them from behind and we hunt them with a fly rod, a loop knot, and Paul Cronin's "Surfin' Merkin" at the end of a nine-foot fluorocarbon leader. That's a tough life for a tough fish!

I began to see fish, or more precisely the shadows and images of fish. At first it was a glimpse of a back fin out of the water, riding in a shallow wave. Then a waving tail, or a puff of sand, or the almost ghost-like feeling of nervous water that did not match all of the rest of the tumbling, foaming, surging, and receding salt-laden H_2O in front of me. And once I began to see the fish, I began casting toward the spot in the foam where I guessed they might be. After a few casts the tip of the rod I had borrowed from Scott simply snapped off. I was mortified, but Kesley said not to worry, it probably already had a crack in it prior to her even stringing it up for me. She offered me her rod, but I declined and after a bit of haggling we agreed to share it, taking turns casting while the other acted as a fish spotter for whomever had the rod in hand. We adapted, like the fish adapt with the tide. It was the natural thing to do.

At one point when it was my turn with the rod, Kesley walked down the beach, looking for corbina activity while I began casting blindly into the surf hoping to get lucky. Aileen was about fifty yards south of me, I assumed, doing the same thing. We had chatted earlier about how we wanted to fish even if we didn't see fish. But when Kesley walked back up to me she asked, "Steve . . . are you casting to a fish?" I said that I was not, but I thought I'd try my luck blind casting into the trough. She said, "Well stop it! You're just jacking off and you want the real thing . . . you want sex! Don't make your move until you see the girl at the bar!" I broke out laughing and so did Aileen. Then Kesley said, "I hope I didn't offend you, but I wanted to say it in a way that you'd remember." I was still laughing when I said, "No worries. I'm a Marine and don't offend easy and trust me when I say, I will never forget that!"

So now I had been told the rules and although it felt a little like having my dentist chastise me for not flossing enough, I knew she was right and that I had no clue what I was doing. Kesley was a good teacher, and I tried my best to be a good learner. We talked gear and technique and how to read the beach and the ocean. And I absorbed these lessons as best I could, not because I felt like I was being coerced to floss, but because I wanted to floss if it was the only way I was going to get the "girl at the bar."

A big part of corbina fishing is walking, walking, walking along the beach and looking, looking, looking for signs of fish activity or good holding areas. Holding areas can include troughs, pools, flats, and rips where currents or waves collide and retreat, often creating slightly deeper channels for beans to travel in as they access the shoreline. Corbina may be present at any stage in a tide or under any light conditions, but certain tides and light lend themselves to more successful sight casting to these fish. We hit the beach at the bottom of an incoming low tide and would fish it as the tide came in and the sun rose up. Once the light gets well overhead, you have better chance of seeing into the water and spotting beans that are actively feeding in the swash.

The sun was still low over our shoulders, so we couldn't see into the water to spot actual feeding fish. But all three of us were seeing fins, wakes, and the dark forms of fish in the surf, and we cast to them repeatedly to no avail. For the most part, Aileen and I stayed focused. Kesley never lets her head get out of the game; she is nothing but focus and determination. Aileen and I fish well together because neither of us is hardcore. We're a bit like little kids, enjoying fishing, but just as happy to watch the seals and dolphins playing in the waves or the black oyster-catchers and white egrets feeding on the beach.

Kesley had the rod, and I was acting as a spotter about the time a young couple walked by, each one picking up bits of seashells and nicely colored stones as they walked. Kesley noticed them and said, "I just don't get these people who pick up shells and stones! I mean, what's the point?" We had all congregated together in that moment, and Aileen and I smiled at each other. Then I showed Kesley the multicolored rounded stones and bits of seashell in my casting bucket and Aileen shared and compared hers and mine as we oohed and aahed at each other's treasures. I'm not sure if Kesley rolled her eyes but I don't think so because a little bit later she walked over and dropped a shell into my bucket and said, "I thought you'd like this one . . . it's a whelk." She was right, I did want it.

◄►

We worked the first beach for several hours and cast toward quite a few corbina, but the sun was still as low as the tide and while the second condition is a fine thing, the first is not ideal. We had the beach mostly to ourselves in the early morning hours, save for the shell-collecting couple and an unhappy-looking jogger wearing baggy blue shorts and a yellow USC shirt. He wasn't very friendly as I said, "Good morning" and seemed a bit annoyed that we were casting on his jogging beach. As it turned out Kesley casually knew of the man and that he was once inadvertently hooked in the ass by the back cast of a fly fisher he was mindlessly jogging behind. Apparently this soured him on anglers in general. Some people have no sense of humor. As the story goes his baggy shorts saved his ass and the Vlahos marbled sand flea never drew blood.

While part of corbina fishing is walking for miles along the beach seeking feeding beans, another part is knowing when to move to another beach because conditions have changed, and the bite is off. We relocated south over toward La Conchita Beach, close to where we planned to have lunch that day at a little place overlooking the ocean. And this was an outside the comfort zone stretch for my friend Kesley because normally she sees food as something to get done with quickly so that it doesn't interrupt fishing. I see food, drink, and music as an integral part of the travel experience. In fact, my friend Maggie Serva once called me the "Tony Bourdain of the outdoors." I took that as a compliment.

To my mind, Bourdain was interested in the entire story of the people and places of his travels. It felt as if his work had little to do with teaching recipes and techniques and a lot to do with how we can eat, drink, and enjoy life together. He found common ground through the food and the breaking of so many varieties of bread. He listened to his hosts intently, not because he had practiced listening, but because he was actually and empathetically interested in what they had to say and share. He was authentic. And I think he felt that food, music, art, and recreation, were all a part of what makes us interesting. This is all speculation on my part, but I can say that fishing for me is not just about catching fish; it's about being present, connected, awake, alive, and grateful.

So, we walked the beach from one end to the other with our rods in hand and our polarized eyes focused on the surf, but we saw not a single bean. There were a few seals on the rocks and a surfing pelican, but no corbina. The tide was getting fairly high and so we broke for lunch and sat by the sea eating crisp healthy salads and delicious golden-brown fries that may have clogged my arteries but sure did free my soul.

Just before we decided to pause on the search for corbina at the southernmost beach, we came across another angler who was wonderfully kind and giving of his time and observations. For the most part, I find the fly-fishing community to be kind and generous, within reason. I must admit when I am back home in my beloved Texas Hill Country and anyone asks me, "Where do you like to fish?" I never give a specific answer to that question. I'm nicely vague about the whole thing and there is a wink and a nod between me and the other angler that we're more likely to give each other the keys to our pickup trucks than we are the directions to our favorite fishing spots.

This guy was different. He was standing in the surf with his extra-wide-brimmed yellowish straw hat, tattered long-sleeved button-up shirt, and old cotton trousers that were so worn by the sun and the wind that they contained no discernable color. His suspenders held the whole thing together along with a sling pack across his back, fly rod in hand and oddly unadorned stripping bucket hanging low on his ultra-thin midriff. I got the sense that he was a serious angler who like Kesley and Scott, might also find the idea of stopping for lunch a bit crazy. Still, he told us exactly which beach he had been to earlier that morning and how many corbina he saw. We thanked him and made plans to be there just as the tide was right.

When we arrived at Recon Beach it felt like conditions could not be better. The sun was bright and high and the tide was turning in more ways than one. By now, Kesley had prevailed upon me to hold on to the rod and I agreed when she said, "Steve, I live here . . . I can come back." We had talked about it over lunch and decided that we'd have backup gear the next day, just in case anything went wrong like a rod, reel, or line breaking.

Kesley is a good friend and an excellent teacher. I got the feeling that she did not think she would be, but her natural passion for angling and her extensive knowledge of this fish and its habitat were all invaluable. I also got the feeling that she was really enjoying watching her friends as we became totally engrossed and enamored with corbina fishing. I am forever grateful to her. We never know how our chosen acts of kindness change another person's life forever.

As we walked down to the beach we passed a sign that read, "No Dogs/Smoke Free Area/Nudity Prohibited." I didn't really think much about the sign until we got down to the beach and I saw a naked man smoking a joint on the beach while dogs ran freely around him. It reminded me of a quote I once read by Terry Pratchett that read, "Some humans would do anything to see if it was possible to do it. If you put a large switch in some cave somewhere, with a sign on it saying 'End-of-the-World Switch. PLEASE DO NOT TOUCH', the paint wouldn't even have time to dry." I tend to agree with Albert Camus when he wrote, "Integrity has no need of rules." If mutual respect and responsibility guides us in our exercise of personal liberty, no sign is necessary.

Once we got past the bundle of beachgoers that were clustered near the walkway to the parking lot, we had the beach mostly to ourselves. I noticed as we walked farther away from the masses of humanity that the beach became cleaner, the water seemed clearer, and nature was all around us here, near a city of twelve million people. We don't have to wander far off the beaten path to feel far less beaten. Peace is just around any corner.

The ocean tumbled rhythmically. The seals and dolphins patrolled the breakers, and the oystercatchers, plovers, and seagulls were far better company than the masses of humans we'd left behind. Lines of prehistoric-looking brown pelicans soared past us, one after another. Brandt's cormorants fished and floated farther out to sea. California mussels and various small sea anemones clung to the occasional stone that protruded from the sand. With the receding of each wave the beach came alive with burrowing sand crabs. Standing in the wet sand and listening to the sounds of the sea, I felt young again.

Aileen looked over at me and said, "I'd forgotten how much I love the ocean." I told her that I was having the same realization. She grew up in Los Angeles and I grew up in Florida. Two oceans; same sense of home. I was at peace, standing at the edge of the surf, next to two dear friends, smiling. Life was beautiful, again. All I had to do was wait for it. Tides always change.

One of the amazing things about fishing with close friends is that you can have your own solitary experience at the same time that you share it with a kindred spirit. Aileen and I were separated by about fifty yards but we were still fishing together. Kesley was being ever so giving as she refused to take the one rod we had between us and allowed me to fish while she acted as bean-spotter and bean-fishing teacher to us both.

The water and beach were perfect in every way. The waves rolled in across a sandscape that included all the right elements for corbina. There were rips, pools, and long sloping flats. There was an abundance of crab beds which showed themselves clearly as the water washed over them, their antennae leaving V-shaped markings in the wet sand. Some of the beds may have been as small as a hula hoop while others might stretch for many yards across a sloping expanse of waterlogged sand.

Earlier in the day Kesley asked me what I loved most about my experience so far and it was easy for me to answer: "I love learning how to read the beach and the water." And with that, "I love learning about these fish, their prey and their predators." I feel the same way about fishing small creeks and rivers for trout. Fly fishing is a perfect pastime for a naturalist. It causes you to enter into the world of the fish and everything it is connected to, and everything that is connected to it . . . just like me.

Kesley had coached me well about the need for pinpoint accuracy when sight casting to corbina. And I was casting well . . . really in the thoughtless, mindless, mushin zone where I saw a fish and instantly cast toward it, but in that instant is where I failed to seal the deal. I was so focused on finding and quickly and accurately casting to beans that I failed to control my propensity for casting directly to the object of my observation. So, instead of presenting the fly three or four feet in front of the bean, I was beaning the bean right on the head. I didn't do it all the time, but at least half a dozen good-sized fish flipped and splashed their way back to the trough after I inadvertently smacked them directly on the head with a Surfin' Merkin! I laughed, but I guess it wasn't funny that I was blowing perfectly good opportunities on some pretty nice-sized corbina. Kesley high-fived me and said, "That's good . . . you're being aggressive!" Now all I had to do was stop hitting them and start catching them.

Looking down the beach I could see that Aileen was having a similar experience of seeing and casting toward a lot of corbina but with no takes as of yet. But the action was intense and I was having as much fun as I have ever had on any fishing trip. And that is saying a lot. I became entranced by these silver-gray sucker-mouthed mystery fish. Just the idea of their summer lifestyle was amazing.

The waves came in and I found myself leaning toward them, staring intently into each wave's wash, and waiting for the sand particles to settle and the water to clear. Sometimes when the six to sixteen inches of water between surface and sand became clear, there was nothing to see but burrowing sand crabs and waving leaves of drifting kelp. Other times the corbina appeared, either cruising parallel to the troughs searching for prey, or ascending the beach using the foam of the wash to carry them toward the crabs and then back into the ocean. In that time the angler has only a moment to cast, present, and give action to the fly. Only a moment, and not another moment longer. It is enthralling.

I forgot to drink water. I forgot about the illusion of time. I even forgot to breathe. All I remembered was to lean forward in anticipation, look forward in concentration, cast forward in breathless hope, strip line backward as enticement, and live forever in the moment. The world vanished as quickly as the fish. I was performing the kata of corbina.

Everything was in motion, and everything was frozen in the reality of its timelessness. Bill Blake's words tumbled through my mind: "To see a world in a grain of sand. And a heaven in a wildflower. Hold infinity in the palm of your hand. And Eternity in an hour." The waves rolled back and in between them; I could breathe again. I walked. I searched. I cast. I walked again.

My friends and I had covered over twelve miles of beach that day, in search of this amazing creature. In the end our feet hurt, our legs hurt, our bodies were burned by the sun and worn by the walking. We caught exactly zero fish, did not get a single tug, and it was worth every mile, every cast, and every anguished moment. There was value in watching my fly land on the water, stripping it toward me as the wave fell away toward the sea. It didn't matter if the fish of my dreams swam by my offering, uninterested each time. I was fishing.

As we reeled in and walked back, passing the naked dope smoker and the free-running dogs and toward the city of twelve million people, I remembered Scott's words from the day before. "And even if you do everything right, more often than not the fish will ignore your fly . . . you just never know." Today, I caught nothing. Tomorrow was another day. Tonight, I knew I'd be dreaming of corbina.

CHAPTER TWELVE

Corbina—The Beaches of Ventura County, California

The Last Day of the Quest

We have lived our lives by the assumption that what was good for us would be good for the world. We have been wrong. We must change our lives so that it will be possible to live by the contrary assumption, that what is good for the world will be good for us. And that requires that we make the effort to know the world and learn what is good for it.

~ WENDELL BERRY, *THE LONG-LEGGED HOUSE*

THERE WAS A CHILL IN THE AIR WHEN WE ARRIVED AT RECON BEACH. The sun was not yet shining through the early morning fog bank that seemed to render both the mountains to our east and the ocean horizon to our west, almost dreamlike. We unloaded the gear from Kesley's "Urban Assault Vehicle." She drives a black Toyota 4Runner with a four-rod capacity enclosed rack on top that looks like a rocket launcher from a

Somali "Technical." And being a true "Angeleno," she takes no prisoners when she's driving down "the 101" on the way to the beach.

Looking down from the bluff we could see the harbor seals on patrol just beyond the breakers. It seemed that we had the beach and the ocean mostly to ourselves. At first we did what any good angler does, we watched and waited to see what nature was telling us. Kesley spotted some motion along a rip at the edge of a deepish pool and told Aileen and me to work either side of the pool, and we did.

A moment later I saw a boil and the splashing flip of a tail and I instinctively cast toward the rip just beside the splash, stripped the line three times and felt the tug. Almost in amazement I set the hook and began fighting the first corbina of my life as Kesley coached me each step of the way. The bean went on a short run and I did my best to keep the tension on with my line hand as I quickly moved backward and farther up on the beach, so as to get him on the reel. Once he was on the reel the fight was on, my rod bent sharply, the corbina kicking and twisting in the surf, and me applying pressure and not knowing how much was too much.

Kesley moved up toward the surf to help me land the bean. "Oh, it's a nice fish!" she hollered. "It's about four to four and a half pounds!" I'm not sure if that made me more excited, or more worried . . . and that's when I felt him pull hard and I pulled back just as hard, and the tippet broke, along with a piece of my heart. The first corbina of my life was gone.

I really did not know how to land that fish, but I knew in that instant that I had pulled too hard when I should have let him run. "If you love something, let it go." I knew better; I just didn't do better. And so, I stood there with this comical look on my face as I cried out to the universe, "Oh no!" with my arms splayed wide, my expression one of disbelief. Norman Maclean once wrote, "Poets talk about 'spots of time,' but it is really the fishermen who experience eternity compressed into a moment. No one can tell what a spot of time is until suddenly the whole world is a fish, and the fish is gone." I was experiencing, "a spot of time." I had come so close to holding that magnificent fish in my hands, and then in an instant, he was free and I was forever bonded to the moment we parted ways. I will never forget him.

When things come undone in fishing or in life, the only thing we can do is learn from the experience, check our knots, leaders, and previous assumptions, remember, and adapt to what we've learned and cast forward once again, in a new direction. I have shared with some of my dearest friends the fact that two Hollywood movies helped to change my life. Now, I will share this story with you, my new friends. The first movie was *Rocky*, the 1976 drama written by and starring Sylvester Stallone.

I saw that film at the Paramount Theater on the island of Palm Beach when I was sixteen years old. My dad took me, and while he found it to be entertaining I found it to be transformative. I was a short, overweight, desperately shy adolescent who had been abused as a child and who was constantly bullied in school. But when I saw that movie, I realized that I could control much about my own destiny and although I could do nothing about what happened to me, I could do everything about my choices in dealing with life's challenges. In short, *Rocky* woke me up to being proactive not reactive and helped me to move myself from "victim" to "victor." It was a lesson I never forgot.

After two years of controlling my diet, working out, running, and disciplining my mind, I became a U.S. Marine who would go on to be four times meritoriously promoted before time-in-grade. I transformed myself through sheer willpower and determination and learned to take each hit as an opportunity to grow stronger. I learned to listen to my own voice and not the voices of others who might wish to impose their limitations upon me. And I have shared that same invaluable lesson with anyone who might have needed it, as much as I did then. Rocky was the perfect lesson for an awkward sixteen-year-old.

The second movie that changed my life was *Rocky Balboa*, the 2006 film written, directed by, and starring Sylvester Stallone, in which a post-middle-aged prize fighter comes out of retirement to prove to himself and others that he still has "stuff in the basement." Rocky Balboa was the perfect lesson for an aging sixty-year-old.

In that movie the character Rocky gives a speech to his son that is the essence of what needs to be said to so many of us, both young and old. It goes like this:

*Let me tell you something you already know. The world ain't all sun-
shine and rainbows. It's a very mean and nasty place and I don't care
how tough you are it will beat you to your knees and keep you there
permanently if you let it. You, me, or nobody is gonna hit as hard as
life. But it ain't about how hard ya hit. It's about how hard you can
get hit and keep moving forward. How much you can take and keep
moving forward. That's how winning is done!*

We all take life's hits. It is in hardship that we are all defined. I have
been beaten down by life many times, but I have never been defeated. I
get back up. And where one person laments losing a friend or a fish, I
celebrate that even for a moment I was connected to either. I count my
blessings, not my burdens. Expectations can lead to a sense of exaspera-
tion that robs us of our joy. Acceptance leads to a sense of gratitude that
reminds us of the many reasons to be joyful.

As momentarily deflated as I was not to land that corbina, I was also
elated to have hooked it in the first place, against all odds. So, I walked
down the beach to the next likely spot, watched until I saw another
corbina tailing in the shallows, and I cast forward again with a renewed
sense of hope and promise. Life was as beautiful, as always. Everything is
forever changing and there is nothing in life that we possess for all time
. . . including life itself. The corbina was never mine; nothing had been
lost.

There was a lot of activity on both ends of the pools and although
the light wasn't bright enough to see into the water we could see the
tails, backs, and V-shaped wakes of feeding corbina. All three of us were
finding fish to cast to and before long I felt another tug, set the hook, and
found myself connected to a smaller but still powerful bean. This time I
tried to do a better job of getting it on the reel and allowing it to run
whenever it wanted to, applying side pressure, and reeling it in whenever
the fish gave its subtle permission. In short . . . I was practicing all that I
was learning from Kesley.

I walked it back on the beach and Kesley excitedly reeled in and came
over to try to help me land it just as she had done before. I could feel
it thrashing along the sandy bottom and was doing my best to keep the

tension on but not make the same mistake I had made on the first fish, and I didn't. Instead, I made a new mistake, allowing the briefest moment of slack which is all that it needed to somehow slip the hook. Incredulously I found myself standing there slack lined and slack jawed with the score: Corbina two, Steve zero. It didn't matter. Kesley and I high-fived each other while Aileen cheered. Kesley said, "Steve, you're on fire!" We were having a great morning!

I looked down the beach toward Aileen and although I don't pray anymore, I made a silent wish to whomever might be listening that she'd be the one to catch a corbina. Aileen has one of the kindest hearts I've ever known, and I wanted to see her holding a corbina with a bright smile on her face. These are the moments that make fishing with friends so precious and perfect. I always find myself taking "snapshots" with my mind. I think that's called making memories.

The chill of the morning had worn off and the sun was beginning to rise up over the edge of the bluff and onto our shoulders. And about the time I was realizing that it was getting warm Aileen saw me looking at her and she called out over the sound of the surf, "Are you taking your jacket off?" I saw that Aileen and Kesley had already stowed their windbreakers into their packs so, I yelled back, "I guess I really should!" Aileen started laughing and said, "I asked you if you were jacking off!" Then we both started laughing and I shouted back, "Yes . . . you caught me just casting blindly into the waves." She laughed and said, "Well stop it! You don't make your move until you see the girl at the bar!"

I noticed that the three of us had our own styles for working the water. Aileen is as patient as anyone I've ever known, and she likes to find good water where she is seeing or has seen activity and work it methodically and completely. She waits and watches, like an elegant egret, standing on the shore. Kesley likes to cover a lot of ground and seems to be always on the move. She had scouted much farther down the beach stopping only when she actively saw fish feeding, sort of like a vigilant osprey, soaring over the waves. I'm somewhere in the middle.

I enjoy working a rip, flat, or pool then taking a few steps down to the next one, sometimes focused on sight casting to a single fish and other times just fishing by casting my hopes into "likely places." I must admit that I did not always wait to see the "girl at the bar." All in all, we made a nice little flock of misfits who smiled and laughed as often as we cast, and that's a good thing.

I began casting to a few corbina that I saw riding the surf toward the crab beds, just about the same time I heard some commotion and excitement coming from where Aileen and Kesley were standing. As it turned out, my silent wish to the universe was heard and Aileen was into a nice-sized corbina. I saw the look on Aileen's face and heard Kesley cheering her on and got so excited myself that I almost forgot to watch the water in front of me.

Before I could do much more than let out a cheer for my friend, I saw a splash in the water and a couple of nice beans cruising through the trough, just down from a crab bed. I was too slow to cast to them as they were in the swash, and just then another wave crashed ashore obscuring the fish beneath the foam. I cast my line toward the most likely place for the fish to be and after a single strip of the line, I felt the pull and set the hook. Now we had a double hookup between me and Aileen with Kesley trying to coach us both at the same time! Kesley was spending so much time and energy trying to help us catch a bean that she barely had any time to fish for herself.

I was like a giddy kid as I backed away from the surf, got the bean on the reel, and began trying to work it in toward the shore. When I lost the last fish, I asked Kesley for some tips on fighting and landing corbina. This time I knew the value of applying side pressure, letting them run and then working them back in, and most of all, allowing the action of the surf to help me work the fish farther and farther onto shore. In a sense, I was trying to "beach the bean."

I was so busy trying to hold on to my fish that I completely missed what was going on with Aileen and her bean, but as it turned out we both came unhooked from our fish at about the same time. We had a double hookup and a double long-distance release. We both moaned with that open-mouthed expression of a kid whose double-dipped ice cream just fell off the cone and onto the sand.

After a moment of disbelief came the laughter and the joy of actually being fortunate enough to have hooked a corbina. I had hooked and lost three and Aileen had hooked and lost another, and from Kesley's reaction, we beginners were having a banner day! This is as good a time as any to reiterate that I fell in love with corbina fishing, and Kesley was an amazing teacher. She is all business when focused on fish which probably explains her string of world records . . . but with us, she was kind, patient, and giving. I will never forget that. I am forever grateful.

⌒〜

We did break for lunch as the tide came in and the sightings of fish dwindled down to nothing more than recent memories. All along I had asked my two friends from Los Angeles to take me someplace that served food that was "quintessential L.A." We had discussed calamari tacos at a shack on another beach, and that seemed interesting to me. But we never made it to that other beach so they took me to an In-N-Out Burger. I'm not sure how quintessentially L.A. it is, but I can say this; it was my first In-N-Out Burger and I savored every calorie-packed moment. And it did feel authentically L.A. as we sat outside next to a busy highway while paying appropriate attention to the various questionable characters who circled around us like seagulls behind a shrimp boat. None of that mattered. After walking over twelve miles on the beach the day prior and about another six miles that morning, we ate our burgers and fries as if it was the best meal of our lives. In lunch as in life, it's all about context.

When we got back to Recon Beach the sun was high, the sand was hot, and the tide was in a better place than it was when we left. I felt myself click into "hunting mode," because now the light was good, and we could see the corbina as they rode the waves up onto the beach in search of sand crabs. This kind of fishing is not unlike searching and sight casting to bonefish except this wasn't the Bahamas and bonefish are definitely easier to catch than corbina. I love sight-fishing in part because it really feels like hunting. Fishing the surf for corbina reminded me a lot of what it was like to hunt for kudu in Africa.

Seeing them is the most important thing . . . stalking them is next . . . setting up the shot doesn't come easy, and following through to the end takes all the concentration and dedication you can muster. To my mind, corbina fishing is a true adventure. It has all the requisite qualities of challenge, complexity, and uncertainty.

For those who are unfamiliar, a kudu is a large, spiral-horned antelope of eastern and southern Africa. They are difficult to hunt, especially the old bulls, and their ability to seemingly vanish in the bush has earned them the name "gray ghosts." I hunted kudu in Namibia, walking endless miles through thornbush and up razor-sharp volcanic kloofs and through tree-dotted grasslands that harbored puff adders, spitting cobras, and black mambas. And I did this for thirteen hard days while carrying my pack, water, ammunition, and rifle while following Bushman trackers who never seemed to grow weary.

Like corbina, kudu can be quite difficult to see as they move and blend with their habitat. And like corbina, they are perfectly suited for the challenge of avoiding the many predators that seek them, including humans. In order to successfully hunt African kudu, I had to consider the conditions of the habitat and the nature of the kudu as a species. I had to pay attention to the wind, sunlight, shadows, vegetation, and structures ... just as I must take notice of the current, waves, light, shadow, and structure of the beach when seeking corbina.

And then there is the problem of the presentation of a weighted crab fly just far enough in front of a moving corbina that is swimming of its own free will, within a moving ocean. The cast must be timed perfectly, so that the fly has time to sink to the bottom of a wave-covered shoreline that varies in depth from moment to moment. And then, at just the right moment, I must give that fly just enough motion to attract and not repel the fish. I might add that you are doing all this while trying to attract a fish that is both easily spooked and remarkably fickle. Easy peasy, right? It's a wonder that we ever catch a corbina.

———

When thinking about corbina we need to also be thinking about why the corbina are in the trough and why they risk life and fin to get up the beach while riding in the shallow slosh of a wave. The answer to this question is contained in one creature that has several names: sand crab, mole crab, sand flea, and more specifically, *Emerita analoga*.

A sand crab spends most of its time buried in shifting sand in the swash zone, which is the area of the beach where waves are breaking, surging, and receding. They are well camouflaged by their grayish shells and are perfectly designed to live in this dynamic environment, absorbing the power of a wave as it washes over their curved, armored bodies. They hold on to their place in the sand with a complement of sharply pointed legs. Unlike most crabs, sand crabs have no claws and can only move backward of their own volition. They also use the power of the sea to move them up and down the beach with the changing tide. As soon as a sand crab washes to a new location with the incoming wave, it quickly burrows backward into the sand with only its primary antennae showing, forming a pronounced V shape in the sand.

As corbina anglers we need to look for "crab beds" where many of these little creatures have gathered because that space on the beach favors them in that moment of time and tide. If you watch closely as a wave is receding over them, you may see the crabs uncoil a second pair of featherlike antennae which they use to filter out tiny plankton that they feed on. The plankton, which consists mostly of single-celled plants called dinoflagellates, may photosynthesize energy from the sun or combine that action with the capturing and digestion of even smaller prey creatures like protozoa.

Everything in nature eats something else, even if that something else is sunlight itself. And the food chain from porpoise to protozoa grows evermore minuscule, which means every large living thing on Earth requires the existence of the smallest living things on Earth in order to survive. Individual death and the transference of the sun's energy are prerequisites for continued life on this planet. To paraphrase the poet John Donne, any death of a species or habitat diminishes the whole.

And it is important to understand that many things in this vast ocean feed on and depend upon the tiny sand crab. They are eaten by various fishes, seabirds, and shorebirds. Some studies have indicated that up to 90 percent of the diet of corbina and barred surfperch is sand crabs, and in turn, seals, sea lions, dolphins, and various larger gamefish feed on corbina and surf perch. It's all connected in one big loop that circles around the sun. We're all in this together. No one is on top.

I am as much a naturalist as an angler, and I find my experience is infinitely richer because I take the time to learn about the creatures I seek to connect with, and in doing so, I learn about the world. I have a long way to go in my knowledge of knots, flies, techniques, and other such mechanical aspects of angling. Almost everyone knows more about these things than I do, and watching me tie a knot with my battered, dysfunctional fingers and aged, malfunctioning eyes can be something between comical and pathetic. But I see and feel more than many, and therefore my life as an angler is never reduced to counting numbers of fish caught or the size of the fish compared to the tippet strength.

The problem with such "goals" is that they are never enough. One artificial "milestone" leads to another, and another, like a drug fix that always wears off. But for me, knowing more about how everything works in the surf, sea, or a mountain stream makes the entire experience of angling richer and more meaningful. I appreciate a fish for the magnificent creature it is, not as a "trophy" or simple source of protein. I'm weird like that.

—❦—

As the afternoon wore on, we walked mile after mile, back and forth across the beach while casting to fish as we saw them and searching for fish when we didn't. Things had obviously slowed down and the tide continued to rise and at one point we stopped searching and just stood together on the beach enjoying each other's good company. That's when Kesley said, "I think we're seeing less fish here today than we did this time yesterday because Steve kept smacking them on the head with the fly!" We all laughed and agreed that somewhere down in the trough was a corbina warning the others, "Dude, don't go up there! Some idiot keeps hitting me on the head every time I swim into the swash!"

The sun drifted westward, the fish shifted outward, and the catching became nonexistent. I was still seeing the occasional corbina cruising through the waves or up the beach in the swash and I cast to them every chance I got, but most of them simply ignored me. Sometimes the beans would be swimming in the trough, parallel to the beach and just ahead of me so that I'd have to run up the beach and get ahead of them so that I could present my cast. More times than not by the time I got in position another wave would wash over the fish and they were gone.

One time I snuck down to an incoming wave to peek in and look for fish just as a nice corbina was coming up that same wave to look for sand crabs. We ran into each other at the same time and both of us leapt backward—me on two awkward feet and she on several elegant fins. In another instance I had a big corbina following my fly up the beach as I stripped it farther and farther into an ever-diminishing wave. In the end the wave began to ebb, the bean refused to commit, and we parted ways as ocean became wet sand once again.

By the end of the day, we had walked another twelve miles and cast more times than I ever have on a single day of fishing. I saw many, many, corbina, and all that effort led to me hooking and losing three, getting three more solid strikes, all of which I missed, and a couple of good follows that led nowhere in particular. Aileen hooked and lost one and Kesley spent most of her time coaching us in her valiant effort to help us catch a fish. We came close, and Kesley was a truly wonderful teacher.

I never leave a river or an ocean without taking a few final lingering looks and taking in all that was beautiful and amazing about that place and time. This was no different. I reeled in and stood there on the beach, looking out and in and occasionally back. I was thinking of my dad who had passed away five years prior and how he loved and lived for the sea. We used to call him "The Captain." And I was thinking of my childhood, growing up along the Atlantic Ocean, and all that I once loved about being there, and all that has vanished from those waters since that time. Then my mind wandered back to the present, as I watched a harbor seal swimming through the curl of a wave. I saw a line of once-endangered brown pelicans as they soared over the ocean and a trio of black oyster-catchers, as they worked their way along the wash of the waves.

They were all seeking bits of life, so as to sustain their own lives a little longer. Every living thing shares a desire to keep living. Inside every corbina, harbor seal, and oystercatcher is a beating heart and a sense of self.

And all I could think of was of how amazing it was to see so much wildlife in one place. There were fish and shellfish, birds, and myriads of marine mammals . . . seals, sea lions, dolphins, and whales. There was so much life here that still remains, against all odds. In that moment, it was so easy to forget that just a few miles away existed a sprawling city of twelve million humans. I wondered, how long can this last? I hope this ocean and this world can prosper, as long as the sun continues to shine.

As I walked from the beach and away from the sea, I recalled the thought that came to me earlier that day. . . . It's all one big loop that circles around the sun. The sun's light sustains the Earth's life. The Earth's life gives meaning to the sun's light. I hope my humble words can help us to tighten our loop, connect to all life, and lighten our mutual path forward.

CHAPTER THIRTEEN

The Crossing of the Santa Barbara Channel

Channel Island National Park and Marine Sanctuary

Time just seems to fly away for a boy. That, I s'pose, is why one day
you wake up suddenly and you ain't a boy any longer
~ ROBERT RUARK, *THE OLD MAN AND THE BOY*

CROSSINGS ARE ALWAYS TRANSFORMATIVE, AND THIS ONE WOULD BE NO different. The history of humanity and of every individual human is nothing less than a story of crossings. Depending upon the crossing and what we find upon arrival in "the new world," we may or may not return. And even if we do return, we are not the same being who crossed over in the first instance. We are forever changed, for better or worse, or both. And if there is no change then we failed to travel, because travel includes more than transportation across geography; travel includes transformation and transmogrification. It is a metamorphosis that alters the way we see the universe and ourselves. It is a gift . . . if we choose to open it.

When Columbus sailed the ocean blue, the Taino natives never knew that his crossings and those of others like him would bring about the end of their world. He was followed by Pizarro and Cortés, Drake and

Rolfe, each bringing with them people, ideas, weapons, and pathogens that ended one way of life and gave birth to another. In viral fashion Europe was replicated, treaties were negotiated under duress and over time one culture supplanted another. More accurately, cultures mingled and became integrated so that eventually the colonists of the Americas, both north and south of the equator, rejected their original homelands of England, Scotland, France, Portugal, and Spain, and they too became "Americans." Crossings are always transformative and all too often, penetrative.

As the ferry boat carried us over the ocean from Ventura Harbor to Scorpion Landing, I was thinking of this transformation of people and places. On a mist-filled morning, my friends Aileen, Kesley, and I were crossing the Santa Barbara Channel to the Channel Islands National Park and Marine Sanctuary. As a teller of stories, I needed to experience this magnificent coastline that even today is so brimming with wildlife that it seems wholly appropriate that these waters be an integral part of "the Serengeti of the Sea."

This coast where my friends and I had sought corbina in the surf is also home to a multitude of fish, fowl, and marine mammals. It contains vast forests of kelp and deep canyons where whales are drawn close to the coastline, and millions of sardines, anchovies, and Pacific menhaden thrive, if we let them. It contains rocky shores with tidal pools filled with wave-washed creatures that cling to the Earth and depend on the sea. It contains estuaries that are the tidal cradles of life, ever changing, ever rejuvenating through the cycle of life, death, decay, and new life. It contains garnet-purple sands that hold communities of microbes and mollusks, crustaceans, and other arthropods. And this is the message that every angler, sea-glass-seeking beachcomber, surfer, scuba diver, and otherwise engaged human being must understand: The ocean is vast but not without limits.

In many ways we Homo sapiens are depleting the sea, almost to the breaking point. That breaking point might be the sad silence that comes when there are no more whales singing in the sea. Or that breaking point might be the all-encompassing silence that comes when there are no more microbes clinging to a single grain of sand. And there is no doubt life on Earth as we know it ends if we kill off the phytoplankton that provides most of the oxygen we breathe.

Repetition creates memory, and I want us all to remember that everything is connected to everything. The biggest living creatures survive on the shoulders of the most minuscule. A world without microbes and phytoplankton is a dead world. It is a world without humans. Nature doesn't need us; we need nature. Evolution is not pyramidal or linear; it is a silken spider's web. With every strand we snap, we come perilously close to collapsing that intricate web, and sending it tumbling into time, and oblivion.

The crossing to Santa Cruz Island took just under an hour. Along the way we saw the massive rolling back of a whale and several arched silhouettes of common dolphins. Pods of hundreds of dolphins are not uncommon in these waters. Marauding schools of tuna live beside sun-loving and solitary swordfish, and this fact alone is reason for hope. They're still here.

At one point the captain slowed the ship to a full stop, and we all wondered why. We wondered if he had seen a pod of whales in his path or perhaps a swirling vortex of tuna and sardines, but no natural wonder had ceased our progress. To his credit he stopped the ship so that a member of the crew could remove a Mylar balloon from the ocean's surface. They are a scourge to marine wildlife who mistake them as food once the metallic paint wears off into the sea.

An especially terrible toll is paid by sea turtles that ingest what they mistake for jellyfish or other food item but turns out to be an indigestible and potentially deadly meal. The death toll includes an immeasurable amount of marine mammals, seabirds, coastal waterfowl, turtles, and fish. Still for every clueless dolt tossing plastic onto the land or into the air and sea, there is an enlightened ship's captain, beachcomber, angler, or hiker ready to do the right thing and pick it up. We could save ourselves a lot of bending if we just stood up for the Earth. As an angler, I'm in love with wild and sacred mountain streams and ocean shores . . . not desecrated canals and waterfront wastelands. How about you?

Santa Cruz Island seemed to appear like some maritime Brigadoon, rising out of a sea that was once much shallower, combining all of the Northern Channel Islands into a single landmass. With more land exposed from the sea, the channel was only five or so miles from the mainland and the crossings of Native Americans and native wildlife came more naturally. The Channel Islands contain endemic species of mammal, bird, reptile, amphibian, and insect that are found nowhere else on Earth. I was hoping to see a few of them as we explored the hills and bluffs that are surrounded by the bluest ocean I have ever seen.

As we sailed into Scorpion Landing, I tried to imagine the Native American Chumash peoples navigating these waters with ease in the small dugout canoes they called tomols. These able seagoing vessels were hand carved out of native coastal redwood or pine. Tomols once allowed the Chumash to conduct trade and transport between island and mainland villages.

Today, huge cargo ships and tankers occupy the same shipping lanes through the channel that the Chumash once paddled. Several endangered or threatened species of whale that travel and feed in the Santa Barbara Channel are at risk of being struck by ships passing through the shipping lane. Marine scientists have estimated about eighty endangered whales are killed from vessel collisions off the U.S West Coast each year, although the number of killed and wounded is likely higher.

One of these massive cargo ships slowly passed by us just before we reached the island. It was a four-story-high, floating parking garage that was returning to Japan after dropping off a shipment of automobiles. It was most likely carrying various raw materials purchased in the United States for use in Japan. The amount of ballast required to keep the ship upright in the ocean must be adjusted depending upon the weight of the cargo. In the early days of maritime trade that ballast would be made up of stones and soil that would be dumped at each destination, thus creating the exchange of not only valuable trade goods, but also harmful invasive species of animals and plants that clung to the stone and lived in the soil.

In these times the ballast will be in the form of sea water drawn into the ship in one part of the world and released back into the oceans, bays, and Great Lakes of another part of the world. With that water come foreign and invasive plants, animals, and microscopic organisms. Few people realize that the international shipping trade is transporting a second potentially dangerous cargo, namely entire aquatic ecosystems, from one sea to another.

We already know the negative impact from the introduction of Black Sea zebra mussels, Japanese crabs, Asian mosquitoes, and stowaway jellyfish, but we have no idea what the impact is of transporting various forms of plankton and their predators from one ocean to another. Yet we continue, unperturbed and with no effort to mitigate the threat. Commerce at all costs is the mantra of the money changers.

Scorpion Landing is the site of an old homestead and cattle ranch and today there is a modern dock, campground, and a small museum. In the time of the Chumash this cove was a natural settlement site, complete with a source of fresh running water. Gratefully, most of this island has been preserved and protected by both the National Park Service and the Nature Conservancy.

Much of the waters around the Channel Islands, including Scorpion Landing, are set aside as National Marine Protected Areas that include 1,470 square miles of ocean, as well as the plants and animals that call these waters home. As an angler and naturalist, I don't mind that I can't fish here with my fly rod; I fish with my eyes. Wherever there is moving water, I am fishing for something. It doesn't matter if my quarry is corbina, bonefish, or simply peace of mind. Even if I never have the opportunity to visit a particular wilderness, whether terrestrial or marine in nature—it pleases me to know these places still exist.

Leaning on the dock railing, we paused to look into the clear, blue-green water, down in between the swaying stalks of giant kelp, into the empty spaces that were intermittently filled with bright-blue surf perch and blaze-orange Garibaldi. We knew there were other fish down there, even if we did not see them at that moment. There are California sheepshead, rockfish, kelpfish, giant sea bass, and leopard sharks that depend upon this habitat. Kelp forests contain and sustain more varieties of marine plants and animals than almost any other oceanic community. The naturalist in me was content with the fish we were catching with our eyes. The angler in me echoed Kesley's sentiments when she said, "I sure would like to take a kayak and cast the edges of that kelp to see what comes up!" That's what happens whenever three anglers go for a walk by the sea. We see possibilities.

Hiking on Santa Cruz begins with climbing up and up and up and ends with a gradual descent until you end up back where you started . . . kind of like life. The day was warm, the sky was blue, and the drifting clouds were few and far between. Wherever clouds did exist they did so in wispy and cotton puff shapes of imaginary running horses, flying raptors, and the occasional winged angel. It was the kind of sky that makes you want to lie on your back in a grassy meadow and just watch the world spin. But we were on our way to Potato Point, which struck me as a stupid name for such a beautiful place.

So, we began climbing with Kesley leading the way, Aileen directly behind her, and me falling backward as if gravity had ahold of my backside, and in a way, it did. But for the most part what was holding me back was something else. My asthmatic lungs were reminding me that no matter how strong my will to climb may be, the trajectory of my life's vigor was downward. This year, more than any before it, I felt my age.

It's not the years; it's the mileage that gets you. It's not time, it's the expansion of the universe that changes you, for all time. Ashes to ashes and stardust to stardust, with only salt water remaining. So, I keep casting forward and onward with increasing urgency. I write these words in the sand with full knowledge of the incoming tide.

As we climbed up the steep, winding trail to the top of the bluff, I tried my best to focus on the landscape, the wildflowers, and the promise of looking once again into the ocean and across the horizon. I focused on the way the grasses bent and swayed in the wind, and the swirling, rising, falling, mystical flight of the swallows. I searched the underbrush for spotted towhees and felt childlike excitement at the sudden scurry of an island scrub lizard. And I noticed how effortlessly the ravens and seagulls floated from rolling sea to ridgetop, as I found myself wishing for wings. Do songbirds ever grow weary of flight? I suspect the older ones do.

When we arrived at the top of Cavern Point, Kesley raised her arms in a gesture somewhere between "victory" and "reverie." Aileen looked back and smiled at me as I made the final labored steps to reach the top and join my friends. I was out of breath when I stood next to Kesley and confided, "I don't know whether I should feel upset with myself for having such a tough time climbing these hills . . . or pleased with myself for being sixty years old and still climbing." Without hesitation and with a sense of compassion she replied, "You should feel pleased." I will never forget that simple act of kindness.

Before turning away from Cavern Point, we stood just close enough to the end of the cliff to look down into the ocean below, searching for rising fish as anglers are apt to do anytime water is near. Close to the rocky shoreline was a vast kelp forest and even from two thousand feet above, we could see the bright orange Garibaldi, the bluish-colored surf perch, and a few nondescript shadows of fish below. A seal raised its head with a large fish in his mouth and he shook it violently as seagulls circled around him, picking pieces of the seal's lunch from the surface of the sea. They seemed like sparrows eating crumbs at a picnic.

I know we were all thinking the same thing. If only we could cast a sinking line into the edges of the kelp, what might we find? But we were looking into the Scorpion National Marine Reserve, and the only legal fishing there is being done by seals and sea lions, pelicans, and eagles. I'm okay with that. This is as close as I might find to a natural seascape, but even here we leave our mark.

Not far from these seemingly pristine ocean waters, scientists from San Diego's Scripps Institution of Oceanography led a mission to map out an underwater dumping site that may contain as many as 100,000 barrels of toxic chemicals. These toxins were disposed of by various companies, prior to any regulations being in place or enforced by the United States government. Now corroded and leaking deep within the San Pedro Basin, no one really knows what the outcome will be to this pending ecological disaster. Seals, sea lions, and other marine life are already showing signs of toxic chemicals in their bodies, with some pinnipeds developing cancer that may be related to this human-caused pollution.

I feel about the ocean as I do of the forest, deserts, canyons, and wetlands. There needs to be places where we try our best to look . . . and not touch. Nature must have a place on the Earth to rest and rejuvenate from the pressure of human extractions and habitation. I want every generation to be able to explore whatever approximates wilderness areas, both terrestrial and aquatic. We will never really know what once was, but we can come to know, love, and value, what remains.

There is no such thing as true wilderness on Earth. Even here the hand of humanity floats in boats, walks on trails, and flies overhead on its way to LAX. From the Amazon to the Arctic human impact is constant and pervasive. But it makes me feel better knowing there still exist a few places that we agree to keep as intact as possible. I want to be able to experience an ocean with some resemblance to the balanced and life-filled waters we inherited, and the Channel Islands National Marine Sanctuary is such a place. These waters support a vast array of marine mammals including harbor seals, northern fur seals, northern elephant seals, Guadalupe fur seals, California and Steller sea lions, sea otters, common and bottlenose dolphins, and gray, humpbacked, and blue whales.

These islands are important calving areas for many of these creatures. The islands of San Miguel, Santa Barbara, and Santa Rosa are vital to the northern elephant seal which at one time was considered to be extinct after decades of overhunting by whalers. Their original range extended from Alaska to Baja California, but in the end, less than one hundred elephant seals survived on an isolated Mexican island. All of the northern elephant seals alive today are descendants of these few survivors. These huge marine mammals spend 90 percent of their lives in the deep ocean, diving up to five thousand feet below the surface to find food. They survive the cold and pressure of the deep sea yet almost vanished under the cold pressure of relentless hunting for the oil that their blubber contains.

Walking along the bluff toward the bay I kept my eyes focused on the deeper ocean beyond the kelp beds, hoping to see some more whales. The single cetacean that Kesley and I spotted on the crossing was an all-too-brief glimpse of a rolling, rounded back as it slid into the depths of the Santa Barbara Channel. I wanted more. It gave me hope to see that some whale populations are on the rise, even as others may seem doomed to extinction.

If you have not experienced being with whales at sea, you must do your best to change this condition. There is intelligence in those eyes, as there is empathy in mine. Each time I see them swimming together I feel joy. Each time I see them swimming alone, I too feel alone. I really do not wish to live in a world without the songs of birds or whales. In nature, the smallest and largest of living creatures are equally magical.

While having our lunch on the cliffs above the kelp-forested cove, we watched a sea lion chasing fish. I wished I could join him. A raven flew toward the cliff carrying something black and cloth-like in its beak. It spread its wings and floated to the edge where it deposited its treasure and began examining it as if to determine its value or potential usefulness. Four other ravens joined in, each picking up what turned out to be a soft cover for sunglasses. After each member of the flock had the chance to consider the object and engage in a lively discussion, they seemed to decide that it was not interesting enough to keep, and so they flew off, no doubt ready to pilfer whatever they could from the backpacks of unsuspecting hikers.

Corvids, which include ravens, crows, and jays, are among the most intelligent animals on Earth. In her book titled, *The Genius of Birds*, author Jennifer Ackerman weaves an intricate profile of just how intelligent these birds are, and why they are so important to the entire ecosystem they inhabit. Ravens are known to have complex social groups where past relationships are remembered, fall apart, and come together again, and where empathy is shown for flock members during difficult times. Ravens provide emotional support for each other by sitting beside, preening, and uttering comforting sounds toward flock members that have been traumatized. Ravens are known to play both with objects and conditions, such as sliding down snowbanks repeatedly with flock mates. They learn through play and have fun while doing so. They understand reciprocity and gift giving, and are able to remember past experiences, relationships, and lessons learned. They are sentient beings, just like us.

The walk back down to Scorpion Landing was beautiful and restorative to my laboring lungs. We clung to the edges of the bluff overlooking the sea, and I found myself transfixed by the blue of the water, the green of the kelp, and the glistening silver-white flashes of sunlight on the sea. It felt good to be alive and as much as I tried to remain in the moment, from time to time my mind wandered back to the feelings that overcame me on the steady, upward climb. I felt my age, and I didn't like it. I wondered, "How long do I have before I can't do this anymore?"

To paraphrase Terry Pratchett, inside every older person is a younger person wondering what the hell happened. I'm not old, but I am older. It's proven to be quite an adjustment for a man who once felt young and invincible and now finds himself wondering if his days of climbing are over. So, what if they are? If in time I find that I can no longer climb, I will adapt from climbing to crossing. After all, the Earth is filled with shorelines that can lead me along the sea, and blue lines on a map, that tumble down toward wherever I might happen to be standing.

Walking through the campground we saw island foxes and ravens sneaking water from a spigot. The ravens have learned how to pull the lever, causing the water to flow. The foxes have learned that staying close to ravens led to access to fresh water. And they've learned that staying close to humans offers the possibility of table scraps or tasty treasures left unguarded at campsites. Both creatures have adapted to humans and found their niche among the mix. This current reality causes me to feel both sorrow and joy. Wildlife that can adapt to the vagaries of ever-increasing human habitation has a better chance of survival. Still, I always feel that the dumpster-diving black bear is somehow diminished. Perhaps his newfound dependence is more reflective of us than of him.

By the time we reached the canyon's floor we were all feeling a bit worse for wear. I had consumed my entire thirty-two-ounce water bottle plus two additional twelve-ounce bottles that I had in my pack, and I was still thirsty. Just before reaching the cove, we came across a bonded pair of island scrub jays. More than any other indigenous animal on Santa Cruz Island, I wanted to see this brilliant blue corvid that is found nowhere else on Earth. Scrub jays are brilliant in more ways than color. They have episodic memories, forethought, and the ability to apply strategic thinking and complex tactics as they cache food items and pilfer it from competing birds. They remember past lessons and plan ahead. They are also incredibly beautiful.

Exhausted, we all decided to lie on the rocky shoreline of Scorpion Landing as we waited for our transport ship to arrive. There is no beach here, but rather, a small crescent-shaped tidal area of round, multi-colored, fist-sized stones. We each wiggled and squirmed our battered bodies into the rocky rubble like a flock of nesting plovers. Never before have I felt so comfortable resting on a bed of stone, eyes closed and ears open to the soft sounds of the sea.

We all fell asleep on our beds of stone ... waking and drifting off intermittently. In my drowsy half-submerged dreams I heard a familiar sound, woke, and opened my eyes to the sight of a bald eagle floating on broad wings, just beyond the rolling breakers. I smiled in kindred recognition. I was happy to see him. After all, he's a seeker of fish and freedom.

Part III

The Gulf of Mexico

BobWhite

CHAPTER FOURTEEN

Redfish

The Estuaries of Mustang Island, Texas Coast

They won't listen. Do you know why? Because they have certain fixed notions about the past. Any change would be blasphemy in their eyes, even if it were the truth. They don't want the truth; they want their traditions.

~ ISAAC ASIMOV, PEBBLE IN THE SKY

I SUSPECT THAT I WAS THE ONLY PERSON AT THE DOCKS THAT MORNING who noticed the golden-yellow sunrise over Padre Island National Seashore and the way the spartina grass moved like ocean waves in the morning breeze. I couldn't take my eyes off it, as if I was fearful that this might be the last sunrise I'd ever see and the final time grass would bend like that before everything on Earth went black. Everyone else was busy loading gear and launching boats and learning of the catching and releasing of the previous day. There was an army of pickup trucks pulling an armada of flats skiffs all preparing to do battle with redfish, speckled trout, and the occasional flounder—and I was once again, a child, amazed at the sunrise, entranced by morning birdsong, happily clueless about the concerns of men.

It's important for any young boy or old man to be brave. At six or sixty we all need to retain the capacity to try new things and not give a damn about falling down or looking foolish. So as a boy I climbed trees knowing I might fall, and I caught lizards knowing they might bite me, and I asked the pretty girl in my geometry glass if she'd go to the dance with me, knowing she might reject me—in front of everyone. (And she did.)

As an older man I've crossed swift-water rivers where my legs could barely hold me upright. And I've walked unarmed through bear country, even though bears make me nervous. And I've stood at-the-ready on the bow of a flats skiff with a fly held between my thumb and forefinger, my eyes scanning hopefully toward the clear, shimmering, water, while the guide shouts out orders toward a novice who is expected to "get it done."

Fathers and fishing guides can be teachers, preachers, or bullies. Only one of these three is actually getting it done. The other two are endlessly trying to fill a hole that can never be filled. In the Marines I learned to be bold yet humble. In martial arts and meditation, I learned the value of a beginner's mind—always open to learning, always willing to teach. When we start from a place of compassion, we come to a place of understanding, meaning, and eventually, mastery.

In my estimation, the best guides in life are all teachers at heart. They remember the days when they first tried to cast into the wind at a living, moving, weary gamefish. They recall the decades they've had to learn how to do one thing with mastery and they delight in sharing this earned wisdom and world with others. And although we were fishing together as friends, my friend William Townsend is a professional guide in the best sense of the word. He is a consummate learner, conscientious angler, and compassionate teacher. As a mere child of saltwater fly fishing, I am grateful for this reality. I have so much to learn, and I'm fine with that.

The morning began with me and my buddy Landon Rowlett getting a quick breakfast before meeting William at his house. This was the first time Landon and I had traveled and fished together, and for all we have in common we discovered our unique differences. Landon is a self-described "night owl" and I am a lifelong early-rising morning person who requires time for breakfast and coffee before I launch into any adventure. I am usually in for the night by six in the evening and winding down with sleepy eyes by ten at night. He is barely functional at six o'clock as he comes tottering down to the hotel lobby with sleepy eyes—just coming into his prime around ten in the morning. Landon is younger than my daughter, and I am older than his father, but for all these differences, we are much the same. We both know the value of a life well lived. We both love our families and deeply care for our friends and hold out hope for the future . . . against all odds. Young men like Landon give me reason to hope.

Placing the morning sun just over our left shoulder, William throttled up the skiff's engine and quickly moved us from static buoyancy to being on plane. He and I sat in the stern behind the transom and Landon sat center front just behind the bow so that we could efficiently get enough lift to ride the bow wave and reduce the drag for our long, twenty-plus-mile ride to our fishing spot. We were heading away from the weekend crowds and hopefully toward schools of willing fish.

The day before, William had checked the area out with clients, and he said there were good-sized redfish everywhere they looked. I never allow my hopes to get up when I hear such reports. Too many times I have traveled far and wide only to be told, "You should have been here last week!"

I love to ride quickly over calm water in a flats skiff. I love the way the world seems dreamlike as the calico patchwork of sea grass and sand slides beneath the hull, the salty spray coming over the bow freshens my face in the warm morning sunlight and the moments of silence we all observe as the shoreline passes behind us and the skyline remains fixed before us. There is magic in these moments, and I always marvel at how "grown" men and women become childlike on the deck of a speeding watercraft. After a while, William took his hands off the wheel, looked at me, smiled and said, "The boat knows exactly where she's going." I smiled back.

When we arrived, our captain and Landon both voted that I had first dibs on the bow. William and Landon are longtime friends who have the wonderful ability to kid each other without malice. William said, "You'll find Landon can be a bit of a bow hog." They both laughed. Friendships like theirs are the best kind of friendships, and I hoped to earn my place in the Corpus Christi Club of good-natured mutual sarcasm.

It didn't take long. Almost immediately William spotted some redfish cruising toward us—fish that I could not yet see from the bow. He hollered out, "Reds about sixty feet out at 10 o'clock!" I was still stripping line out onto the deck and for some reason got flustered and managed to cast in the wrong direction when William said, "Left! Left! . . . no, your other left!" Flashbacks of Marine boot camp came to mind where every recruit sooner or later ends up doing a "right face" on the command of "left face" just because they got flummoxed under pressure. I adjusted but realized that my mistake was also my opportunity to enter the club. I laughed and said, "I promise I do know left from right and how to read a clock face, when my brain is functioning."

The water around us was less than clear so the redfish were sometimes appearing right next to the bow or blowing up out of the sandy bottom because they sensed us before we sensed them. Three big reds started my way and I cast in front but a little short of them. I stripped the line, got a follow and then an immediate rejection.

William was doing a masterful job of poling us into range of several nice-sized reds, but I did a less than masterful job of reaching and enticing them. So, once we began to see fewer fish and ultimately no more fish, we decided to move to a new area and give Landon a shot. After all, I did not want to be known as a bow hog. (Landon . . . I'm smiling as I write this, my friend.)

As I previously mentioned, we had traveled over twenty miles by boat to get to this spot between the barrier island and King Ranch. It was a beautiful journey across bright green water and under a clear blue Texas sky. And it was worth the wait because what looked like a massive coastal bay from afar was actually a wide, shallow flat that contained the possibility of redfish, speckled trout, flounder, juvenile tarpon, snook, jacks, skip jacks, and the extremely challenging sheepshead fish. Against all odds the Texas coast is a vast and varied ecosystem of fish and fowl. If not for the mixture of oil wells and windmills this coast would seem pristine. It's not.

With Landon standing at the ready on the bow and me sitting in "time out" on the cooler, William began pushing the skiff across a new area of flats that felt even more promising than the last. I say this because the water was skinny and clear and the visibility much better as the sun rose from its early morning horizontal to its mid-morning angle that lit up the water like the incandescent lamp of an aquarium hood. Whereas sight-fishing off the bow of a boat was fairly new to me, Landon had it dialed in from the get-go.

We came to an area with a brackish water inflow, where the water was only about two feet deep with a mix of sand and sea grass on the bottom. A big, speckled trout blew across our bow, then a sheepshead and then another trout. They were already wise to our presence and too alarmed to cast toward. But then something wonderful happened. A school of redfish that may have been one hundred strong began to circle the boat. Landon cast and got a follow and a take that he missed. It was a soft, half-hearted take. Then he cast again and again, sometimes getting ignored and sometimes getting a follow and rejection. And just as fast as they appeared they seemed to drift away. William kept poling forward and then out a little deeper in hopes of locating the fish.

In short order we began seeing redfish swimming into range and Landon was getting quite a few opportunities to connect and did a good job of getting the fly in front of the fish, but they were reticent at first and we began to contemplate a change of flies—just in case these were discriminatory fish. He tied on a little brown shrimpy-looking thingamabob with wiggly legs and googly eyes and began casting toward every pod of fish that wandered within range. It didn't take long for him to get a follow and a take and soon he was into a nice redfish that gave a solid fight before being brought to William's waiting net. We were all ecstatic!

It was a stunningly beautiful fish with brassy tones of silver-gray scales and a luminescent glow from gill plate to tail. That's when Landon said, "Let me get in the water and hold it while you take a photo." William looked at him incredulously. He said, "You don't need to get in the water to get a photo . . . you'll scare away the other fish." Landon seemed insistent but in the end the wishes of our captain prevailed.

Now it was my turn again. William had decided at the beginning of the trip that he was not going to fish until I caught my first redfish. He knew that although I'd pursued them in Texas and South Carolina, I had yet to catch one on a fly. He seemed to be determined to be the one who guided me toward my first redfish landing. I didn't want to let him down.

It takes a while for me to get my eyes adjusted to see fish in new water, but I was beginning to see them with a bit more proficiency, even if William was so much better at it from his perch on the poling platform. I cast to a few cruising redfish and got a couple of follows without a take. Then I cast to one directly in front of the boat, got a follow and a take, and blew the hookset. Finally, we all saw the shadow of a big fish heading directly toward the boat. I made the cast, stripped the line as fast as I could and the shadow descended upon the fly like a predatory torpedo! It slashed at the fly, I set the hook, and that's when we realized it was a skip jack or ladyfish! Still, it fought well, jumped several times, and eventually came boat side. It wasn't what I was hoping for, but I was still happy to have caught and released such a strong, elegant predator.

My friends decided I should stay on the bow since I'd not yet found my first redfish, and who was I to argue? The truth is, I wanted to break the spell and follow Landon's lead ... and I did. It wasn't long before William called out that he saw a fish coming toward me at about ten o'clock and this time I saw the fish, made the cast, got a follow and a take, and finally set the hook! I was so worried that I'd lose the fish that I held on a little too tight at first, but soon adjusted and got it on the reel. The fish pulled left, I went right, and we played that dance back and forth for a while until it was at the gunnel and in my hands. Catching it was a thrill; releasing it was a joy. Another first of a species for this sixty-one-year-old kid who is trying so many things for the first time. I was grateful to Landon, William, and the Laguna Madre.

Laguna Madre is Spanish for Mother Lagoon and that is no misnomer for what is in fact the largest hypersaline lagoon in the world when measured with its sister system south of the Mexican Border, the Laguna Madre de Tamaulipas. As an ecosystem, it is considered a negative estuary because seawater flows in, rather than out, due to there being less freshwater inflow than positive estuaries which have a consistent and substantial flow of fresh water entering them and eventually becoming part of the ocean, sea, or gulf. This makes these waters unique and much more ecologically sensitive than a normal estuary, and damage caused by human or natural events can take decades or longer to recover.

This area is home to various threatened or endangered species of birds including piping and snowy plovers, reddish egrets, brown pelicans, peregrine falcons, white-tailed hawks, and the only naturally occurring breeding population of whooping cranes. Almost 80 percent of the redhead ducks of North America winter here, and it represents the largest continuous expanse of suitable habitats in North America for migrating songbirds and shorebirds between their breeding ground in the north and their wintering grounds in Central and South America. And it contains vast colonial water bird rookeries for such amazing creatures as the snowy, great white, and reddish egrets, tricolored, great blue, little blue, and green herons, roseate spoonbills, white-faced ibises, black skimmers, and more.

The beaches of Padre Island National Seashore are one of the last refuges for breeding Kemps Ridley Sea Turtles—the most endangered sea turtles in the world. Almost 80 percent of sea grass beds along the Texas coast are within the lagoon, and these along with the vast areas of critically important spartina grass marsh are key nurseries for one of the most diverse fisheries in America. For all these reasons and more, the Nature Conservancy designated the Laguna Madre as a high-priority conservation area in 1998. Padre Island and the Laguna Madre's coastal beaches and dunes, wetlands, salt marshes, riparian zones, coastal prairies, and live oak forests need to be protected and restored on both sides of the water. This place is not only a national treasure, but also unique in the world.

As soon as I released that fish something happened that made me just as happy, if not more. William finally stepped down from the poling platform and stood on the bow with my rod in his hand. And that's when I said, "Wouldn't it be poetic if after Landon and I both worked so hard to catch a redfish, you make a couple of casts and bring one boat side?" And he did.

It seemed like mere seconds had passed since I released my fish when William spotted a nice red that was far out and against the wind from our location. I should mention that William is an amazing distance fly caster who soon demonstrated that he could cast out almost all of the line on my reel and reach a faraway fish with accuracy, as if it were the easiest thing in the world. I know that I cheered louder for him than I did for me as he brought that fish to the net and lifted it briefly from the water. As far as I was concerned, this had already been a perfect morning. We had shared a stunning morning on a body of crystalline water, and we all caught redfish!

William fired up the engine and motored back to the area where we had first started the morning's quest. The water had cleared and the wind had picked up and Landon was on the bow trying for a second red. He cast toward a few without result, and then stood at the ready, waiting, searching and hoping for something beautiful to happen—and it did. When I saw his rod tip bend and watched the fish's bright, blue-tinged tail clear the water's surface, I knew this was a good one. I've never seen a more lovely and prismatically colorful fish in my life. We were all so happy for Landon and even more joyful about watching that fish swim powerfully away. I will never forget it.

After the fish was released, we decided that we'd move toward the docks at Bird Island but stop along the way to try one last area on the King Ranch side of the lagoon. That's when Landon decided to confide in us as to why he wanted to get in the water with the first fish and why he NEEDED to get in the water now. As it turns out, he said, "I can't pee off a boat. I want to but for some reason, I can't release!" I will admit that I had a good laugh at that one, but then admitted my own phobia. I said, "Well, we all have something like that my friend. You know that public restroom you used this morning at the docks? I'd rather be in a firefight than walk into a place like that!" Even the seagulls seemed afraid of it! We all have something that bothers us and for me, dirty public restrooms are my kryptonite. We all laughed as William got us moving quickly north toward our final fishing spot. It was my turn.

When we arrived and I got on the bow, William began pushing the skiff along the shoreline as he told me about the possibilities of redfish, black drum, speckled trout, flounder, jacks, skip jacks, snook, and the occasional juvenile tarpon. I'll admit that now that I had connected with my redfish, I was hoping for a tarpon. That's not very Zen of me. I know better. I know that I need to accept life as it comes to me and let go of artificial expectations. But I'm an imperfect Texan Buddha and as such, I sometimes do sin. Forgive me . . . I have lusted for gamefish before and in my dreamworld of angling I am a master caster who sets every hook with perfection and lands every fish as if it were second nature—but then reality arrives. And it did.

I was half-gone in my baby tarpon daydreams when William shouted, "Big trout dead ahead!" By the time I snapped out of it that speck was long gone. Then the same thing happened when a redfish blew past us and then another trout. It had been a wonderful long day and although I did manage to refocus myself, deep in my heart I knew that I was done. I was content to just watch the roseate spoonbill feeding in the shallows, sweeping its paddle-shaped bill rhythmically from side to side. I was happy to just feel the rocking of the boat and the rolling of the tide. Like a child who's already filled his bucket with bluegill, I was satisfied.

On the way back to the docks I absorbed every sight, sound, smell, and nuanced feeling of us skidding across the water, sunlight warm and comforting against my shoulders, salt spray refreshing against my face, and the cooling, bracing, invigorating feeling of the wind as it pushed against me like a sweetheart's embrace. I was happy—or to be more precise, I was joyful. They are not the same thing. Happiness is too often dependent on our perceived conditions and expectations, while joy is a simple choice. Life is so short; I always choose joy.

We needed to be back up on plane to hasten our return to the docks, so I sat in the stern with William and Landon, who is a taller and bigger man than I, was sitting forward of center. I felt grateful to share this time with my friends. And I enjoyed watching Landon as he waved to tugboat captains, and I thought of the value of keeping a youthful spirit.

William and I shared moments of peaceful silence and reflection mixed with conversation about this beautiful fishery and its fragile nature.

I was asking questions as I always do about what the threats were and what the solutions might be, but William gave a soulful, blunt, honest response that no one else has ever given me. He said, "I appreciate the passions of many of my fellow guides and boat captains who talk about the need to control the underregulated oyster and shrimp harvest, improve the quantity and quality of fresh water entering the estuary and the many other challenges we face—but in truth, without people of money and power behind protecting these waters, nothing will ever change for the better." And you know what? I think he's right.

All the well-meaning words in the world are worthless without effective action toward win/win solutions. Until such time that we pull together, this world will continue to come apart. We're all on "Spaceship Earth" together.

As I looked out across the last view I'd get of those hallowed waters and salt marsh prairies, I envisioned them with more fish and less fishers. I pictured a time when we might put some limits on ourselves so that we might experience an unlimited wild coastline. And as I looked out and pictured the lagoon that is described by old-timers with sorrowfully dim lights in their eyes, I wondered—am I just daydreaming again? I hope not.

CHAPTER FIFTEEN

Snook, Redfish, Jack, Snapper, Ladyfish
Texas Coast—South Padre Island

Whenever I gaze up at the moon, I feel like I'm on a time machine. I am back to that precious pinpoint of time, standing on the foreboding—yet beautiful—Sea of Tranquility. I could see our shining blue planet Earth poised in the darkness of space.
~ BUZZ ALDRIN, AMERICAN ASTRONAUT

THE SKIFF SLID JUST BENEATH THE LOW-SLUNG BRIDGE AND WE COULD see the scrapes and scars on the concrete from those who came before us and neglected to protect their fishing rods and boat antennas. My buddy Aaron Reed has passed this way many times before and so our gear and our heads were appropriately lowered for safety's sake. As the bow of the boat began to protrude out the other side of the bridge, the sunlight illuminated a nautical scene complete with shrimp boats and pelicans that stood watch from the whitewashed pylons and piers. The shrimp boats swayed, with air-dried nets and empty hulls. The pelicans posed motionless and statuesque in their feathered suits of grayish brown, their yellowish white heads and their comical yet practical gap-mouthed faces.

Early mornings on a skiff while crossing saline waters just as the sunlight peeks over the horizon make me feel hopeful, grateful, and filled with wonder. I love the smell of the sea and the sounds of shorebirds chattering from atop the mangroves. I love the way the wind feels against my battered sunburned face as the bow of the skiff rises and falls to the rhythm of the sea. And I love the quiet times when a dear friend is at the helm guiding us across waters they might know and love, but that are new to me. That's how I was feeling that day. . . . I was in love with being alive in the here and now. I felt at peace in a world all too often lacking that quality.

Aaron Reed is a good man, and that's a good way to begin any story about fishing and friendship. He is a father and a son, an angler, author, an Army veteran who served in Bosnia, and a tugboat captain who's based out of Corpus Christi, Texas. He is an aficionado of distilled spirits and distinctive folk music, and fortunately for me—he is my friend. These days, I seem to be lucky that way.

On the previous day I drove down to Rockport from my home in the Texas Hill Country so I might spend time with Aaron in his hometown. That night we enjoyed dinner at a waterside café while sipping a cold beer and listening to Jimmy Buffet music—not a bad way to start any adventure. We talked about this unique coastal landscape with its imperiled prairies, isolated oak forests, and vast, shallow, water-filled habitats. He told me of how he loved growing up here, roaming free as a kid, hunting, fishing, and sailing his small boat across the bay. And how the advantage of knowing everyone in town could become a disadvantage for a teenager—where everyone also knows you.

Just before dinner we went to a little bridge that spanned over what looked to me like a polluted drainage ditch filled with runoff water from an oil refinery, but to Aaron this was an angling honey hole to be cherished and protected. Everything is a matter of perspective. In fact, it was such a special place for him that whenever a vehicle came down the dirt road leading to the bridge we'd stash our rods and just look out over the railing like two friends having a chat about nothing—which of course, we were. It's not that there was anything wrong with us fishing there, but rather, we didn't want anyone else to get the idea that this was a good place for them to come back to and fish—which of course, it was.

That evening, Aaron managed to hook and prematurely release a nice juvenile tarpon and I managed to hook and land a stout adult ladyfish. The tarpon was impressive; the ladyfish, not so much—but it all counts. None of this was part of our actual planned adventure but rather, just something we did the night before heading down to Port Isabel, South Padre, and the Brownsville Ship Channel.

And now as Aaron's father's skiff slid past the docks of shrimpers and bait fishermen we hoped to target snook and a variety of other native gamefish with our fly rods, using nothing more than a bit of fur and feathers attached to a stainless-steel hook which we'd drag enticingly through the deep, dark waters of the Brownsville Ship Channel. Like the son of a son of a sailor he is, Aaron deftly eased us out of that particular harbor, rounding the edge of a spoil island into more open water. As we crossed the Intracoastal Waterway into the shipping channel we left the "no wake zone" but still took our time passing a bird rookery that was brimming with avian activity.

A love of birds is one of many things Aaron and I share in common. On the drive down from Corpus we stopped to photograph green jays, hooded orioles, a chachalaca, and some invasive but lovely Eurasian collared doves. And now as we slowly passed the mangroves adorned in egrets, herons, ibis, and spoonbills we watched as they went about their daily lives, as their ancestors have for countless generations. I silently hoped they would still be here long after I am gone.

The Gulf Intracoastal Waterway is a navigable inland waterway running approximately 1,000 miles from Carrabelle, Florida, to Brownsville, Texas. The Brownsville Ship Channel is the southern terminus of the Gulf Intracoastal Waterway. It acts as a deep-water port located not far from the mouth of the Rio Grande in the Lower Rio Grande Valley, only eight miles from the border of Mexico and the United States. This valley and these waters were first inhabited by Native Americans and then "owned" and fought over by Spain, Mexico, the Republic of Texas, the United States and briefly, the Confederate States of America. Over the years humankind has fought and fished here—the first venture tragic and the second often magic. I wish we'd stop fighting and start fishing more often.

What if war became a "catch and release" and "no kill zone" endeavor—more of a sport like paintball where people bet on the outcome and in the end members of both sides shook hands and went out together for dinner and drinks? What if all proceeds from each battle were earmarked for restoring and revitalizing the environment of humans and nonhumans alike? What if we stopped killing each other and instead, just went fishing and broke bread together?

As a Marine I am keenly aware that every true warrior understands the stupidity and waste of war. These days, all I want to do is live in peace. And here we were on our way to a warship's graveyard as we motored past Elon Musk's space center launchpad at Boca Chica. I was struck by the irony of this spaceport being placed so close to the ship channel where naval vessels from my country's past were being disassembled for scrap metal. Aaron called the channel a "ship-breaking yard where old instruments of war are recycled into either plowshares or razor blades." How tragically poetic and true.

We had been traveling at speed for a while, trying to get down to our fishing area in the ship graveyard before the sunlight grew too strong. When he cut the engine we took a moment to hydrate, starting out with our Texas spring water before we got to the Texas beer we had on ice for later. Normally, I like to fish with only the sounds of nature around me, but the shipping channel is a place largely devoid of birdsong and replete with the noise of piledrivers and boom cranes that swing from side to side like dinosaurs feeding on the hulls of decommissioned ships. All around us the gray, metal skeletons of once-grand vessels were being cut into bite-sized pieces and hauled away as scrap. There was nothing of nature in the air beyond the various shorebirds and the slapping of the water on the many empty hulls and seemingly immovable seawalls. So, when Aaron attached a small speaker to his phone and asked, "Do you mind if I play music while we fish?" I was more than pleased to say, "Go for it, brother." A moment later the sounds of deconstruction were replaced with the wonderfully poetic music that I had come to expect from my friend's soundtrack. Acoustic guitars and soulful songs go a long way toward tightening my loop and widening my smile.

We motored down the waterway to the voice of Buddy Guy singing, "What Kind of Woman Is This?" His mighty Stratocaster blues rang out over the drone of the motor as he sang about a woman so beautiful that she brought sight to the blind and speech to the mute. I could almost see the twinkle in his eyes when he slowly called out, "Sssshucks!" and asked the title question, "What kinda woman is this?" By the time Aaron cut the engine so we could drift past our first fishing spot the music had mellowed and Dobie Gray was singing about getting lost in the soul freeing beat of the music while drifting away. How perfectly and poetically poignant. As we began to drift toward the target we stripped out line for the first casts of a long day and night of fishing.

Snook are ambush predators that prefer low light conditions and lots of structure to hide within. As we came up to a section of concrete and metal seawall I got on the bow with my eight-weight fly rod and Aaron was casting his C. Barclay 7-weight. 777, the "Jackpot." from the stern. When I asked him why he was using a light rod for potentially big saltwater fish, he said, "I think most people use a heavier rod than they really need." Since Aaron has caught numerous snook, snappers, redfish, black drum, and juvenile tarpon with that little rod, I can't dispute that claim. I felt a bit more comfortable with my eight-weight when tossing that big, fluffy Seducer toward the docks, seawalls, riprap, and mangroves along the shore.

I don't know if it was the good music or the great company but I was relaxed and casting as if I knew what I was doing. I love it when everything just comes together; a condition I don't find myself in all that often. There was natural native rhythm to everything from our casting to the sound of Lynyrd Skynyrd singing "Simple Man." That song held a lot of wisdom for me in my youthful summers, and it still does in my late autumn season. We drifted. We cast. We retrieved. We cast again. Two wounded warriors who are poets by nature.

As we cast silently into murky waters, we listened as the Michigan Rattlers sang a song of longing, love and loss, and the purely mortal fear that our journey might end—all too soon. I thought of how much that song might fit Aaron and me—two travelers who've made it a long way down life's road, never knowing which cast is our last cast. Making the most of every single loop.

We made several passes along the seawall, and I felt a few hopeful bumps and tugs which I was unable to convert into a fish at the gunnel. The water here is dark and dirty with who-knows-what leaking out of the shipyards, so I couldn't see what smacked at the fly. We took another pass and just as we drifted around the area of the last tug I saw a swirl and felt the weight of a fish which I firmly strip set and solidly hooked. With the first silver-flash of fish flesh I wondered if I'd lucked into a baby tarpon, but with its first of many leaps I knew I had connected with another ladyfish—something I was trying to avoid. Don't get me wrong, I have nothing against catching ladyfish, which are also called "skip jack." It's just that while they are fun to catch, they are also not a snook. I set that one free and we moved down to the next spot, which was a long shoreline of black riprap between two massive ships.

Aaron insisted that I get the bow which I believe gave me a big advantage since I got first shot at every bit of structure or shoreline we came to, and I appreciated his kindness as I methodically cast and retrieved my feathery offering—each time hopeful of it being engulfed by a snook. There were plenty of forage fish swimming all around us and in short order there was quite a bit of splashy predation going on just in front of us. I cast out into the carnage and almost immediately hooked another skipjack which jumped and fought with conviction and attitude before I was finally able to land it—which made me wonder, "Why are they called ladyfish?" There was absolutely nothing delicate about that fight. Still, I must admit I wished it had been a tarpon or a snook, and that's not very "Buddha-like" of this Imperfect Texan Buddha. I guess I have a long way to go to realize I have nothing to achieve and nowhere to arrive.

Even with all the industrial hubbub around us, I'd have to say this was one of my most relaxing and thoughtful fishing trips in a long time. We started working a cove that was rimmed in black mangroves and a few more ladyfish were the result. After I had caught about half a dozen of them Aaron said, "I think I'm going to start calling you 'the Lady Killer!'" "Please don't," I replied. Then after a moment I said in my best bad Austrian accent, "I'd rather be the Snookinator." We both laughed but in truth, I was now actively avoiding casting toward anything that looked like a ladyfish. Six was enough, and I didn't need to exhaust any more of these beautiful, bright creatures.

We were quickly losing the coolest hours of the morning, so we headed toward a shoreline that had a little artificial cove cut into it that was filled with ladyfish at its opening but looked quite "snooky" around its rocky edges. I saw something snapping at the water near a couple of half-submerged boulders, so I lined up a quick cast, landed it where I wanted, made a couple of short strips and connected with a nice mangrove snapper. Knowing that those teeth are nothing to be careless with I was exceedingly careful when removing the hook and setting it free.

The sun was up now, so we decided to try fishing in the shadows of a bridge that Aaron said was known for having snook. As he motored up to the bridge, I made random casts and back-casts toward the overhanging mangroves on either side of the narrow creek. Like everywhere I've fished, this bridge offered an opportunity for anglers of little means to cast baitcasting rigs in hope of putting food on the table. There'd be no grip-and-grin photos going home with them, just dinner. Still, I had to wonder if anyone should be eating the fish from these industrialized waters. I suspect the answer is "No." If these fish came with an ingredients label it might include: mercury, dioxins, chlorinated pesticides, polychlorinated biphenyls, and polybrominated diphenyl ethers. Not appealing or healthy.

I guess this is what was running through my mind as I watched a young family fishing for their dinner, just as our soundtrack switched to Uncle Lucius singing the tale of a man suffering the effects of poisoning from the coastal petrochemical plant he worked at to "Keep the Wolves Away." A haunting rhythm guitar and woeful sound of whistling in the graveyard told the tale of health and life being sacrificed for the profit of a few at the expense of many. Should shareholders share in the misery, I wonder? There was nothing I could do other than keep casting seaward my line and lines of thought—with determination and hope. Is anyone listening?

I switched to a shrimp pattern fly and I think Aaron was tossing something similar as we homed in on the smacking sounds of big predators eating something under the bridge. Aaron put his rod down and said, "I'm going to ease us under there so you can cast between those pylons. That last splash was a snook." It felt right. It looked good. I stood hunched over—at the ready.

We crept in under that low bridge like commandos on a mission and I was side casting between the pylons as quickly as I could. I'd cast to the front and we'd hear a splash behind us. I'd cast to the splash and we'd hear only silence. I tried fast retrieves, slow retrieves, allowing it to sink and skidding it across the top. I would have done a hula dance if I thought it would help because we knew there was a snook down there somewhere—and it was feeding on something. But in the end all we got for our efforts was a little shade in midday and another memory of two friends giving it their best and still feeling fortunate in our defeat. This is fishing. If it were a sure thing, why would we do it?

We left the bridge and motored farther down the ship channel to a dock that had a massive cargo ship attached to it. I could hear the Allman Brothers Band singing, "Let Your Soul Shine," and I was doing my best to follow their lead. Aaron was eager to get me into a snook and had decided to stop fishing himself. Although the sun was up, shaded places like this dock gave us a few additional chances.

Aaron pointed to a shaded spot near a pylon and said, "Cast in there! I think you're gonna get one." So, I made the cast and stripped the line and felt a tug pulling hard and downward. I tugged back just as my rod tip bowed and I stood up for the fight. But the fight was short lived because what I had hooked was once again not a snook but rather, a smallish jack crevalle. I brought the fish boat side and we quickly returned it to its home beneath the docks. It was a nice fish and I was as happy to see him swim away as I was to catch him. I guess the pointlessness of catch and release is exactly the point. Everything is transitory. The Zen of fly fishing never eludes me.

―‿‿―

We found a sheltered cove brimming with mangroves and anchored the boat so we could enjoy the last sunlit moments of the day. Aaron popped the top on a couple of ice-cold Wild Texas Kolsch beers. The brewer describes it as "an easy drinking beer that's perfect for enjoying the Texas outdoors." I can't argue with that description one bit because it tasted soft, cold, and as golden as the evening light. We weren't eating fancy—just a few gas station sandwiches and a bag of chips but it felt like the perfect combination along with the sounds of the water lapping against the shore and Aaron's music wafting through the evening air.

I had begun to fall in love with the music and lyrics of Florida's own J.J. Grey and his band Mofro. Guitars, horns, harmonica, and Hammond organ all blended with his soulful southern voice as he sang of his deepest questions about the existence of God and the significance of humanity. I've asked those questions too, and I won't know the answer until I cross that final river. Perhaps not even then.

J.J.'s voice spoke to me as a fellow son of the South who never knew the hateful world I hear about in the media. Each pleading tone bled through the open wounds of my beloved Southland ... all too often, self-inflicted wounds where slave and slaver pray for redemption and forgiveness. There is no reason for division and yet no region free of those who would divide us. In every generation of every tribe there are those who love and those who hate. Love needs to prevail, one blended voice at a time.

For a while we just sat there in relative silence as the light of the sun faded and the lights of the shipyards came on, one by one until they blotted out the stars. We hoped snook would come toward those lights, and then toward our lines. But for now, we listened to J.J. Grey singing "I Believe (in Everything)"—his song of wisdom and faith.

Faith is a funny thing. It's based upon nothing provable and everything immovable. Nobody ever learns anything they don't want to learn. After all, you may put your faith in something, that may be nothing; and nothing can remove that faith—but you. I'm not saying the stories aren't true; just that it's true that they are stories—not fact. And over time (whatever time is), I've come to believe that almost everything in life is faith. Reality is questionable.

Every song we heard was of longing and aloneness. Every note that played was like the evening call of a bird. Like a "Last Call." And yet within all that longing and aloneness was the commonality that unites us. Namely, we are not alone in feeling alone. We don't own the only eyes that ever cried, or lips that ever smiled or voice that ever sang. There have been billions before us and there may be billions more yet to come. Who knows?

In between sips of Texas Wild brew, we watched the setting sun and spoke in tones of poetic tragedy and hope. We spoke of this place, its people, and its harsh beauty. When I asked Aaron for his thoughts about this lost and found landscape, he said, "The border region is a sort of between place, a liminal space. The vast watery wilderness of the Lower Laguna Madre, the Tamaulipan thorn forest and its fauna are unique in the United States. South Bay was the first designated state scientific area in Texas, of interest due to the sea grass meadows and black mangroves and the high salinity-tolerant oysters that grow there. Seems like an unwise place for a rocket launch pad. The entire area has been trampled, trammeled, burned, storm-ravaged, fought over, contaminated, and ignored and still somehow manages to surprise us with its beauty and bounty of wildlife. In Texas, we use the natural environment hard, but somehow enough survives to surprise and delight us. The border wall is an ecological disaster, interrupting gene flow for species like the ocelot and jaguarundi. It also pisses off the locals, most of whom were never all that worried. The port is just doing what it was designed to do, and the fishery there wouldn't exist without the industry that created it." My friend Aaron is a philosophical, tattooed, widely educated warrior-poet, with a halo of smoke and heart of gold. I'm grateful for our friendship.

I listened in silence—but running through my mind was the idea that this place was either a lost land or a forgotten one—or both. I wondered as I have so many times before why we can't just all get along—humanity and nature. Why can't we have a port without the poison? Why can't we build cities that are filled with fresh running water, native plants and public fruit and vegetable gardens and at least some amount of wildlife to "delight us"—against all odds? Are we so small a species that we can't pursue such a big life?

When darkness fell we did what men like us do and gravitated toward the light. We followed the lights along the ship channel until we came to the swill-filled turning basin. We cast our lines in hopeful loops toward illuminated seawalls, pylons, and rock piles. We tried again and again as Aaron shared stories of the big snook he had caught before in this place or that place. But we did not find any of them waiting for us under those lights or in the darkness. It's as if we were alone—together. J.J. sang through the night about "The River." The lyrics reached out with the haunting plea of a man who was trying to find the meaning of his life.

It's a waste of time, you know? Trying to find the meaning of life is a waste of time. The meaning of our lives is whatever meaning we give it through our choices and actions. For me, kindness, empathy, courage, and a search for wisdom, drive me forward—even as I have nowhere to go.

We never connected with a snook. We never even saw one. Over the course of this day and night we caught ladyfish, snapper, and jacks but no snook, and I'm fine with that. It took nothing away from the taste of cold beer or the feel of the warm sunlight. It took nothing away from the silent, starlit run back to Port Isabel. It could not erase the joy of casting side by side with a good friend, on his father's boat. And it left me wanting more—not in some silly mournful, regretful way . . . but in a completely joyful and meaningful manner. In fact, this trip was so perfect, it made me envision another. The trick is to live in the "here and now" while being open to the "there and then" of life. It's a loop—not a line. If you miss your mark, just pick up and cast again. You simply do what you can to connect the circle.

PART IV

THE SOUTH ATLANTIC
AND CARIBBEAN SEA

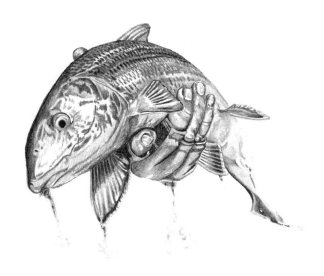

BobWhite

Chapter Sixteen

Bonefish
Turks and Caicos Islands

In every grain of sand, there is the story of the Earth.
~ Rachel Carson, environmentalist,
author of *The Sea Around Us*

I'm not sure what's my favorite part of any adventure. Adventure is not always pleasant. Sometimes the best part is the sense of accomplishment after climbing a mountain in Italy, completing a trek through the Peruvian rainforest, or successfully tracking that kudu through the South African thornbush. The joy of an adventure isn't just in the doing; it is in the striving. My daughter Megan earned a master's degree in outdoor education from a prestigious international university. Once while we were climbing a mountain together in the Scottish Highlands, she told me that there are two types of meaningful outdoor experience. A type one experience is relaxing, easy, and even restful. Type two is when you must struggle and suffer to complete the adventure, but after, you are grateful that you did it—even if you would never want to do it again. I've had both kinds of adventure, including while chasing bonefish.

I love the planning and the anticipation of an adventure. I love selecting my gear and guide and even the flood of memories from past adventures. I love daydreaming of all the different places I've been and things I've experienced. My mind wanders across East African plains and West African rainforests. I recall diving wrecks and reefs across the Caribbean and the way the surface of the sea looked from ninety feet below. And then I flash back to the sunrise over the Incan Gate of Machu Picchu in Peru or the way the snow blew over the edges of the Scottish Highlands as I finally reached the summit. But the first moment that any adventure feels real and imminent for me is when I see my destination materialize under the wing of the plane that carries me there, and then the wheels touch down and suddenly I find myself in a new world. This adventure was no different.

The Turks and Caicos Islands are somehow unique from all the other island nations I have visited. Perhaps the beaches seem whiter and the skies seem brighter, but really what is different is the people. The people of these islands are "Belongers." Everyone else is from somewhere else. Yes, I know that is true everywhere, but this is different. There is something special about how the people of this cluster of coral islands feel about their home. I've gone to other islands where I think, "This is so beautiful, I wish I could stay." But this is different. When you meet the Belongers of TCI you don't yearn for their beaches; you yearn for their belonging. You wish you could be one of them. I had come here to chase bonefish. I caught something else.

As a boy I used to love to sit on the bow of my father's boat as we skidded across the ocean's surface, the salt spray in my face, flying fish and leaping dolphin keeping just beyond my reach. I loved to do this until the chop of the sea picked up and the bow of the boat began to crash against the water in bone-jarring repetition. This is how I felt as we rounded the western edge of Provo Island and crossed over to North Caicos. Having grown up part of my childhood on the edge of the Gulf Stream, I knew all too well the violent possibilities contained within the flat-black thunderheads that were drifting across the Turks Island Passage. I wondered what the weather was like at that moment in Cockburn Town and pictured wind and rain-blown cruise ship tourists running for their lives.

Then I envisioned me and my guide, Jon, tossing on a windswept sea in a sixteen-foot flats boat.

I had just one day of fishing planned as is often the case during one of my quick reconnaissance trips to new places. Today would be that day no matter the vagaries of weather. Looking to the shore I saw the massive, rusted steel hulk of a cargo ship that was sitting high and dry among the mangroves. I looked over at Jon and motioned to him. He smiled and said, "Hurricane." I held on as the boat rose and fell with the chop of the windward side of the island.

The Turks and Caicos Islands are a British Overseas Territory. They consist of two major island chains which are separated by the pelagically deep Turks Island Passage. Whales use the passage in their migrations, north and south. Shallow coral banks surround each island making them meccas for shallow water species like the bonefish I was hoping to connect with on this trip. Miles of white sand beaches and hundreds of acres of sand and turtle grass flats make this a perfect place to cast a fly in front of you, while leaving everything else behind you.

The first set of islands include Providenciales, called Provo by Belongers. Provo is the hub for accessing North, Middle, South Caicos, and Parrot Cay. Across the Turks Island passage are the islands of Grand Turk and Salt Cay. The capital, Cockburn Town, is on the island of Grand Turk. Almost 90 percent of Belongers are Afro-Caribbean with a small Anglo-Caribbean population and a scattering of expatriates from everywhere. The expats are not Belongers and never will be. Like Rick Blaine in *Casablanca*, they will tell you they "came for the waters." Belongers stay because it's home.

～⌣～

We brought the boat to a stop and anchored in a lovely sandy bay at the mouth of a brackish stream that tumbled into the sea. Wading in knee-high water, we stalked slowly across the sand flats, walking and then waiting, looking and lingering, searching for any sign of our quarry. As is so often the case, this sand flat was surrounded by submerged turtle grass beds in slightly deeper water, and the shadow of a large barracuda along the edge of that grass caught my attention, but I wasn't here for barracuda.

Stalking bonefish is much like stalking kudu. You and your guide must move in sync, each aware and awake, communicating on a primal level, often without words. We were both searching for any sign of uplifted tails, puffs of sand, or silver-flashing shadows. We worked our way across the flat and then began walking slowly, almost heron-like, up the brackish stream. I felt the soft sand swallowing my footsteps as we moved slowly forward. We saw nothing but the stilted roots of red mangroves and the occasional sideways scurry of crabs. Jon shook his head. "I don't understand it," he said. "They should be here." We moved on.

Our next stop was a crescent-shaped bay that contained a mixture of sand flats and turtle grass. We had faced a stiff wind all the way up, but as we rounded the far side of the island the wind became a breeze, and I was hopeful. I will never forget this beautiful spot. Sand dollars were scattered everywhere, and a myriad of tiny glistening minnows sparkled in the morning sun. At first, we walked the flats, and then I stood at the ready on the bow of the boat as Jon poled us across the turtle grass flats, but to no avail. It was stunningly beautiful but seemingly devoid of bonefish. Jon seemed worried that I was disappointed. "I don't understand it," he said again. "They should be here." I smiled and said, "Jon, no worries . . . it's fishing. If it were easy, why would I do it?" We moved on, again.

To be a guide means that you are forever going fishing with strangers. I suspect some may become friends, but most will not even become memories. To be a client means placing your faith and no small amount of time and money in the hands of someone whom you've never met, and likely will never see again. Usually, it all works out. It's a win-win situation where you get to learn from someone who truly knows the lay of the land and water, and they get to make a tough but meaningful living in the place they love, doing the thing they love. It's all good. That's what I was reminding myself as we crossed out of the shallow flats and into the open ocean in Jon's tiny boat. I reminded myself that he's been doing this for a long time, and my research into his operation indicated no reports of any of his past clients vanishing at sea. No worries. Right?

Still, after what seemed like an eternity without seeing any landfall, not an island, not even a flying shorebird, and nothing but miles and miles of seemingly open ocean, I did begin to wonder. What does he have in mind? Where are we going? Finally, I had to ask, "Where are we? I don't see any islands out here." Jon looked at me and smiled, "It's called Red Bank. Don't worry, you'll see. It's a good place." We motored on, for perhaps an hour across deep, dark water. I noticed frequent sightings of sharks moving across our bow. I thought of his last words, "It's a good place."

When Jon cut the engine, I noticed that we had come to a place where the water suddenly changed from a deep indigo blue to shallow and lightly green. I'd never seen any place quite like this before. It was a vast expanse of sand, coral, shells, and turtle grass, no more than two or three feet deep, and it was in the middle of the open ocean. As soon as we stepped out and I held my eight-weight at the ready we saw them coming. Everywhere I looked I saw three things: bonefish, barracuda, and sharks. Everyone was hunting everyone. I felt connected to it all. We were all predators on the hunt, the sharks, barracuda, bonefish, and me.

Jon smiled. "See . . . I told you, it's a good place." And it was, except for the wind. The wind was impressive. I don't mean bring your casting A-game impressive; I mean the type of wind that forces you to find some bonefish that are downwind kind of impressive. I mean the kind of wind that bends your rod like a blade of grass and bows your head so that you don't blow over. I knew it was serious when a blast of it hit us and Jon leaned into it laughing and said, "Oh mon, dis is bad!" I looked through my tear-filled eyes at the many silver-gray fish swirling around us and replied, "No, my friend, this is good . . . this is good!"

Stepping out of the skiff I realized that beside the wind and the slosh of the ocean, the other challenge was going to be simply keeping my footing as I waded across a substrate of broken coral, limestone rubble, and bristling spiny sea urchins. All around us moderately sized sharks circled, each looking to eat some of the same fish we had come to catch and release. I took a mental note that it was up to me to protect any bonefish I hooked from the opportunistic feeding practices of the sharks and barracuda. That's not always easy to do, but I always do my best. I travel to connect with these fish, but also to set them free again, relatively unharmed and hopefully the wiser for the experience. That too is a challenge.

We started wading down a sandy strip in the middle of the rocky bottomed flats. Every once in a while a few six- to eight-foot-long sharks would come cruising up the strip toward us but once they saw us they swam quickly away, seemingly annoyed at the competition. Barracuda drifted in and out of the area like toothy torpedoes with bad intentions. A stingray burst from the sand in front of us and everywhere we looked life and death ebbed and flowed as it danced to the music of the sea. All was in motion and Jon and I stood motionless, taking it all in.

In time we saw them coming. It was a school of feeding bonefish, each about three or four pounds in size, slowly making their way toward us. The wind was in my face at this point, pushing against my left cheek, but the shot I had was the only one I could take so I gave it my best, which was barely good enough, dropping the fly too far in front of them, but not way too far. I let it sink and waited for them to come into range of the Gotcha, hoping the fly would live up to its name as it has so many times before. When the fish fed to within a few feet of the fly, I gave it a strip and the lead fish turned, followed, then rejected and spooked! The entire school swam quickly away. *Merde!*

Jon pointed and said, "Look!" A large barracuda had moved in toward the bones just as I was stripping the line. To this day, I'm not sure if I screwed up or it was just the luck of the draw. Life and death unfold as they will, and all we can do is pick up our lifeline and cast again.

The wind was such that we had to turn and move in the opposite direction. Gone was the smooth white sand. Now we waded through an area of rubble and turtle grass, but at least the wind was quartering across us from behind. There were good-sized bonefish everywhere. I saw one feeding toward us and it got pretty close before I fired off a short cast, stripped the line, watched it tip its tail up and face down, felt the tug and strip set the hook. That's when all hell broke loose!

I knew better, but I still failed to move my left hand away from the reel before the handle rapped my knuckles harder than Sister Mary used to smack them when I was a boy in Catholic school. That bone put me into my backing in a swollen handful of seconds, and just when I became concerned about the amount of line I had left on the reel, it turned and came at me like a pit bull on a postal worker. And I was still reeling in line as fast as I could manage, about the time it turned again and headed out in the general direction of Cuba.

I really can't even recall how I eventually got that fish landed, but once I did, I saw that it was a chunky, long rocket of a fish. He slimed me good as I lifted him from the water, unhooked the fly, and sent him back on his way. Jon and I laughed and shared a high-five. Finally, I managed to connect with a Turks and Caicos bonefish! And this was not the last of its kind I would meet that day.

Fishing for bonefish while wading in sand, grass, or coral-studded flats in shallow water is one of my favorite things. It is both strategic and tactical. It causes you to become immersed in the world of the bonefish—its predators and its prey. It's as much hunting as it is fishing, and in order to be successful you must stalk the flats in heron-like, quiet, patient, mindful slow motion. Your eyes focus up close—searching for a moving shadow, and then they scan farther out watching for waving tails or cruising V-wakes. You stand at the ready, fly held between thumb and forefinger, rod low so as to not cast a shadow—mindful and awake. Bonefish become skittish in clear, calm, shallow water, but today, we had both the challenge and the benefit of the wind. The challenge was in the casting and presentation of the fly. The benefit was in the slight chop on the water, which can make bones feel a bit safer from overhead predators.

I think my friend Randall Kaufmann said it best when he wrote, "In streams, the water moves but the fish do not. In lakes, the fish move, but the water does not. On saltwater flats, both the fish and the water move." Tidal movement is key, and observing tidal movement while understanding its impact on bonefish behavior will go a long way toward greater success. Bonefish don't live on the shallow flats as much as they use them as "feeding areas," and although the distinction may seem slight, it matters. When the tide is coming in, it provides the fish with access to prime feeding grounds as they search for clams, snails, and small fish on the sandy flats or among the stilted roots of mangroves. They use deeper passageways into these areas as the tide rises and then out of them as the tide recedes. This allows you to work the shallows and the deeper passages as the fish's behavior allows. Every angler is, by nature, a student of nature.

The essence of fishing is learning and understanding how everything fits together, and why.

Jon and I worked our way across the flats while paying special attention to the sandy cuts between the coral heads. I picked up another smaller bonefish, and then another, and another, before we saw a lone big boy pushing his way toward us in about a foot of water. I pushed my back cast into the wind and sent it forward so the fly landed about four feet in front of the fish and after allowing it to sink I gave it a twitch and in an instant, I saw the fish pounce and felt the line stop. After strip setting the hook, the fight was back on with the backing ripping off my reel and the sizzling sound the line makes as the bonefish pulls it across the shallow sea. I raised my rod tip high, trying to keep my line off the rocky rubble and coral heads, and just when I thought he might take it all he turned sideways and started across the flats toward deeper water. I managed to stop him and slowly work in more line until we closed the distance and landed him into Jon's skillful hands.

He was another big fish, at least by my standards, and although I usually try to keep them in the water and release them quickly, I must admit, I held him for a brief while, just to admire his powerful sleekness and burn the image of him into my mind. I was happy to watch that beautiful bonefish as he swam briskly from my grasp and back out to the perilous but beautiful place where we found him. I felt both elated and a bit melancholy, as I often do.

I guess my half-Irish poet nature kicks in whenever I have to part ways with someone, something, or someplace I have come to love. I'm a romantic, I guess; always falling in love. I'm just being me. Quite like Annie Dillard: "I am a fugitive and a vagabond, a sojourner seeking signs." Fishing isn't just fishing, for me. It's poetry, alchemy, and mystery all at once. It's a "spot in time" where the universe is revealed, vast and ever changing if we pay attention to the music of the spheres and the rhythm of the tides—and I do.

After a morning of seeking bones in beautiful bays and sandy flats to no avail, we now had an afternoon of casting and catching until my arm hurt. The smallest bonefish I hooked was in the two- or three-pound range but five of them ranged closer to seven. The runs were powerful and explosive and on several occasions the bone that I had connected with blasted into a school of other bonefish which in turn exploded across the flats in sprays of salty water like some sort of aquatic fireworks display. It was without a doubt the most amazing and magical place I have fished for bonefish thus far, and all the way back to the docks that evening, neither of us could stop smiling. My shoulder ached along with my back, arm, wrist, and legs from fighting the incredible wind and these amazing fish. I did not seem to mind and as we pulled into the docks, all I could think was, this was a "type two experience" that I very much want to do again.

———

Back at my bungalow on Provo I sat outside and watched the evening fade as the sun drifted over the horizon. I had been on the island for several days exploring the beaches, coves, and wooded trails on foot and on horseback. I was trying as best I could to soak up what made this place so special and the people so joyful. I sampled the food, tasted the rum, and listened to the imported reggae rhythms that felt as native as the bonefish. I walked among the brightly painted, multicolored buildings with the slanted tin roofs and slatted wooden shutters. I tried my best to feel deep down inside me what it meant to be a Belonger.

On my last day on the island, I woke before sunrise and walked down to the beach to watch the new day's light come to life. I've missed way too many sunrises in this lifetime, and I wasn't about to miss this one. Grace Bay Beach is long and slightly curved with a barrier reef about a quarter mile offshore that keeps the surf gentle and the sea's surface calm. Intricate lines of colorful, broken seashells told the stories of the tides. The low, waxy vegetation where rare iguanas lived defined where the sand beach ended and the limestone island began.

It was like this before Columbus arrived, enslaving the Taino native peoples and exterminating much of the native wildlife. Sea turtles and Caribbean monk seals were easy targets. The turtles managed to endure and persist, but the last monk seal passed into history long ago. It was like this before the arrival of slavery and sugarcane with the resulting exported wealth and imported poverty. And it was like this before the condos and estates lined the beaches and before the airport came to Provo and the seaport came to Cockburn Town. I wondered what it will be like if someday in the not-too-distant future, nature calls our bluff and humanity is diminished . . . or extinct. I hoped it will not come to that, but if it does, I hoped that this beautiful blue planet would heal. After all, the world would be fine without us.

The sand beneath my feet was as white as any eggshell and as bright as the sunlight on the glistening sea. But in these early hours when the sun is only a soft luminescent glow on the horizon, I could sit on the beach and closely explore the nature of the sand. I could see every tiny grain and marvel at the wonder of its existence. I could hold it in my hand and allow it to sift earthward through my fingers, taking note of all that was observable to my aging naked eye—and I did.

Sand is Earth transformed by a living planet. It reflects not only the light of the sun and moon but also the life of the Earth itself. Sand forms in many ways, but most often it is the result of terrestrial stone being broken down in the process of weathering and eroding over millions of years. The bedrock decomposes over time and washes down a million rivers toward the sea. The brook trout in Appalachia spawns over the same gravel that will itself be reborn in the tidal zones of the Gulf of Mexico. Everything is connected to everything. Earth, Sky, Ocean, and every living thing, are interdependent. We fit like a puzzle whose pieces breathe, feed, and replicate, pushing our essence forward in time. The loss of any piece diminishes the life of the whole.

Many anglers count success in fishing by numbers and poundage of fish—I do not. Don't get me wrong, I love to catch fish and catching a big fish is always a wonderful challenge. But I am more inquisitive than that, so I guess I'm not only a "catch and release" angler, I'm also a "catch on to what's going on" angler. I want to learn about the fish and the place it calls home. I want to know what it feeds on and how it interacts with the tides and why there are tides—in the first place. I want to know what eats them, what threatens their future existence, and what I can do to mitigate that impact. I want to dive in and swim with them and find out what they're up to down there! If the only time I see a fish is in my hand or on a plate, I'm missing out on a lot of the adventure that is "fishing."

I'm the same about the Earth, and everything from soil to sand amazes me. Both soil and sand are living communities of microbes and algae that live out microscopic dramas of predators and prey. Without these tiny building blocks, our whole world collapses. And the important thing to realize here is, these building blocks are so tiny that we can walk right over them, never knowing that we might be killing off our own future, one chemical spill at a time.

Most people who walk the beach notice the sameness of sand and sea yet miss the differences that are all around them. I try to decipher the beach and read the water. I notice what might be dying in the drift line and what might be living in the swash. I explore tidal pools and pay attention to the way sand crabs burrow in as corbina dig them out. There is so much life and history of life on any beach. Sand fascinates me.

White sand in some places such as the Gulf Coast beaches of northwest Florida, Alabama, and Mississippi are the result of ground-up quartz crystals that travel with the rivers from Appalachia to the Gulf of Mexico. But the sandy beaches of the Turks and Caicos have their origins as the result of the feeding habits of tropical parrotfish. These beautiful buck-toothed fish feed on algae that live on rocks and corals, grinding up the inedible calcium carbonate in their guts and excreting pure white sand. A single parrotfish can produce hundreds of pounds of white sand every year of its life. I wonder what will become of these beaches once all the parrotfish are gone. They are vanishing quickly in many places.

Black sand beaches in Hawaii, Iceland, or the Canary Islands are the result of volcanic activity, as are the green sands of Hawaii's Papakolea Beach where the mineral olivine washes down from the Pu`u Mahana volcano. The purple sand beaches of California's Big Sur Coast are the result of eroded manganese garnet that is carried to the sea by the Big Sur River and its tributaries. And the tan-colored sands of so many beaches are the result of iron oxide that tinges the quartz and feldspar as it washes from mountain streams to coastal waters.

I have yet to see the pink sand beaches of Bermuda but have wanted to fish for bonefish there and hope to do so in the not-too-distant future. Bermudan beaches are tinged pink from the single-celled animal known as foraminifera. The red-colored "foram" mix with white-colored calcium carbonate sand to create a pink hue. There are even red sand beaches, due to having a concentrated iron content, along the coast of Prince Edward Island in Canada. The point is, don't just look down; look in.

Look into the water where the fishes live. Look into the sand, where a myriad of living creatures and transported minerals tell the story of life on Earth. And look into yourself to realize how insignificant we are and how significant our choices have become. When I think of bonefish, I think of sand. And when I think of sand, I think of life on Earth. It's all part of the same magical gumbo.

After my morning on the beach, I decided to charter a catamaran out to the barrier reef to do a little snorkeling. I dove into the waters I'd been fishing in just a day prior, and I swam over the barrier reef and collected a live conch for fresh conch salad. Since I had spent part of my childhood living off the sea across various islands in this stream, I took responsibility for my meal and chopped the conch out of its shell myself. It's not an easy thing to do, not because of the shell but because often, the living conch is looking at you as you cut it out of the shell. But this is the way of things when you are a participant in nature and not an observer. Life and death and responsibility for both, are all outcomes of our choices. And there is something else we gain when we take responsibility for the food we eat—namely, a greater degree of respect and admiration for the living things that sustain us and the living places that sustain them.

When I was a kid growing up on the edge of the Gulf Stream, conch were plentiful. Now, I am worried about their future and that is why I allowed myself to eat a single conch, and why I insisted on killing it and cleaning it myself. I didn't want it showing up in a bowl next to a cold beer without me being keenly aware that I should be grateful, and act accordingly. That conch is now a part of me, and I will forever be committed to the survival of its kind.

Coral reefs remind me of some of the best days of my childhood, fishing and foraging, scuba diving and free diving, off the coast of Green Turtle Cay. Back then we lived for a week on the water we collected from rain and the fish, conch, and lobster we collected from the sea. Back then the reef was brilliant with color, vibrant with life, breathing with the sway of the sea.

I remember the many species of multicolored corals: staghorn, elk-horn, rose, brain, fire, and pillar corals mixed with yellow and orange sponges, mere feet beneath the surface. Grouper, snapper, hog snapper, and parrotfish swam over the reef, while French, queen, and black angel-fish did the same between the sheltered branches of staghorn corals. And wherever the water was deep enough along the reef's edges, amber jacks, barracuda, and sharks patrolled, always ready for the next opportunity to consume some living creature, so that they too might continue to live. We are all consumers of life, and in time we will be consumed. It matters not if we are eaten by fish or fungi—every living thing is destined to the same end. Life is a transferable state of being, endlessly in flux.

The Bahamian coral reef that I knew as a boy no longer exists. When I returned as an adult, I found the coral had turned to bleached white and gray rubble, and the sandy pastures of queen conch were no more. Most of the fish seemed absent. A lonely French angelfish and a couple of wrasses milled about like the last survivors of a scorched-earth war. There were no crabs, spiny lobster, or coral shrimp to be found. There were no cuttlefish, octopus, or seahorses, anywhere. There were no sponges or gorgonians and the brightly colored flamingo tongue seashells had van-ished with the sea fans they once lived on. I was heartbroken. And even as I write this, I try to remove these images from my aging memory and replace them with those of a young boy who once swam like a fish over a kaleidoscopic heaven.

In the Turks and Caicos Islands the reef is still alive. It's not quite what it once was, but it still contains the hopeful promise of rebirth. As I swam over the living corals off the coast of Provo Island, I saw that they still reflected the colors of their photosynthetic algae partners. The reef still contained a vibrant community of mollusks, crustaceans, and fish. The bonefish I sought still had healthy populations of crabs, clams, and shrimp to eat, and these prey animals had a healthy environment in which to survive and multiply. Drifting facedown and breathing air through a snorkel, I could see that the creatures that breathe water were still alive and well in these islands, but I wondered . . . for how long?

Most reef-building corals contain a type of algae called zooxan-thellae within their living tissue, and this mutualistic plant/animal relationship becomes the basis for the survival of both living entities. The algae give the coral polyps food via photosynthesis while the coral provide the algae with shelter from which to access the carbon dioxide, water, and sunlight energy required for that process. The algae also provide the coral with pigmentation, and this is why "coral bleaching" is the beginning of the end for coral reefs. Anthropogenic (human-caused) changes to the ocean such as warming, pollution, siltation, and acidification result in the death of the beneficial algae, the corals lose color and then lose their lives. As the reefs vanish, so do the fish from wrasse to wahoo.

Everything is a part of the whole, including us. We are all bits of carbon and water molecules, temporarily rearranged. We depend upon each other, like the zooxanthellae and the corals. I think we could learn a thing or two from a bit of algae that eats the sunshine and shares its meal. There is hope if we pay attention and act . . . together.

Someday, I know I will feed a tree or become part of the detritus of a stream that will take me ultimately to the sea—where I belong. This pleases me. I held that thought as I enjoyed my fresh conch salad and Turks Head Beer. I closed my eyes and felt the ocean sea breeze on my face while reliving the memories of fast running bonefish in my mind. I opened my eyes and thought about my newfound love for these islands and its people, forever in my heart. In fact, for a moment, I felt as if I belonged here. And in that moment, I felt truly happy.

As I placed the cold bottle of beer against my still-aching knuckles, I was reminded of the challenging and ultimately wonderful day casting toward ethereal shadows and silver-gray dreams. I was reminded of those wild bonefish, sharks, and barracuda that thankfully still swim atop that mystical flat. And I was reminded of the feeling of the sand firm beneath my feet and the sun warm against my face. I recalled how the wind blew the ocean's surface into a chop and my line into places unintended by me. And I felt fortunate, indeed . . . simply to be alive.

Jon had guided me to a lot more than good fishing. He led me toward new experiences and understandings of an amazing creature and a timeless place. The sand flats I have come to love would be deserts without the living things that inhabit them from barnacles to bonefish.

I don't want to live in a time where this stark vision comes true. Instead, I want to see the time where we learn the same art of mutualistic living that a tiny coral polyp seems to understand. I want to come back and watch the drama unfold—the swimming, swirling, tidal world of the living sandy shallows. Standing on these sand flats looking out toward the depths, I am reminded to never choose to be a fish, when I can choose to be the ocean. By understanding the tiniest of things, I become vast. Whenever I am casting seaward, I am reaching out for home.

The fresh conch and lime tasted bright and bold as the Turk's Head brew tasted crisp and cold against my sunburned lips. The surf rolled in as the tide rolled out, and the breeze blew softly with the dying of the day. Looking out to sea, one last time, I raised my glass and smiled as I said aloud, "Ya mon . . . this is a good place." And for a moment, I almost felt like a Belonger.

CHAPTER SEVENTEEN

Bonefish
Grand Cayman Island

You have brains in your head. You have feet in your shoes. You can
steer yourself in any direction you choose. You're on your own, and you
know what you know. And you are the guy who'll decide where to go.
~ DR. SEUSS, *OH, THE PLACES YOU'LL GO!*

WHEN I WAS A KID, A LONG, LONG, LONG, TIME AGO, I USED TO WATCH
two kinds of shows without fail. The first was nature shows such as *Wild*
Kingdom, with an unlikely host named Marlin Perkins and his trusty
sidekick Jim Fowler. (I feel sure that Jim would prefer not to be called a
"sidekick.") I have to admit even as a kid laughing when Marlin would
calmly explain from the comfort of his television stage something like,
"And now Jim will leap from the swiftly moving Land Rover onto the
back of the angry hartebeest." (Hilarity would ensue for everyone except
perhaps Jim and the animal he was riding.)

The second kind of show I watched as often as possible is the
"Outdoor Sportsman" style, where some lucky bastard was hunting or
fishing in some part of the world that might as well have been Mars to

this young boy whose entire outdoor world was the woods, streams, and ponds that surrounded his house and whose "gear" included a Zebco rod and reel and a .22 rifle. I loved all the shows about hunters chasing down tigers, lions, and bears, but the one show that truly captured my imagination was of a man casting to and catching bonefish on a fly rod. I loved the sound of his reel screaming as the fish seemingly left him helpless to do anything other than pray to Poseidon that the fish would tire or turn before his backing ran out! Even then, I knew I had to be that guy, someday.

When I arrived on the island, I called my guide, who we will call Ziggy. He was pleasant but had that lackadaisical way about him that I came to see again and again in quite a few Caribbean fly-fishing guides. (Maybe it's just me?) It goes like this . . .

Me: "So, I'm really looking forward to fishing tomorrow!"

Him: "Yah, maybe we go, maybe we don't."

Me: (Trying to sound relaxed about his reply) "The weather looks pretty good . . . a few clouds maybe."

Him: "Yah, well, you never know. We will see in the morning."

I've decided it's a test to see if I can chill . . . go with the flow . . . roll with the tide. I do. I just let it unfold. Then again, maybe there's something in my voice that makes them think that sleeping in might be a better use of their time, I don't know.

Ziggy was a laid-back, chain-smoking Afro-Islander with an easy smile, impressive dreadlocks, and round beer belly of which he seemed quite proud. He was sober upon arrival at my hotel but from our initial conversation I gathered that he'd been out on the town into the wee hours of the morning of our adventure. I try to take people as they come as long as they're not hurting anyone and Ziggy seemed to have a heart as big as his belly. I liked him . . . in fact, I'd go with him again. I'd even hang out with him if I wasn't concerned about the effects of all that sec-ondhand smoke, being arrested, or being killed by an angry husband—of which I suspected there were several.

When Ziggy picked me up, we began driving around the island in his quirky yellow Volkswagen van, stopping here and there to check out a few hidden coves and make blind casts into likely spots that were still too dark to see into. The sun was just a sliver of light on the horizon. By the time we had enough sunlight to see, we'd arrived at the place he had in mind, a stunningly beautiful sand flat in a wide-open bay with turtle grass forming the western edge and a barrier reef forming the northeastern edge. True to Ziggy's nature, he parked on the road directly in front of a "No Parking" sign. I asked, "Is this going to be okay?" "No worries, mon." he replied. He lit another cigarette and we waded out onto the flat.

Of all the places I have fished for bonefish this little bay might be my favorite. I've traveled to various other islands and I caught more bonefish there than I had ever dreamed of as a kid, but this sandy bay holds beauty like no other. I am completely aware that every bonefish I've ever caught was a tribute to every one of those laid-back, knowledgeable guides—and not my own knowledge or skills. Still, it is a goal of mine to someday chase bonefish on my own.

Ziggy wore baggy shorts with pockets that bulged with packets of cigarettes and a single box of flies he had tied "while drunk." He wore no shoes and only a tattered and stained T-shirt over his round belly, and he carried with him a wonderful sense of humor and an attitude that immediately put me at ease. He was never without a lit cigarette between his lips, even as he spoke. What I have not mentioned is that I am asthmatic and allergic to cigarette smoke, and once I shared this fact, even in his somewhat wobbly state after a night of debauchery that he delighted in telling me of in detail, he was a true gentleman and always tried to stand downwind of me.

—◦—

The one peculiar quality I noticed about Ziggy is how his accent changed whenever he spoke to me, and then when he spoke to a fellow islander. For example, speaking to me he would say, "Bonefish coming at two o'clock." And he would say this softly while using "the Queen's English." Based on the sound of his perfect diction and stately accent, he could have been a member of the Royal Family. Then once when a fellow local absentmindedly began wading toward us in splashy, tipsy curiosity, the conversation went something like this:

"Hey mon . . . Whatchu fish'n for?"

"Bones mon!"

"Bones?"

"Yah mon, we be fish'n for bones!"

"Whatcha use'n for bait, mon?"

"A fly!"

"A fry?"

"No mon . . . not a fry . . . a fly!"

His curiosity quenched, our inebriated friend turned and splashed his way back toward shore while my hungover guide shook his head and declared in a voice not unlike Sir Ben Kingsley, "Bloody drunks." I laughed. I love irony. Humor is our best adaptation for survival in this uncertain universe and all too often upside-down human world. I laugh often and most often I am laughing at myself.

— ‿ —

The sun was up at an angle now, which helped me to see the shadows of fish coming onto the sand flats from the turtle grass. It seemed a perfect morning as we faced outward across the flats hoping for a steady parade of traveling and tailing bonefish. We had an incoming tide and with it came the sleek silver-gray fish that are so perfectly adapted to this ever-changing waterscape.

When the tide comes in, bonefish gain access to food sources that were beyond their reach prior to the flooding of the flats and mangroves. When the tide goes out, bonefish lie in wait in channels, cuts, and depressions for the various shrimp and crabs that are drawn out of the mangroves and sand flats by the pull of the ocean and the topography of the submerged seascape. With bonefish, corbina, and many fish of the coastal flats, estuaries, and mangrove forests, the tide is a major influence on behavior. In general, bonefish move into shallow water pursuing food items like mollusks, shrimp, crabs, and minnows on a rising tide, and swim out to safer, cooler, deeper water on a falling tide.

Tides are basically "long-period waves" caused by the gravitational pull of the sun and moon. Tides originate in the ocean's pelagic waters and move toward the coastal areas where they appear to us as the rising and falling of the sea's surface that regularly floods and drains sand flats, estuaries, beaches, and mangrove forests. Tides are a vital part of the process of bringing fresh, oxygenated water into the flats and estuaries while pulling excess nutrients and potential prey items out to sea.

With climate change being greatly accelerated by humans burning fossil fuels, polar ice is melting at an alarming rate, leading to sea-level rise that threatens to topple condos and ecosystems alike. Global and local sea levels are changing at different rates depending on many factors, but the end game is, things are being submerged that used to be dry and this causes habitat to move and vanish faster than living organisms can adapt. Mangroves retreat, sand flats decrease, bonefish and everything they are connected to are adversely and perhaps irreversibly impacted.

As Ziggy and I stood in the calf-deep, salty-clear waters of the sandy flats, I scanned the middle distance for signs of approaching fish—the fly held firmly between my left thumb and forefinger, the rod handle softly held in my right casting hand, poised like a heron at the water's edge. We moved ever so slowly, almost imperceptibly forward closer to the edge of the turtle grass. Above was a phalanx of pelicans that flew quickly by us, and the dancing flight of terns in the near distance. Just below the water's surface I saw the occasional starfish or stingray on the hunt . . . the scurry of crabs and shrimp that were being hunted, and the empty open shells of bivalves that had been caught. I absorbed every sight, every sound, every aroma of this shallow-water Serengeti. And even before the arrival of the first bonefish, I felt fortunate.

One of the challenges of catching bonefish is being able to cast to them accurately, quickly, and with some degree of stealth. Another challenge is being able to see them in the first place, before they see you. Clear, thin, water works both ways, and bonefish are well adapted to this shallow-water habitat where everything is eating everything else. It should be obvious that you need a good pair of polarized sunglasses as a starting point—but that is only the start. You may not have ideal light, but if you do, it will be with the sun between eleven and one o'clock overhead, with minimal cloud cover, to reduce shadows that you might cast on the water but increase the likelihood that you can see the shadows of the fish as they swim over the sandy flats searching for prey.

Many anglers learn to "read a river" but fewer experience the joys of reading a beachline or sand flat. It's even more dynamic than a river. Topography, sunlight, wind speed and direction, tides, currents, all play a role in locating and connecting to bonefish. We were searching for any signs such as wakes, tails, shadows, or even "nervous water." Before long, we began to see all of these and with the incoming tide and rising morning sun, a seemingly barren sand flat became a swirl of action and drama.

We saw them coming at about the same time. At first, I saw only the shadows of the fish as they hunted the transition zone between the grass and the sand flats. Then, the fish themselves materialized, sleek, silver, shimmering, and iridescent, moving from right to left about sixty to seventy feet in front of us. I set up the cast, keeping my body and casting arm low so that my shadow didn't spook the fish. I made the cast, landing the fly slightly short of their path as they continued forward, yet unaware of our presence. Letting them pass, I picked up the line and cast again this time about four to six feet ahead of their rooting lips. The fly sank, and as they approached I gave it a twitch and two of the four fish in the group turned and one began to follow. I let the fly settle a moment then twitched it again and braced for the bite as one of the fish raced forward. At the last moment, it turned and swam away, leaving me deflated and yet elated, all at once.

It felt so close, I could feel my breath catch and my heart hold a beat, and just as he turned away, I was breathing once more. We were just getting started. Like my quarry, I adapted. We pursued them slowly, methodically, and quietly, as other schools of bonefish were entering the flats from all sides. It was exhilarating.

Scanning the flat, we spotted half a dozen bones tailing in the shallows closer to shore. We never saw them enter the flats but lucky for me, they hadn't noticed us either. We stalked into casting range and I let it fly, doing my best to drop the little shrimp pattern as softly as I could. Once again I let the fly sink in front of them, allowed the fish to get within sight of the fly, twitched it as best I could to imitate a fleeing shrimp, got a follow and then another rejection. This pattern played out again and again over the next few sunbaked hours and after a while, I was running out of water and Ziggy ran out of cigarettes.

Sometimes the cast was at the limits of my abilities and other times the fish would feed within thirty feet of us, and I'd make cast after cast, right on target, or at least, close enough to do the trick. We changed flies a number of times, trying to unlock the mystery of why these actively feeding fish were rejecting each presentation—but the bonefish were having none of it. We had more chances at bones than I can count, and I managed to get a couple of follows but for the life of me, not a single take. Each time my round-bellied buddy would say, "I just don't understand . . . everything is just right but we can't get a bite."

He lit another cigarette and adjusted his position beside me so that the caustic smoke drifted away from me. For that, I felt grateful. There was a kind man under that tattered, beer-stained T-shirt. I don't recall what was printed on it but it should have read, "Live and Let Live." I think that's exactly what he was doing . . . and there's not a damn thing wrong with that.

$$\sim\!\!-\!\!\sim$$

We decided to abandon this beautiful flat with its glistening clear waters, glaring white sands, and gorgeous but reticent bonefish. Arriving at a cove on the south side of the island we bailed out of the bright yellow Ziggy mobile and waded into another flat that was filled with turtle grass and contained pockets of open sand here and there. The wading was difficult here, but we could see tailing bonefish in the distance and another group of bones were swimming randomly through a sandy cut. We tried them first since they were the closest to where we were standing. I looked down into the water near my feet and saw a brightly colored octopus looking up at me with a face that seemed to recognize exactly who I was and what I was doing there. He didn't look hopeful.

Casting into the sandy cut I dropped the fly among the school of bones and they never even adjusted their pattern of movement. Cast after cast elicited no strike or even, a reaction. I wondered what the octopus knew that I didn't. Ziggy decided we should change flies yet again and he tied on something that looked like an irradiated half-crab / half-shrimp that was made out of pieces of old shag carpet from some cheap motel. I'd never seen anything like it before or since. In Ziggy, I put my trust.

With all the stealth that a happily hungover Caymanian fish guide and a hopeful but somewhat flummoxed Texan angler could muster, we moved into position in front of a half-dozen tailing bonefish. The fish were about seventy feet away from me, and with the wind in my face, the cast was at the edge of my comfort zone. We let them move closer and at about sixty feet I dropped the fly in front of the two bones on the far-right edge of the line of fish, so as to not spook them all. There was no response. They fed on, tails up, heads down. This should have been easy.

I cast again, allowed the fly to sink and twitched it just enough to elicit a turn, a follow, and a rejection. The gig was up as the bones moved off just out of range at about the same time a noisy flock of Cayman Island parrots filled a tree at the water's edge and the rumble of thunder filled the sky. The wind picked up. Lightning flashed in the near distance. The storm was moving toward us, and, as always, nature had made the call. I'm okay with that.

We had a beautiful day of fishing, Ziggy and me. Sure, I wanted to catch a few bonefish but the fact that I hadn't did not ruin the fishing trip. The water was as blue as the sky, the sand flats as bright as our spirits and the bonefish were lovely as living mercury. I cast and I cast, and we changed flies and we changed places but no matter what we did, I could not get a bite. In the end, I assured my new friend that I had a great time.

He seemed a bit downtrodden that we could not connect, and his voice was kind as he said, "It's notchu mon . . . da bones were fuck'n crazy today." It was not lost on me that Ziggy had relaxed and was no longer speaking like Sir Ben Kingsley with me. This pleased me immensely.

Maybe what Ziggy said was true and I had done all I could do to connect to a bonefish, or maybe it *was* me. Either way, we parted ways smiling and I found myself hoping that he wouldn't end up driving headlong into a palm tree or falling victim to an irate spouse. I liked Ziggy, human flaws and all. He was a generally decent guy living a pretty good simple life as best he could manage.

When I was a young man, life hadn't yet taught me the lessons of humility and acceptance. Falling down and getting up teaches more than persistence, resilience, and balance. It teaches us empathy and understanding. It teaches us kindness and forgiveness. And it reminds us that a world without the possibility of redemption is a world without hope. We all fall down.

Since then, so many tides have washed across the edges of my life. I have learned that how I view and accept other people often reflects my own level of spiritual evolution. As a more evolved soul, I am a more accepting soul. This doesn't mean I don't have boundaries or core values; it simply means I understand now what Oscar Wilde meant when he wrote, "Every saint has a past, and every sinner has a future."

When Ziggy and I parted ways, I remember thinking that I wished he'd stop smoking, drink a little less, and lose a bit of that magnificent round belly of his. I'm not judging him; not a bit. Who am I to judge anyone? No . . . it's just that deep under the dreadlocks and constant haze of smoke and after-buzz was a man of kind heart and good intentions. And I'd like him to stick around for a while.

Maybe next time we fish together, we might catch something. Then again, I can hear him now as he takes another drag from that glowing tube of death and says, "Yah, maybe we catch one, maybe we don't." I think there's a lot of Zen in that dreadlocked island man.

Expectations are the root of suffering and I did not suffer a bit because the bonefish eluded me during my day with Ziggy. All it meant is that I'd come back and try again. I'd learn more and improve my skills, and most of all, I'd never allow myself to lose my sense of wonder and gratitude for just being able to be alive—out in nature.

A few days prior I had rolled off a boat's gunnel into the deeper sea on a scuba dive over a reef in about forty feet of water. Even though I have lived most of my life in Texas, I grew up in old Florida before the circus came to town and the Everglades was replaced with drainage canals and golf courses. I was thirteen years old when my dad and I became NAUI

Certified scuba divers, and from that day on we dove about two tanks a week off the coast of Florida and the Bahamas. Back then, I recall swimming over vast colorful corals, sponges, sea fans, and gorgonians. Fish, conch, and spiny lobster were so plentiful we could go to the islands for weeks on end and live almost completely from the bounty of the sea.

I was serving in the Marines when Dad went diving off the coast of Grand Cayman. He came back raving of the vast forests of bright living corals and the swarms of swimming multicolored fish. But when I got there some thirty years later, it was all but gone. Those coral-filled fields of my father's dreams had been replaced by bleached skeletons of staghorn, elkhorn, and brain corals and the burnt orange ooze of fire coral growing like crabgrass in a once healthy lawn. When I saw this, all I heard was the sound of my breath rising toward the surface and all I felt was empty. How can we allow this?

The next morning was stunningly beautiful and the dreamlike day of casting and wading had become a wonderful life experience I'd happily relive. Ziggy will never know how much his laid-back kindness meant to me. It was as valuable as the beauty of the water, sky, and windswept palm trees. There is something of value in everything we do in life. Sure, I wish I had caught one of those beautiful bonefish on Cayman, just like I had done many times before in other places. I am grateful, nonetheless.

I had some time before needing to get ready for my flight, so after having coffee on the beach of my hotel I put on my mask, snorkel, and fins to have one last swim in the warm sea. It's meditative to hear your own breath drawing in and out of your snorkel tube. It's peaceful to watch sea fans sway and parrotfish swim and tiny creatures crawl across the rippled-sand.

I kicked across the sea in big looping circles, first over the reef and then over the sand and that's where it happened. I could not stop laughing into the mouthpiece of my snorkel—I had suddenly found myself surrounded by bonefish. There must have been a hundred of them circling around me in four feet of water like a silver-colored whirlpool, and I swear that I can see them to this day in my mind's eye and absolutely every one of them was looking directly at me, smiling. Cheeky bastards.

I have never spent a day fishing and then felt as if my time was wasted. If you contain a love of mountain streams and windswept sand flats, it matters not how the catching is, because the fishing is always beautiful. I fell in love with Grand Cayman, its people, and its molten-glass water teeming with sarcastic bonefish. And as for me not catching a single thing on this trip . . . no worries, mon. I'll be back. I wonder what Ziggy's up to now?

Chapter Eighteen

Snook, Jack Crevalle, Moonfish

Rivers, Mangroves, and Bays, Florida

The angel cried with a loud voice, saying, Hurt not the earth, neither the sea, nor the trees.

~ The Bible, Revelation 7:3

The boat was sinking, or at least it had more water flowing in than seemed appropriate or healthy for a vessel that was never designed for subsurface operation. My new buddy Terry Gibson was at the helm of a borrowed sixteen-foot-long, four-foot-wide micro-skiff with a water-logged white deck and shallow-draft blue hull with the name *Prop Scars* painted across its bow, complete with dripping blood descending from each letter. We were crossing the Indian River Lagoon heading toward a long line of red mangroves where we hoped to find snook and perhaps some juvenile tarpon, jack, or snapper. Mangroves harbor so much life among their propped-up roots and outstretched water-shading branches that you never know what to expect, and that is part of their charm.

We made it across the lagoon and beached the boat on a sandy strip just long enough for Terry to find that the plug wasn't quite as tightly affixed to the hole in the hull as we'd like. It was a quick fix, and we took a bit of time to allow the bilge pump a chance to do its thing and drain the lagoon back out to where it belonged. It didn't take long before we shoved off and Terry was on the stern poling us forward along a line of mangroves and sandy beaches. I was casting Terry's seven-weight glass rod, which felt soft and slow in my hands. It took me a bit to settle down and get into the rhythm of casting, stripping the line, and recasting to likely places along the way. I have a bad habit of getting a bit of the jitters when I first step up to the casting platform or unfamiliar boat bow with any new rod in my battered old hands. But soon we were both moving like music across the flats—Terry poling the little skiff and me pushing the little rod. It was all good water with red mangroves, freshwater runoff flows, and a bit of structure here and there in the form of fallen trees and rocky debris.

Terry and I had spoken many times, but the first time we'd met was just a few hours prior when he picked me up at the West Palm Beach Airport. The last time I was here was the last time I saw my father alive. Although I am a Texan at heart and have lived most of my life in the Lone Star State, I grew up in "Old Florida" when there were more gators and gopher tortoises than people, the fishing was phenomenal, and we all said "y'all" and not "you guys."

I was introduced to Terry by our mutual friend Brandon Shuler who is, among other things, the Executive Director of the American Water Security Project. Brandon is also someone whose life has traveled in the reverse order of my own. He is a Native Texan who has made Florida his home, and I was a boy from Old Florida who made Texas my home.

Terry has made his living as a professional fishing and hunting guide and editor of several major outdoor magazines and has served a decade and a half working as a consultant for various conservation organizations across the fields of fisheries management, water management, climate change, public lands, clean energy, and Everglades restoration. He currently serves as the Florida Program Lead for "Deploy-U.S." which describes itself as a "bipartisan climate leadership" "convenor and accelerator." Terry is also 100 percent Floridian, but he has fished and hunted

Texas so we are all connected by common places and passions for outdoor living and protecting the places we love.

Although my childhood had the challenge of an abusive and ultimately abandoning mother it also had the blessing of a loving and devoted father. My dad invested many days and years with me outdoors in nature between the Everglades and the Gulf Stream. Dad used to call it "church in the woods" and "church at sea." All I know is, if I've ever seen the hand of God it's been in the intricacy of nature and the intensity of my dad's devotion and love.

Just prior to our crossing on the waterlogged micro-skiff we'd stopped at a little angler's restaurant and bar in Jensen Beach called Lures. It had plenty of oversized replica lures hanging from the rafters, and kitschy signs like the one that read, "Bait Your Own Hook, Clean Your Own Fish, Tell Your Own Lies." Another sign advertised, "Free Beer—Tomorrow." Jessica brought me my "Lures Burger," fries, and sweet tea as I listened to the comforting sound of classic rock and the banter of locals who all seemed to know each other, and who never tired of talking about fish, fishing, and the way "things used to be—back then."

I've heard that same conversation in every angler's hangout from Alaska to New York. It's somewhere between a melancholy recollection and a prideful badge of honor: "I was there, back then when the fishing was amazing and the lagoon was clean." It felt like a homecoming for this Texan who grew up among the slash pines and palmettoes of the Loxahatchee National Wildlife Refuge. And from the waterside café to the lagoon, I was flooded with memories of a childhood where brackish waterways and a salty ocean were part of my everyday life. As Terry pushed the little skiff along into the wind I tried to focus on the mission at hand but often wandered to memories long ago.

Terry kept placing me in front of some great holding waters as I shot cast after cast into notches between mangrove roots and along creases in the current. One of the issues along these barrier islands is that runoff water flows directly into the Indian River Lagoon complete with whatever pesticides, petrochemicals, and poodle doodle they might pick up on the way from condos to culverts. But those outflows also become a good ambush site for waiting snook.

Terry directed me to cast toward one of the outflows and almost instantly we saw a modest-sized snook following my fly. I should have accelerated my retrieve but instead I paused, and that's all it took to cause the fish to turn and swim away. When you mess up like that all you can do is try to learn from your mistakes and keep casting. That's true in fishing and in life. We're all guilty of zigging when we needed to zag, but guilt and regret are a waste of time and energy. I know this intellectually, but I must admit a moment of weakness when I thought, "I wish I had retrieved it faster."

Sometimes when I'm fishing I make sure to pick my head up and just look around at the beauty of the water, landscape, and sky. This time when I looked up I saw an anhinga, which is also sometimes called a snakebird, darter, or water turkey. Fond memories came to mind of my many years as a boy on these waters, watching these amazing birds. The anhinga might have been hunted to extinction if not for the Migratory Bird Act of 1918. In fact, so many of the shorebirds I have come to love would most likely have gone the way of the Carolina parakeet long before I was born if not for us finding the wisdom to codify the idea that, "This, we will not destroy." I think we need to do a lot more of that. Either we will control our own behaviors or eventually Mother Nature will do it for us. If humans vanished tomorrow, the Earth would breathe a sigh of relief.

The name anhinga comes from the language of the native Brazilians who speak the Tupi language, and it means "snake bird." It got this name because of its long snake-like neck and sharp slender beak that it uses to spear fish as it swims underwater with webbed feet that are perfectly adapted for its lifestyle. What isn't adapted well is that the snakebird's feathers are not waterproof, which is why this one was standing on a dead mangrove branch with outstretched wings—drying in the wind and the last of the evening's sunlight.

Before long we were rounding a corner where we could see a snook smashing into forage fish along a conflicting current on the edge of the mangroves. Terry pushed us into place and I began casting from the depths to the shallows with no result. "Damn, that cast deserved a fish," Terry said. "Yeah, well, life has nothing to do with what we deserve," I replied. And it's true.

I'm not being a pessimist, just an Imperfect Texan Buddha in that I know expectations truly are the root of all suffering. Nature and life aren't kind or cruel; they are both ambivalent to our existence. The gift and the joy is that we get another cast . . . another breath . . . another chance to make new choices. As long as we can stay afloat we can stay in the game. And once our last cast finally does come, all we can do is say, "Thank you" to the universe for all the back casts we've known. We're all crossing the same river—together.

The west horizon was awash in yellow, golden, and purple tones of dying sunlight, and the docks that lined the seawalls behind multi-million-dollar mansions and immaculate mobile homes became illuminated in lights of green and white. Each one of these lagoon side structures was another ill-conceived construct, waiting for the next big blow. Although hurricanes were a part of life on this coast when I was a kid, they are becoming more severe and frequent with the warming seas and slowing Gulf Stream.

Oceanside condos stood silent in the dusky half-light just waiting for the day they become uninhabitable with climate change and rising seas. I envisioned them as artificial reefs, lying on their sides in the ocean's surf like unintentional piers with porches. Would there be any fish to inhabit their crumbled rooms and fallen roofs? I wonder, what will the ocean and world look like when my daughter is my age—long after I am gone?

I decided to switch over to my own graphite eight-weight and my casting began to get in the groove. It felt good. Like walking with an old friend down a well-known path. But as comfortable as I was with my fly rod, this kind of fishing was all new to me.

Terry coached me in the nuances of battling snook under the dock lights and around the pylons. He said, "When you set the hook there will be a moment in time . . . just a few seconds where either you win or the snook does. As soon as it feels the hook, the fish will power forward into structure—mangrove roots or pier pylons—and try to break your leader. So, the trick is to immediately lead the fish away from the structure and into open water." I burned that advice into my lizard brain, wanting my casting and catching to come naturally, like breathing and a beating heart.

Terry's trolling motor wasn't working, and due to the pandemic-related supply-chain issues, replacement parts have been hard to come by—so we had to drift past the docks, get off a couple casts, and then circle around again for another try. We moved up to the first dock and could clearly see several nice snook smashing into something on the surface, just at the light's molten edges. I cast my shrimpy-looking fly and got an immediate follow and rejection. So, I picked it up and sent it back out getting another follow and a half-hearted strike that missed the target. I was thinking like a frightened crustacean as I did my best impression of a fleeing shrimp and pulled the fly quickly away from the fish. Not actually what I wanted to happen.

We decided to give that spot a rest and moved down to the next set of well-lit docks. Almost immediately we could see feeding activity under the lights and in the darkened water just beyond it. This time we had to drift in from the opposite angle, so I made a half-blind back cast in the general direction of boiling black water. After the first strip of the line, I felt the tug of a fish, strip set the hook, and the rod bent heavy for a moment and then popped free just as I was putting the pressure on a yet unseen gamefish. Terry said, "It's okay, go again!" I did and immediately got another hookup and began pulling for all I was worth to get the fish away from the pylons—and it too came unglued.

"You pulled too hard," Terry said. "You want to guide the fish away from the structure, not pull it." Another note to self. There is so much in fly fishing and almost every artistic life endeavor that must somehow be translated from the conscious to unconscious mind.

We made another pass and I back cast again, this time a little to the outside of the lights on the water, stripped the line a couple of times, felt the fly stop, strip set the hook, and consciously said to myself, "guide—don't—pull." And I did, but the first fish of the night was not a snook but rather, a small jack crevalle.

All along this part of the lagoon the natural shoreline was almost nonexistent. The stretch of mangroves we fished at dusk was part of a meager remnant that had only avoided extermination because a golf course abutted that shoreline. Beyond that small strip of native greenery, most of the natural mangrove forests and coastal hammocks had been replaced by concrete seawalls and lawns that required constant irrigation and fertilizing, all of which ended up in the lagoon. Native sea grass has been replaced by toxic algae and the endangered manatees are dying of starvation throughout the Indian River. Old memories of wild and native waters mixed with new realities of seawalls, stormwater runoff, and unintended consequences.

I recall traveling up the river as a child with my dad, moving ever so slowly while trying to avoid those peaceful marine mammals. We were just becoming aware of the dangers our boat propellers could be for manatees and other marine creatures. Back then, almost all of the shoreline north of Jupiter, Florida, was mangroves above the water with oyster beds and sea grass beneath the surface. Now, almost all of it was concrete and steel and although I was happy to see so many snook beneath the dock lights I'd give up every cast to bring back the place I once knew.

Thomas Wolfe was right: "You Can't Go Home Again." Perhaps it's the way of things that his novel was published after his death and the story of Old Florida is being told only now, when it's been relegated to memory and fragments of forgotten real estate. Somehow I knew that coming here would feel like the death of something—a plaintive and poetic eulogy for a long-lost love. But there is also a hint of joy in seeing those fragments that remain and knowing that all is not lost.

I could easily become addicted to fly fishing for snook and doing so at night on a micro-skiff added an extra degree of challenge. There were quite a few factors to consider as I set up each cast—all the while trying to get used to standing on the somewhat tippy, narrow bow of the little boat. One of the things I had to get used to was casting in total darkness but after I let go of the desire of seeing my airborne fly line and simply "feeling it," it began to feel more natural.

We also had the challenge of an ever-increasing degree of wind, but Terry did an awesome job of putting it to our advantage as much as possible as we moved from one dock to another while casting toward the fish in not-so-clean "well-lighted places." It didn't come easy and more often than not the result was, "Nada, por nada." So, we tried again,

We came upon a smaller dock lamp that had a big spotted sea trout under it and I began working the little shrimp fly in front of it, but to no avail. With the snook and the trout, we got passive follows and half-hearted strikes, but nothing like the crashing predation unfolding naturally in the water. The snook were at every dock and every light aggressively feeding on something. We strained our eyes trying to see what it was—shrimp, minnows, mullet? But we could see nothing. I kept tossing the fly under the docks, got a follow and a take of a snook that was heading directly at me but my attempt at setting the hook ended up pulling the fly out of its mouth. *Merde.*

The water continued to boil with feeding fish and we began to talk about changing flies. I cast one more time with the shrimp pattern and got a tug that was solid but too soft to be a snook. The result was a moonfish or "lookdown fish" which was quite a surprise. The moonfish is a disk-shaped, slender, metallic silver fish that has a distinctive steep, sloping face that terminates in a tiny mouth. They are often a schooling fish that is able to communicate at some level by making grunting sounds with their swim bladders. They feed on marine worms, small fish, and crustaceans, so my shrimp fly was a good match for this unusual fish to catch on a fly. They're also reportedly delicious table fare, and when I carefully unhooked and released it I said, "I don't want to hurt it" to which Terry said, "Don't worry, if you do I will take it home and eat it!" I can report that it lived to be eaten another day.

We decided that I needed to change flies, and after several tries we finally figured out what the snook were feeding on—glass minnows. I tied on a sparse, slender, almost translucent Clouser-like fly and prepared to make good on my last chance at snook that night. The problem was that the tide was going slack and we could see the feeding activity turning off as if "the word" had been passed from dock to dock, one fish to the other. It was also past midnight and the wind was picking up, just as the tidal current was dying down. So, we went back to the first dock light we'd come to that night and positioned the skiff so that it could drift into range of the lights and the snook we'd seen earlier, hovering just inside their warm green glow.

I have always felt an affection for snook as a completely wild fish that has done an amazing job of adapting to human construction and deconstruction. For the longest time these fish were somewhat imperiled by our lack of understanding that they need both time and space to exist. We might see them in the ocean surf or in the depths of bays or beneath the stilted roots of red mangroves, or even far upriver in places we might expect freshwater bass. But we need to understand that snook don't live in any one of these places—they live in all of them depending on where they might be in their life cycle.

Snook habitat ecology ranges from fresh water to salt water and everything in between, because they have a physiology that allows them to use the process of osmoregulation to control the amount of saline in their bodies. The snook's ability to move freely from fresh to brackish to salt waters and back is sometimes called "habitat plasticity." And this ability is vital for snook to be able to spawn in the ocean, have their eggs carried inshore by the tides, and allow their young to grow and ultimately move from fresh and brackish waters to more saline habitats.

Why is this important for anglers, naturalists, and anyone who cares about the Earth and oceans to understand? Well, it's important because just like the coho salmon in the Tongass of Alaska, snook in the American tropics remind us of the need to save and protect *all* of the habitat. Once again, everything in nature is connected and if we lose any part of the snook's required habitat, we lose *all* of the snook.

Snook have another lesson to teach us. They are a hermaphroditic fish that changes sex from male to female only after growing to about thirty inches in length. So, if anglers focus on taking the biggest fish from any population, what we are actually doing is dooming the species to extinction. So many things can impact the snook's ability to spawn from rainfall, salinity, temperature, and even the moon cycle . . . but the final factor is that they need both male and female fish to make new fish. These tiny fish will all be born male. In this case, snook remind us that we need to protect portions of *each* generation and make sure that some of them will live long enough to get in touch with their feminine sides!

It wasn't long before my arrival in Florida that I had first tried to connect with snook on a trip to the Brownsville Ship Channel with my friend Aaron Reed. We worked hard, and I cast for hours but no snook were caught or even found. And now here I was again, weary and wet after many hours of casting my cares toward this line-sided predator.

With the tide going slack, Terry and I both knew that this was going to be my last shot.

As he cut the engine and allowed the skiff to be caught in the tidal current and begin drifting slowly toward the light, I readied myself for my last casts of the night. It was about then that I turned toward Terry and said, "Wouldn't it be poetic if I caught my first snook of my life, on the last cast of the night?" Terry looked at me with a less-than-hopeful face and said, "That would be poetic. You've worked hard for it. You deserve it! These fish are just being assholes tonight." I laughed as I launched the cast toward the light's edges.

The little glass minnow fly landed perfectly on the up-current edge of the waterborne ring of light. I let it drift into the illuminated circle and gave the line a short quick strip that immediately provoked a committed strike! I set the hook and guided the thrashing fish away from the pylons and toward the boat where Terry plucked it from the water and placed it into my arms and with a big smile on his face said, "You earned that fish!" I was so happy to hold him and even happier to see him swim away.

That's when I turned to Terry and with a big beaming smile on my battered face I said, "Wouldn't it be poetic if you took a cast in there and caught a snook right away?" He smiled and said, "Yes, that would be poetic."

Once Terry had circled the boat back around so that it would drift one more time toward that same well-lit dock, I handed Terry the rod and said, "Go show me how it's done, my friend." And he did. We could see snook crashing into forage fish just under the docks and Terry slammed a cast right among them, got the bite, and set the hook like it was the easiest thing in the world. We cheered as I held the skiff away from the pylons and he set the fish free. We were both wet, sweaty, weary, and completely content. As Terry started up the engine and we began to cross the lagoon in the phosphorescent darkness, I felt a sense of peace and satisfaction wash over me. It had been a perfect and poetic ending to a long and lovely night of fishing and living—truly.

I remember the first time I ever really saw the stars. It was on Green Turtle Cay in the Bahamas. It was the first time my dad and I went there to spend a week at a friend's beach house to go skin diving, fishing, exploring, and living largely on the fish, lobster, and conch we harvested from the sea. Our fresh water came from the evening rains, collected in a rooftop cistern and drained into the house by force of gravity. We showered outside whenever the rainstorms came, and when the evening sun returned I would play my guitar on the veranda that overlooked the sea. It was a rustic house where we had to strain the mosquito larvae out of the water and boil it before we drank it and the only air conditioning we had was a trade wind coming off the ocean. And I remember that by the end of the week I was sick of eating lobster and fish every day—a problem I can only dream of having now. But it was an incredible adventure with my dad, filled with hummingbirds and bananaquits, and hours of drifting over multicolored living coral reefs that no longer exist.

On the first night on the island, we walked from the house up a small hill—I wasn't sure why. I remember noticing that I could just barely see the trail in the darkness as it wandered and wove between sea grapes and flowering agave plants that filled the night air with perfume. When we reached the top of the hill my dad touched my shoulder and said, "Look up." When I did, I stopped breathing, for just a moment.

Above me was the Milky Way and more stars than I'd ever seen in Florida. I was still a kid and looked up at my dad's smiling face and said, "Dad, where did they all come from?" He said, "Steve, they've always been there—we just couldn't see them. The lights of houses and highways blind us to them. But here, there are no highways and the only lights are above you." I will never forget that moment—the day I learned that there is more to the world than we might see back home.

I'd see those stars again later in life, first as a U.S. Marine in Africa, and later as a father trekking through the Peruvian Andes with my daughter. Now as Terry and I crossed the Indian River Lagoon through the seemingly darkened night, I looked up and realized, it wasn't dark enough. There were almost no stars visible in the night sky. Yes, I know, they were there. I just couldn't see them anymore.

Isn't it tragic when the things we choose to do causes the things we naturally love to vanish? Isn't it magic whenever we learn to make better choices? These days, I think about that often. Don't you?

CHAPTER NINETEEN

False Albacore, Bar Jack, Yellowtail Snapper
Florida—Offshore

Since oceans are the life support system of our planet, regulating the
climate, providing most of our oxygen and feeding over a billion peo-
ple, what's bad for oceans is bad for us—very bad.
~ PHILIPPE COUSTEAU JR.

THERE WERE SHARKS ALL AROUND US. TERRY HAD JUST CAUGHT A BAR
jack and I was hoping to catch one right behind him but as quickly as we
were into the school of jacks they vanished and the sharks appeared in
their place. The sharks off Palm Beach County have learned that fishing
boats are good places to catch struggling fish. Like the dolphins in South
Carolina, these apex predators had adapted to the influx of human predators into their world.

Even though I grew up on these waters and have spent countless
hours at sea, I have never before seen so many sharks at one time. Most
of them were bull sharks including one massive fish that swam repeatedly
under the boat as if it was contemplating exactly how it might get at its
contents—us. There was no chance of getting another bar jack here and

even if we did, it would never make it to the boat, so the captain started the engine and off we went to another part of the reef—hoping to avoid the sharks.

Terry and I had hired a guide friend of his who specializes in pelagic fly fishing off the coast of the Palm Beaches. Captain Scott Hamilton is originally from New Jersey, and his many years of honing his considerable skills as a Florida offshore fishing guide has not taken a bit of the New Jersey from him. There was no chance that a "y'all" was going to pass through those lips. He is skillful and knowledgeable, and I enjoyed listening to him and Terry kidding each other throughout the day. It was obvious that those two had been helping each other for years in the fly-fishing business and that they're fast friends.

Scott chose a wonderful initial target for an offshore fly-fishing neophyte like me. Bar jacks are relatively small as pelagic fish go and we started catching them on a three-weight rod that Scott loved and I was doing a lousy job of casting across these wide-open waters. I just wasn't in the groove yet and had a bit of the "first cast in new waters jitters." I think this is a "training scar" from my years in Catholic school. It's almost like the guide is wearing a habit, sensible shoes, and holding a ruler while saying in the stern voice of Sister Mary Moppet, "Now Stephen . . . execute the cast and don't screw it up! God is watching!" The only difference was that this time Sister Mary had a New Jersey accent and was smoking a stubby cigarette.

After a couple of deep breaths and a "Hail Mary" I began to settle down, and although I was yearning for the added power of an eight-weight I managed to get my act together and cast out far enough to hook and land a jack. I was grateful that Scott never smacked me in the knuckles with a ruler when I flubbed a cast, and in time, I started slowing down both my heart rate and my casting stroke so that the soft glass rod could do what it was designed to do. I could still hear my sixth-grade teacher whispering in my ear, "Be a winner not a sinner." I told her to go sit in the corner, and I began to relax.

<hr />

We were following a shallow reef that extends south to north along the coast of Jupiter Beach in about sixty feet of water. There was also a sargassum seaweed line that was attracting the bar jacks because of the multitude of tiny shrimp and fish that live among the drifting brown algae. We were hoping for the arrival of dolphin along the weed lines farther out toward the Gulf Stream, and Scott was in communication with boat captains who were already out there but so far there wasn't enough activity to justify the journey. I must admit that when I was daydreaming of this trip I inserted visions of landing dolphin, kingfish, and even a sailfish . . . but the one fish I most wanted to find was false albacore, and there was a better than even chance that we'd make that daydream come true.

The water was so clear and blue that we could see all the way to the bottom where the reef appeared among the sands as patches and lines of dark rocky ridges. The hard corals that I knew as a kid here were long since gone, sitting bleached on a bookshelf somewhere up north—a once living memento of a summer vacation in the Sunshine State. Still, the clear blue waters allowed me to see so many fish beneath the surface, and the frequent passing of loggerhead and green sea turtles added to the near perfection of the day.

When I was a young teenager my father and I would come out to these same reefs every weekend to scuba dive. We'd dive one tank's worth of air in deeper water and another in more shallow water, and in between we'd decompress while fishing and eating lunch. When it was just me and my dad, lunch was a simple affair of a sandwich, chips, and a drink. But when my dad's friend Carlos would come with us, I knew it would be Cuban sandwiches, Cuban cookies, and Cuban coffee . . . all of which were such a treat for me. To this day the taste of slow-roasted pork, cheese, and pickles on Cuban bread send me back to those childhood moments with our Mambo instructor friend. Carlos was one of a kind.

Back then the reefs were alive with brain and rose corals, sea fans, and multicolored sponges. There were thousands of small colorful reef fish among the corals, angelfish, butterfly fish, grunts, snapper, and parrotfish. Spiny lobsters seemed to fill every crevice and we'd collect our dinner of hog snapper or grouper with a single shot of my dad's speargun. I can't imagine doing that now, with so fewer fish, lobster, and conch—and so many more human-habituated sharks.

Still, it could be much that way again. We can turn that wheel and move this vessel in a new direction. The smallest trim-tab turns the ship. The slightest breeze can become a fortunate wind. We simply need to first envision and then commit to that new destination. As Seneca once wrote, "If one does not know to which port one is sailing, no wind is favorable."

It didn't take long for us to come across more bar jacks, and Terry and I took turns catching them on the little three-weight. They are beautiful little fish with an electric blue bar running horizontally along their backs from head to tail. With their sleek, silvery sides and classic jack-shaped bodies, they make me wonder why reef fish and songbirds are so beautiful. Does that beauty serve some practical purpose, or is it just a gift we should accept and enjoy?

In between our search for bar jacks Terry spotted a triggerfish swimming leisurely up from the bottom with a look of curiosity toward the boat. The fish had a "sneak thief" look about it, as if it were trying to get close to us, undetected, hoping for a bit of bait tossed over the gunnel. Scott said, "I'd cast to that," and Terry did. He allowed the fly to sink and then gave it a bit of movement to get the triggerfish's attention. I stopped casting and began watching the on-and-off interest the fish paid toward the twitching fly. Eventually the fish lost interest and began to swim ever so slowly back toward the reef.

While watching this spectacle I had a flashback to a time I was a teenager scuba diving with my dad just south of here, off the island of Palm Beach. I was focused on catching a spiny lobster that was backed into a hole in the reef. The methodology was to slide a lightweight aluminum "tickle stick" behind the lobster and tap it on the tail so that it would come forward enough to be grabbed at the base of its antennae and pulled out of the hole. After getting it out of the hole you'd hold it firmly, look under its tail to make sure it wasn't a female with eggs, measure it with calipers that were tied to your buoyancy compensator, and if it was legal in every way, you'd place it in a mesh bag. Later, dad would broil the tails with drawn butter and we'd eat them with fresh baked bread and a side salad. Wonderful memories, one and all.

Usually, this process of teasing a lobster from its hiding place would go swimmingly, but this time, just as I was poised to lunge toward the lobster, a triggerfish lunged toward me and gave my left earlobe a vicious bite. I will never forget the feeling of being struck in the head multiple times as the big female triggerfish thrashed its body while tearing at my earlobe. I turned and saw it coming after me again through a greenish cloud of my own blood. I knew it was blood because I was at a depth where the color red can no longer be seen—it appears green. It took me many kicks of my swim fins to get the triggerfish to stop pursuing me and return to the hole in the reef from which it came. On my way back up to the surface my green blood turned reddish and a small shark appeared below me. It was tracking the trail of my bleeding earlobe!

Each time we'd get into a school of jacks and begin catching them, the sharks would reappear and we'd have to move farther along the reef. Whenever we hooked a fish, we did our best to land and release it before the sharks gathered close to the boat. If a shark did start after a hooked fish, we loosened the drag on the reel so that the fish could "run" freely and have a chance of escaping. The bull sharks were being joined by sandbar sharks, a smaller but close relative who has a far-less-lethal reputation in its encounters with swimming humans.

Bull sharks may be responsible for most of the attacks on humans in shallow waters, and they are attributed to having the strongest known "bite pressure" of any shark. Peter Benchley's 1974 novel *Jaws* was in part inspired by a series of attacks off the coast of New Jersey that were most likely attributed to bull sharks and not a great white shark. We are always fascinated and horrified by natural predators that might consider consuming humans, but in reality, sharks are a woefully maligned and mistreated group of fish that rarely harm humans and even then, most often do so in a case of mistaken identity. Even as I was watching our boat be repeatedly surrounded by sharks, I knew that the sharks are in much more danger from humanity than humanity is from them.

At one point as we were casting to and catching bar jacks Terry saw a sailfish swimming by the boat and called out his sighting to Scott. I turned as fast as I could hoping to catch a glimpse of it, but only saw water, weed, and the waving hand of Scott as he hollered, "Bye, bye!" toward the fish and said, "All we can do is wave it goodbye because I don't have a rod rigged for it now." I had visions of catching my first sailfish on a fly but would have been happy just to see it. Still, I was glad it was out there and Terry told me that sailfish numbers were on the rise along the Florida coast due to regulations and a community ethos of catch-and-release that includes the use of circle hooks. Also, climate change may be sending fish up from the warming Caribbean as well.

Scott moved us out to another reef, away from the weed line, bar jacks, and sharks and toward a chance at some reef fish. We switched to full sinking lines and eight-weight rods. I really came to love this kind of fishing, it was new to me, but felt understandable and almost natural. The trick was to cast or simply drop your line and then feed out as many feet of it as you needed to reach the bottom without dragging on the reef. Scott called out the depth to us, and Terry and I would estimate the amount of line we'd feed out to fit the known depth. I began simply allowing the line to flow out of my guides until it lost tension on the line, then I'd bring in enough to eliminate any slack and begin stripping it in with fast and slow strips, varied until we found what was working.

Terry hooked a nice fish that gave a solid fight and turned out to be a yellowtail snapper which was unlucky twice—first for being caught and second for being delicious. That one went into the cooler. Terry said, "If we get three we'll have them for dinner tonight!"

I wanted to contribute to that meal so I was sending out and retrieving line as quickly as I could manage. I hooked a potential meal after about three tries but it turned out to be another bar jack, so I set it free. Then, Terry caught another yellowtail which joined its unhappy partner on ice. The sharks were nowhere to be seen so I kept casting, snaking out more line until reaching the bottom and retrieving it hopefully with a burning desire for yellowtail snapper.

The water was unbelievably clear and although I could see the reef directly below us I could not see what was attached to my line farther out, but it was fighting quite like the last two yellowtails did for Terry. The excitement was short lived as whatever it was came unbuttoned. I guess I needed to set the hook a bit more solidly . . . either that, or something ate my fish. I looked for a sleek, toothy predator, but saw none.

I still had hope and time to catch that third snapper for our dinner, but the activity had died down over the reef we were drifting across, so

Scott started up the engine and we moved on toward a place where he had noticed several kingfish leaping from the water in the near distance. I saw one jump just in front of the boat and was getting excited about the new possibilities. Scott tied a wire leader to each line and had Terry and I cast blindly in the direction of the last sighting of kingfish, but nothing took our offerings and no more kingfish were seen leaping from the sea. It would have been nice to land one, but fishing is always just a series of improbable possibilities. Therein lies the adventure.

As we were crossing the rolling blue water just off the Juno Beach Pier, my mind kept drifting back and forth from the stunning beauty of the here and now and the inevitable longing for those long-ago times with my dad. One of the things I always loved is when I would sit on the bow of his boat and watch the flying fish sail over the surface of the sea and then hit the water with a splash so delicate, that it might invoke feelings of envy in any Olympic diver. I was hoping for a repeat of that show and the ocean did not disappoint me.

Everywhere we went the tiny metallic fish burst from the surface, sailed with outstretched and oversized pectoral fins on thin waves of air . . . until they returned to the same ocean that gave them life. I knew this was something that Scott and Terry saw almost every day, but for me, this was a magical memory of my youth. It was a comforting confirmation that some things remain unscathed along this beautiful coastline— and that all the condos and golf courses had not yet extinguished them. Life has indeed, "found a way." Like the snook around the dock lights, and the sharks around the boat, at least some of nature is adapting to us. I wonder, can we begin to adapt to nature? Every shoreline doesn't need a seawall.

━───

False albacore are one of my favorite saltwater fish to target and connect with no matter if they are here in the subtropics or in the cooler waters of Montauk. They have it all. They are consummate predators and eating machines. They are sleek, fast, strong, and beautiful. If they have one shortcoming as a gamefish it's that they are also quickly susceptible to the stress of being caught and handled. And since I do not want to cause any permanent harm to these fish, I am ever so careful in releasing them quickly and appropriately.

Fish like yellowtail are both plentiful and edible, so I see no problem in putting a few on ice. Albies are not a mainstream food fish and so catching them is sport not sustenance fishing and yes, even though I do catch fish that I do not intend to consume I also sometimes ponder the ethics of what I'm doing. But we humans only save the things we come to know and love, and fly fishing is the best way I know to come to understand these fish and their habits and habitat. Still, I do my best to handle fish with care and respect. They need to survive that encounter, whenever possible.

We began drifting across a shallow reef that was in about forty feet of water just off Juno Beach. Long ago in my youth I served as a police officer in that little town and even then I remember being more interested in saving baby sea turtles than catching drug dealers. For a while I was assigned to beach patrol and let me tell you, that's not a bad job at all. One morning I was rolling down the beach on the ATV when I noticed some people crowded near the water's edge, as if someone was in distress just beyond the waves. I moved up there quickly and discovered the focus of their attention was a pygmy sperm whale that was trying to beach itself. I pulled off my gun belt and locked it in the saddlebag of the ATV while asking the dispatcher to contact the Marine Patrol. Then I waded out to the whale and many of the others followed as we each surrounded it and held it in the surf away from the potentially damaging sandy bottom. In time, marine biologists arrived and transported the little whale to a tank at SeaWorld, but I was told that it died soon after.

Everything I did as an officer was intended to "make things better" and mitigate the suffering of others, but no matter what I did I could not save that whale or society. Still, I did manage to save a few baby sea turtles that had gotten turned around by the luminescent lure of road lights. We do what we can do.

Scott knew that this reef was a good place for false albacore, and it didn't take long for us to locate them. There were plenty of them feeding on forage fish about midway in the water column and occasionally breaking the ocean's surface. Many of the guides in South Florida use chum to bring albies in, but Scott fishes exclusively without chum, and that pleased me. I'd rather use the knowledge of the fish's habits and habitats than resort to bait. After all, the skill comes in the ability to find and reach the fish on its own terms and then to approximate the fish's food source with artificial materials—namely, a fishing fly or lure. I wanted to test those skills.

Terry and I took turns with the eight-weight, casting to the albies, hooking up and hopefully landing them. Albies can take you on finger scorching runs well into your backing and that's why I have gotten into the habit of wearing gloves. I have found that bleeding all over your fly line is not the best idea, especially in shark-filled waters.

Earlier that morning Scott had given me some direction as to how he wanted me to fight these fish, with the rod tip low so as to avoid breaking the rod on a sounding fish, while applying sideways pressure and always opposing the will of the fish. He said, "You can either end up helping them breathe or slow them down and we want to slow them down." I've fought albies before but the technique here was a bit different than up at Montauk so I adapted to what Scott was telling me.

It didn't take long at all for both Terry and me to hook a few false albacore. They were as voracious as ever, hunting down your fly like a pack of wolves as you stripped it back toward you as fast as you could manage. Once they strike and you set the hook you soon find yourself in a battle that flows back and forth from holding on for dear life and reeling in as if your life depends on it. They circle the boat and then run out to sea, then turn and run directly back at you until they turn away yet again.

Eventually we got them to the gunnel one by one and Scott would quickly unhook them, flip them face-first toward the water, and drop them straight in so that their gills would receive a refreshing burst of oxygen. He did this so fast it seemed like something a bartender might do with tequila bottles while showing off for pretty girls. As neither Terry nor I are pretty or girlish, I knew this bit of stylish flair was all about the fish . . . mostly.

Like other members of the tuna family, albies need to keep moving in order to push oxygenated water through their gills, rather than pumping it through the gills as many other fish do. Dropping them into the water face-first helps them to revive, and we want them to survive. Albies are short lived as it is, reaching maturity in about a year and having a maximum life span of about five years. Between predatory sharks, seals, and seagoing anglers, these fish need all the help they can get.

After we got a few false albacore to the boat we decided to give that spot a break and travel up to the site of a scuttled ship that was acting as an artificial reef. As a kid growing up in these waters, my dad and I used to dive wrecks with some frequency. It was always fun and interesting to have to switch on our dive flashlights as we explored the inner passages and rooms of sunken tankers and decommissioned naval vessels. I remember that these sunken ships were the only place where I'd see the otherwise infrequently found "spiny clams." I wonder if there are any of these beautiful bivalves remaining on the wrecks along the Palm Beaches. That thought makes me regret the empty shell of one I have sitting forever on my bookshelf. I just didn't know any better back then. Now I do.

I have fond memories of watching the bubbles rise up from my regulator while I was exploring the inside of a submerged tanker ship. They'd get temporarily trapped in the upper bulkhead of the ship's structure, only to eventually find their way through cracks and crevices—bubbling toward the surface like an aquarium aerator. I have a wonderful underwater photo of my dad peeking through the porthole of a submerged ship. The only time I recall my dad being happier than when he was on the ocean . . . was whenever he was under the ocean.

When I was a kid I remember thinking that artificial reefs like scuttled ships, piles of construction debris, and other human-made objects were a perfectly good thing for the environment. I knew that over time they'd accumulate algae, corals, mollusks, and crustaceans and smaller fish that eventually attracted bigger fish like the amber jacks we were hoping to find. And while scuba diving with my dad I remember seeing all the jack, grouper, snapper, barracuda, and even hammerhead sharks that were constantly on the hunt for the smaller fish that inhabited the artificial reef.

But later I learned that they actually act as fish aggregating devices bringing in fish from other natural reefs and concentrating them in one area, often surrounded by empty sand flats. This can make fishing and overfishing easier, while not actually increasing overall fish numbers. Artificial reefs also have the propensity to release toxic chemicals into the water from things like paint, plastics, and other petrochemical based materials. I'm not saying that artificial reefs are all bad . . . just that they're not all good. We need to pay attention to what we're dumping in the ocean.

As we drifted over the sunken ship Terry and I began dropping our lines to the edge of the wreck and retrieving them in a quick, successive, halting manner, so as to give our best imitation of a wounded fish. Scott said that the jacks were swimming about twenty feet from the bottom, but I was still hoping for a chance at a yellowtail so I fished from the sand all the way to the surface. We knew they were down there, but neither Terry nor I were connecting with amber jacks or anything else, so we turned back toward the reef near Juno Beach, hoping to end our day with a few more false albacore. Since albies are a favorite of mine, I was happy with the plan.

❧

I'm not sure that there was any way for my friend Terry or our guide Scott to realize how much this single day on the water meant to me. It wasn't just a fishing trip—it was so much more than that for me. And I've had this kind of moment before in life. Like that morning in Kenya having my coffee at the base of Mount Kilimanjaro. And the last evening in Rome, just before taking the late-night bus to the airport. And the time my daughter Megan and I were at the top of the mountain in the Scottish Highlands . . . or when we watched the sunrise over the Incan Gate of Machu Picchu. And then there was the time when my wife Alice and I were tracking kudu in the thornbush wilderness of Namibia—and when we went snorkeling in the Blue Grotto of Malta.

All of these moments that become memories are about how we connect a place with a person we love. This is when the little voice in your soul tells you, "Don't miss any part of this moment and all it means, because you'll never be here again." It's times like this when you do your best to burn the images into your mind's eye, and breathe in every aroma, feel every breeze, and taste whatever words are lingering—just on the tip of your tongue. And I was about to have another such golden, timeless image burned indelibly into my memory.

Terry had just done a wonderful job of fighting a big albie to the bow. It had taken him into backing on several occasions, and I ended up hooking into an albie at the same time. Scott acted as stage director as we both were run in circles around the boat. First, with Terry on the bow and me on the stern; then he'd be pulled portside and I'd end up starboard. Next, I found myself raising the rod tip high so the line could go around the twin engines of the boat as Terry battled his fish back on the bow. Eventually, Scott ended up unhooking and quickly releasing two fish, but this time we did stop long enough for a quick photo because both fish were so damn beautiful.

A barracuda had moved in from the outer edge of the reef and Terry took a few casts toward it before the big torpedo with teeth decided to swim back to from wherever it came. We turned our attention back to the last casts of the day. Both men were gracious to me as they knew this was my one last shot and they could come back out almost anytime they wished. So, Terry said, "Take another shot at an albie, Steve!" And I did.

It's both beautiful and a bit nerve-racking whenever I feel that a lot is riding on my next few casts and I know I have one or more people on the boat cheering for me. I find myself wanting to catch the next fish—for them. I realize and respect the fact that my compadres both have so much experience at this kind of fishing. What they can do with ease I might do with effort. But I also remind myself that not too many people are willing to throw themselves into uncharted territory in the hope of experiencing and learning something—for the first time.

But everything in my life had a first time—an awkward moment, and an ultimate victory over fear. This for me is what living is all about. So, I cast in hopes of catching one more fish—the last albie of the day. There was just one additional problem to overcome. After the last two landings we once again found ourselves surrounded by sharks. This time, they were all sandbar sharks with their extra tall dorsal fins and sleek bodies that were built for speed and maneuverability.

When I hooked my fish, it was still quite a ways from the boat but already the sharks had become excited, swimming maddeningly around and under the boat. I was doing my best to land the fish quickly so that we might release it and get it out of harm's way as soon as possible. But in an instant we knew that a large sandbar shark was on its tail so I quickly released all of the drag and let the albie swim for its life. What came next will not leave my memory, until life's waning takes my memories away.

It all happened in timeless slow motion and the quickest of speeds all at once. It was as if I had become the albie—and the shark. One fleeing for its life and the other pursuing for its life. This was not sport for them, and there was no intention of catch and release. This was life and death. This was nature. Neither kind nor cruel—simply ambivalent.

The albie had sounded as soon as I let go of the drag and the sandbar shark was in hot pursuit. In an instant, they were both out of sight and everything was silent. And just as quickly, I saw a pressure wave pushing along the surface—and a then a high arching dorsal fin slicing the water directly behind it. Scott pointed as the albie's blue-green back broke the surface with the shark's sandstone dorsal fin not far behind it. Then all at once they were next to the boat, swimming circles around each other in plain view beneath the clear blue water. They spun and thrashed with the shark's tail slapping the chop and spraying salty mist into the air. Just as quickly they both fled to the depths, out of sight but not out of mind and that is when everything went still and silent. Scott was standing beside me and said, "I think the shark got your fish Steve. You can reel in all that line now. That was the last fish of the day." But it wasn't . . . not really.

I began reeling in the long slack line and backing that was drifting in the current after the incredible drama that unfolded before us. I remembered to use my little finger to move the line level across the spool as I reeled and reeled, trying to get it all back on the big reel. And that's when the line stopped, and then it began steadily moving out to sea.

I said, "I might still have that albie." Scott said, "Is it like an unstoppable steady force?" It was. "Think you have the shark, Steve—or rather, it has you." After a bit of effort, we were able to break off the leader against the shark's teeth. I doubt the shark ever noticed. I'm sure the albie was beyond caring. That's life—and death, in the ocean.

Sometimes the sun's energy passes though the teeth of a sandbar shark. Eventually, it will travel through the gut of a microbe. Life is a circle, not a line. We are all connected in one way or another, and in this knowledge there is hope. Within each of us is the power of the sunlight. All we need to do is use it wisely, while we still shine.

—◦—

The ride back to Jupiter Inlet was a thoughtful one for me. I could hear Scott and Terry chatting by the helm, but I was silent on the bow. I was reliving every time my dad and I passed through this inlet on his boat—the *Triton*. How animated with joy and excitement he was when we went out to sea, and how quiet and thoughtful he was whenever we came back in. The Jupiter Lighthouse became a beacon of adventures yet to come and an enduring echo of those that slipped behind us. They weren't always easy. Often the sea was rough and we'd return soaking wet from salt spray and exhausted in a comforting way.

I thought of all the human history that lighthouse has seen since its construction and first illumination on July 10, 1860. For the first years of its life the lighthouse consisted of the original brick that had been laid under the direction of George Gordon Meade, a colleague and fellow officer of U.S. Army Engineers with Robert Edward Lee whose ancestors signed the Declaration of Independence, and who would be defeated by Meade's Army of the Potomac at the Battle of Gettysburg. I knew that the lighthouse survived attack during the "Billy Bowlegs" Seminole War, and that for a while its light had been stolen and stashed by Confederate sympathizers. It survived the passing of German U-boats and the landfall of countless hurricanes and tropical storms. I knew that this guiding light was a survivor.

Over time the humidity and sea air discolored the brick and it was painted red around 1910. We all need a little touch-up now and then. And that was the red brick tower and golden glowing light that greeted my father and me, every time we came home from the sea. As we passed the light, I felt sure that this was the last time I would ever see it, in my current lifetime. I don't know what comes next—and neither do you. The edge of this world is uncharted territory. It's hard to trust letters in a bottle. You never know who really wrote them, or how long they've been floating out there . . . adrift.

I burned the image of the ocean and the light into my memory and when I did I could almost hear my father's laughter as we sailed out to sea, once more. The light flashed in my eyes and salty water filled their corners. With the ocean behind me, softly I said, "Fair winds and following seas, Captain . . . I miss you."

Chapter Twenty

Up the Loxahatchee River
and Down to the Sea
Florida

Naturally we would prefer seven epiphanies a day and an earth not so apparently devoid of angels.

~ Jim Harrison

It has occurred to me that as a child of six and now as a man of sixty, I am still struck by the experience of waking in the dark, truly alone, with that deep empty feeling—that hollow aloneness from which I cannot shake free. As a boy I remember how the silence scared me whenever the bedroom door was closed and all around me was nothing but darkness. I guess that's why to this day I love the sound of rain falling. Back then whenever it rained I would lay on my back with my eyes open, as if I could see the rain as it hit the tin roofed awning outside. The rain kept me company. It still does, sometimes.

When I woke alone in the darkness of my hotel room, it took me a moment to remember that I wasn't in Texas anymore. I had traveled from my beloved Texas Hill Country home, back across a time zone to the home I once knew. I wanted to see what remained intact, of the water-filled world I loved as a boy.

When I was young, "Old Florida" was still fully alive. There was still plenty of clean water flowing in the Everglades down to Florida Bay. The seemingly endless fields of sawgrass contained massive alligators, diminutive deer, and birds of every imaginable shape and size. The waters were filled with Florida bass, bowfins, garfish, and pickerel in the fresh parts and tarpon, snook, and redfish in the salty parts. There were no pythons from Burma or snakeheads from China or butterfly peacock bass from Peru. There were panthers of pure Floridian bloodlines not yet mixed with the transplanted cats of Texas. There were native green anole lizards instead of non-native iguanas and agamids. Back in the days when I grew up here there were only forty thousand residents in all of Palm Beach County and you did not need a road sign to tell you when you had crossed from one small town to another. Pompano was a small fishing village, and Kissimmee a cattle and Florida cowboy town with a good rodeo.

But now my once rural homeland is forever transformed into an uninterrupted metropolitan chain of concrete and steel that extends from Miami to Tequesta and contains over six million humans. Now there are countless condos, millions of gas-swilling automobiles, and more thirsty lawns, golf courses, and swimming pools than you'd find in any continent of the global south. As I lay there half awake in the predawn darkness, I hoped that something of my former home waters remained. I was going to see two such places—perhaps for the last time in my lifetime. I didn't come here to mourn what has been lost. I came to celebrate what we are preserving and restoring. I came for glimmers of hope. And there is hope—if we choose it. There is hope and that hope resides within us.

Terry picked me up in the late morning, which was not our original plan. Last-minute changes came in the form of Terry needing to work in the morning and pick up his six-year-old son, William, from summer camp, in the early afternoon. So, we adapted by deciding to include William in our journey and by turning our breakfast into an early lunch.

When I first conceived this adventure I asked Terry to help me to accomplish four things. First, to be able to fish for snook among the mangroves and nighttime dock lights. Second, to fish for pelagic species off the coast of the Palm Beaches. Third was a boat ride up the Loxahatchee River with the possibility of finding some juvenile tarpon in the mangroves. And fourth, a walk through the restored subtropical hammock of the Nature Conservancy's Blowing Rocks Nature Preserve with the possibility of snook in the surf. Both of these final places loomed large in my best childhood memories and both had become an example of the good "We the People" can do when we put our minds and actions toward it.

When I climbed into the truck, Terry turned and asked, "Do you like barbeque?" In my best flat, emotionless, and humorously sarcastic tone I replied, "I'm from Texas and a son of the South—what do you think?" I smiled. Soon after, we were sitting in Sweet Southern Barbeque, where the Florida-style pulled pork was indeed sweet and the Southern-style iced tea was even sweeter. And in between visits from the sassy red-haired server who came by frequently to refill our teas, we talked about Florida, fishing, and family, while reminiscing about "the way things used to be" and the way things were going—good, bad, and ugly.

The predictable sound of Nashville's current brand of formulaic pop-country music was playing in the background. The blaring sounds of electric guitars, banging drums, and nonsensical lyrics made me wonder if Merle Haggard would have a chance in these shallow water days. I guess it comes with age, this tendency to reminisce. And if we're honest with ourselves, we all tend to recall what we want to recall. We leave in the shiny things and take out the tarnish. Even as I lamented the losses—I knew better. Life is what we make of it—a culmination of our choices and perspectives. So, I chose to enjoy the barbeque, sweet tea, and good conversation and let the river unfold in front of me, without expectations. It will be what it will be . . . after all, that's the way of rivers and lives. They just flow.

After picking up William at summer camp we launched the micro skiff from a dock in the small town of Tequesta. I've always liked Tequesta but could never afford to live there. As we turned the boat inward with the tide I sat on the bow watching the part of the Loxahatchee that did not gain legislative protection from the State of Florida or the United

States of America. Seawalls contained the river as it flowed up toward multimillion-dollar homes, each with its own dock, boat, and bright green irrigated lawn. I knew that snook, tarpon, and even bull sharks would pass this way, just as we were. The bull sharks would birth their pups and the snook and tarpon would feed among the mangroves as they have for a million years. But they had to swim much farther now to get to suitable semi-natural habitat.

The Loxahatchee was declared a National Wild and Scenic River on May 17, 1985, just before I left the Marine Corps, and long after the days of my youthful adventures on that river. Loxahatchee is a Seminole word meaning, "River of Turtles," and there are a lot of turtles living in that river, and sunning along the length of every half-submerged palmetto log. But it might have well been called, "The River of Alligators" or be named after one of the many other forms of wildlife that have depended upon its waters for thousands of years. White-tailed deer, bobcats, armadillos, gopher tortoises, indigo snakes, Eastern diamondback rattlesnakes, alligators, Florida panthers, and black bears all once lived here in abundance—although those days are long gone.

The Loxahatchee River flows for about eight miles from its source until it mingles with the waters of the Jupiter Inlet and ultimately becomes a part of the Atlantic Ocean. Saltwater fishes such as tarpon, snook, and even bull sharks travel up the Loxahatchee from its oceanic outflow to its brackish water mangrove forests. With human-induced climate change and its accompanying sea level rise, salt water is intruding farther inland on the Loxahatchee and every coastal Florida river—killing off cypress, palmetto, and slash pine trees as it does and replacing them with red mangrove. Ironically, as we destroy the mangrove habitats and replace them with seawalls, we also cause the mangrove to replace the cypress, and there's nowhere else for those freshwater wetlands to go—or for the deer, gators, and turtles who rely upon them.

When I was young, I used to paddle my canoe up the Loxahatchee from the State Park Headquarters all the way up to Trapper Nelson's Landing. I'd tie my boat up at the palmetto wood docks and walk among the now empty buildings of the encampment of the "Tarzan of the Loxahatchee." Vince "Trapper" Nelson was born in New Jersey, ran away from home when his mother died, hopped freight trains to Colorado, Texas, and Mexico, and ultimately settled at an encampment on Jupiter Beach, not far from the lighthouse. He became increasingly disillusioned with society and in time moved out far into the woods along the Loxahatchee, where he made a living trapping, hunting, and fishing, eating the meat and selling the furs.

In the 1930s he began making money by promoting his "Trapper Nelson's Zoo and Jungle Gardens," which became a popular tourist attraction for wealthy people from Palm Beach. They would take boat cruises up the river to see his zoo and watch the 6'4" man wrestle alligators for their entertainment. But as time passed the man who once entertained movie stars became more and more reclusive and distrustful of government and people. He blocked off access to his camp and carried a shotgun everywhere he went. Sadly, it was that shotgun that killed him. It was deemed a suicide by the county sheriff, but many locals shared their suspicions that "Trapper" had been murdered by one of several enemies he had made along the way. All this drama and suffering in a place that I came to as a boy, to find peace.

I used to sit out there on the edge of his palm-thatched chickee just envisioning his life unfolding in front of me. I often wondered if he was lonely—because I would have been. Even during the times when the boat captains brought out throngs of tourists to "see him," what they were seeing was a caricature of a man. They saw him as he played his role as the "Jungle Man," but they were neither friends nor family. They were caricatures too.

We've all had that feeling of being unutterably alone in a crowd. And as much as I love being out in nature, the nights that I have camped in the wilderness alone were lonely nights indeed. I find that camping, fishing, and living all can feel more complete when you have someone you love beside you. Humans are social animals and in these times of internet "relationships" and toxic distrust of everything and everyone . . . I wonder if we are not in danger of driving ourselves out to the wilderness of madness—alone in the crowd of eight billion strangers.

And I have to confess that as we cruised down the river together, I was often alone with my thoughts. I felt relief as we passed through the portion of the river that was wrapped in concrete and surrounded by tropical vegetation from faraway places. Most of the foreign-born palms, frangipani, screw pines, casuarina, and tropical gum trees thrive here in the ecologically sterile, manicured lawns because nothing in Florida has evolved to eat them. Isn't it ironic how we humans have such a strong proclivity to find a new place to live and conclude, "This is nice . . . let's change it!" We're like beavers without the whimsy.

William decided he wanted to have a turn at driving the boat and he did a pretty good job, save for the occasional turn toward the mangroves that might have scraped me off the bow. But he is a super smart boy and for all I know, he'd thought the whole thing out. It was so obvious how close he was with his dad, and I was getting in the way of some real father and son time. But in truth, they were on their own most of the time, because I was feeling quite alone on the bow, immersed in my memories of youth and meandering feelings about what it means to be getting older.

Terry and I have seen a world that William will never know. And William may grow up in a world that I don't want to live in. But neither is a foregone conclusion. There is still just a little time to turn the wheel and set a more steady course.

All the way along the river I was watching for signs of tarpon, and we saw a few hopeful swirls and the frequent sight of leaping finger mullet, but the swirls were inconclusive, and the mullet seemed too carefree to be fleeing in fear from anything dangerous, So, we kept motoring slowly upriver toward our destination of Kitching Creek. I was watching for any chance to see one of the many alligators I was so used to seeing here, but the tide was high enough to flood their basking places, so they remained elusive.

Jonathan Dickenson State Park is named after a Quaker merchant from Port Royal, Jamaica, who decided to travel with his family and his ten black African slaves and resettle in the city of Philadelphia, where he became the mayor of that city—twice. (Yes, a slave owner was the mayor of "The City of Brotherly Love.") While on the journey north along the coast of Florida, a hurricane drove their ship onto the beach near modern-day Hobe Sound in 1696. He wrote a journal describing their harrowing ordeal and their encounters with the coastal indigenous tribes including the Hobe tribe, for which the area is named. In his journal he gives details of the frequent acts of cruelty and infrequent moments of kindness they experienced during their brief captivity and long arduous journey up the coast of Spanish Florida to the settlement of St. Augustine.

Before the colonial conquest of the peninsula by Spain, and later by England, this was a water-filled landscape dominated by indigenous people such as the Hobe, Tequesta, and Ais tribes in the southeast, and the Calusa in the Southwest. It's tragically ironic that the Spanish and English interlopers, as well as the native tribes, engaged in various forms of human slavery. None of us are without the stain of past human folly. We are in fact, just human, and all we can do is choose to learn from our past and do better in the future.

The fact is that all of these peoples practiced their own form of religion and systems of social order. Apparently the possession of Protestant crosses, Catholic crucifixes, or Calusa statuettes did not prevent the darker impulses of human nature from rising to the surface. Then and now we seem to justify our lack of empathy and endless supply of apathy by the simpleminded designation "other." We tend to treat the Earth and ocean that way too. Will we ever learn that there is no "other"?

Terry and William were together at the helm, but I was alone with my memories and thoughts. This place was where I so often came when I felt empty and needed to be made whole again. I remember the serenity I felt as my paddle dug into the tea-colored waters, and I watched as the shoreline slipped behind me like so many fears and troubles ... let go. I recalled how once as I paddled along Kitching Creek, I looked up into the treetops and saw a group of barred owls looking down toward me. We just sat together, me in my boat and they on their branches.

Wildlife never fled from me when I was alone. Deer used to stand within arm's reach and birds sat on twigs beside me. We'd look into each other's eyes with a sense of recognition and understanding. This river was my childhood Garden of Eden and only the "sin" of "growing up" seemed to separate us. In my young teenage years, I invested countless hours and days on this river, alone but never lonely. Nature never left me, and I have never left nature.

When we arrived at Kitching Creek the time had finally come for me to cast a few times toward the stilted roots of mangroves in the hope of connecting to a snook or tarpon. I wrote in my first book, *Casting Forward*, that to me any trip where you bring a fishing rod with the intent to fish is a "fishing trip," and I still stand by that definition. But we knew up front that we had gotten out too late in the day, and we'd done so with a weary six-year-old boy who had already had a full day of swimming at camp. We knew that the purpose of this journey was for me to see one of my favorite childhood places—one last time.

I stepped up to the bow of the micro-skiff and began making a series of short casts toward the mangrove. Usually when I fish I do so with the expectation that every cast and any cast brings the possibility of adventure, and although this was still true, somehow it didn't matter to me if I caught a fish or not. I was here . . . on the Loxahatchee. That was enough.

Terry pushed us forward down the creek that was wider and deeper than I had ever known. As part of the restoration efforts the government has established minimum flow guidelines and so more fresh water was coming down river than in my childhood days. This is a good thing. But the other reality is that with anthropogenic accelerated climate change and quickly rising sea levels, during high tides, more salt water was pushing farther upriver than ever before.

As a boy I remember the shoreline of the river near Kitching Creek being a freshwater habitat of sable palms, slash pines, and live oaks. Now as we moved up the creek all I saw on both sides were the brackish water habitats of red mangroves and the dead sentinels of old sable palms and oak trees. It was still beautiful but it wasn't truly natural.

Every place on Earth is now a historical landscape. Nothing is left untouched by the once minor species, Homo sapiens. Even Antarctica is melting into the sea. With my own eyes I have seen the glaciers melting in Peru, Tanzania, and Alaska. With my asthmatic lungs I have breathed in the smoke of burning rainforests. With my own heart I have yearned for our better souls to prevail so that we know when to "snip off" and declare, "That's enough." So, I stood on the bow with my fly rod in hand, but it felt a little like trying to play checkers with someone you love, knowing this was the last time you'd ever see them. The game seemed, unimportant. It was almost a distraction.

At one point we turned a corner in the creek, and we could clearly see where the tideline met—fresh water and brackish. A small tarpon splashed, just around the bend. I tossed out a cast but my heart wasn't in it, and it showed. I was too busy being in awe of the power of water to shape the world.

Just beyond the tideline, the mangroves ended and we found ourselves surrounded by ancient cypress trees, dripping in Spanish moss and the bright, blue-green fronds of healthy, thriving sable palms. With each bend in the creek, we saw more cypress, sables, and live oaks. Then, on higher ground, there were armies of slash pines surrounded by palmettos and myrtle oak. And from memory I knew, if we could see just beyond the palmettos and onward toward the sea, the sugar-white sandhills would be covered in the increasingly rare sand pine scrub that is home to gopher tortoises, indigo snakes, and Florida scrub jays.

I felt at peace seeing that pieces of the places I once called home still existed, even if in miniature. Memories flooded my mind of a younger version of myself paddling these waters among alligator hatchlings that looked like baby dinosaurs and pileated woodpeckers that flew like pterodactyls. Just for a moment, I felt young again. And just for a moment, I felt hopeful. After all, if even fragments remain of the world I once loved, then there is still the opportunity to make it more intact, once again.

Terry asked, "Do you want to go any farther?" I knew it had been a long day for him and young William. I looked forward toward the evening sun and backward toward Terry's weary son. I considered all we had yet to do on my final day of remembrance and reunion. I knew we had a long boat ride back to the dock, and then one more stop before the day came to an end. So, I snipped off the fly and reeled in the line and then turned back to Terry and said, "That's enough."

On the way back toward the dock and away from the Wild and Scenic River, we saw tarpon rolling to either side of us . . . but I had no desire to cast to them. Simply knowing they were still there among the mangroves was satisfaction enough. I was content.

When I was a young boy here, Blowing Rocks Beach was a shadow of the place it has become. The Nature Conservancy's Blowing Rocks Preserve is a perfect example of the best of humanity shining through—and why I implore you to not give up hope and never cease to act upon that hopeful vision. After all, we humans are as capable of planting a garden as we are of supplanting one. We can use our ingenuity to extract from or restore the Earth and oceans. It's a choice, but it's a choice that requires wisdom not greed.

By the time I was growing up here in the 1960s and 1970s, Blowing Rock Beach had already been disfigured by invasive plant species like Brazilian pepper and Australian pine. Nothing wild or native lived here in what once was an amalgam of subtropical hammock, mangrove wetland, and sand dune scrub. Only along the rocks themselves did I find creatures from the native seas—unaltered by humanity, save for their increasing rarity. But so much of that has changed—for the better.

When Terry and I arrived at Blowing Rocks Preserve, we had the fly rods in the truck but chose not to take them with us. Instead, I wanted to simply be with my "old friend" who once was on "death's door," but is so much more healthy and vibrant now. The invasive species have been eliminated and replaced with a thriving native subtropical hammock, quite like the one that Jonathan Dickenson and his family would have seen when their ship ran aground here in 1696.

We walked down the hammock trail through a tunnel of sea grapes, cabbage palms, gumbo limbo, and pigeon plum. Just behind us was the Indian River Lagoon complete with its restored red, black, and white mangrove wetlands that shelter everything from snook to queen conchs and support the nests of ibises, egrets, and herons. As we walked farther down the trail, stepping upon patches of sugary sand and blankets of fallen sea grape leaves I looked up into the treetops to see the intricate webs of golden silk spiders—it was so magical how they caught the evening light and my imagination. And there was birdsong, as one might expect in this vital habitat along the East Atlantic Flyway . . . but as a boy walking among the foreign trees and shrubs the only birds I remember were pigeons. Somehow along with the hammock they have been transformed into warblers and wrens. All I could do was smile.

As we walked, I could hear the sound of the crashing waves upon the rocks. As a boy I came here to search for living seashells among the rocks, as well as the empty vessels of once-living mollusks brought up with the tide. I remember finding living chitons, keyhole limpets, and bleeding tooth shells affixed to the rocks, and augers, olives, chestnut turbans, knobby tops, alphabet cones, and the occasional fighting conch washed up on the sandy beach.

Later, I learned that I was contributing to the demise of these shells and the beach habitat by collecting them, and I never did so again. But as a child, walking this beach, searching among the rocks and tidal pools gave me a lifetime of understanding about nature and sealed my fate as a lifelong naturalist.

Now as an angler I am quite as I was then as a young explorer of everything living in the sea. I want to learn about the life of the fish I seek. It's not enough for me to know that there are snook and tarpon in the surf during certain times of the year—I want to understand why they are there and what their presence means for everything else. As a naturalist angler, I am always learning and therefore, forever young.

At the end of the trail are dunes and then the shoreline where ocean meets land and so many living dramas unfold. I noticed that the sand looked unfamiliar—not the golden color of the Florida Suncoast I knew, but rather, a gray, dingy grit from somewhere else. All across Florida massive dredge-and-fill operations are being euphemistically labeled, "Beach Nourishment" by government entities, corporations, and others. In fact, what they mostly do is cover up the impact of anthropogenic erosion and risk further destruction of habitats for fish and other wildlife, from coral reefs to tidal zones. Concealing symptoms never cures the patient. We still have a lot to learn.

These restored dunes and protected dark skies of the preserve are an important nesting ground for the endangered or threatened loggerhead, green, and leatherback sea turtles, and we found a freshly opened nest where the boardwalk meets the beach. The hatchlings probably just began their life's journey the night before. From that nest they struggled into the surf and out beyond the reefs into the open ocean. Few will survive to return here and reproduce, even without the obstacles we've put in their way. But here along the sands of this coastal preserve, they have a chance.

We chose to heal what we once hurt. I walked down the beach and touched the same limestone just as I once did, so long ago. Memories flooded in like an incoming tide of images and emotions . . . and for once, they weren't all about loss. "We the People" did a good thing here.

Looking around me, I remembered that there was once a rutted dune buggy track along this formerly damaged dune. But now, after twenty years of effort by the Nature Conservancy and its volunteers, that road had been replaced with a healthy sand dune landscape. Now, that sandy scar has been healed, and beach sunflowers are surrounded by the many butterflies and moths that come to pollinate them. The flowers cannot survive without the pollinators, and the pollinators cannot survive without the flowers, and we cannot survive without them all. The existence and future of humanity rests on the shoulders of microbes, the petals of wildflowers, and the wings of native bees, butterflies, and moths. It all matters—more than we do.

For the most part, nature doesn't need humans, but we humans need nature. The only exception to this is perfectly demonstrated by places like the Nature Conservancy's Blowing Rocks Preserve, where human choice and action led to the restoration of much of what we had destroyed. And yet, it's only seventy-three acres of what once was a coastline of mangrove wetlands, maritime hammocks, coastal scrub, living dunes, and vibrant healthy littoral zone that extends from the shoreline areas that are permanently submerged, through the spray zone high-water mark, which is rarely inundated.

In my daydreams, as the sea level continues to rise, we finally realize that building condos and mansions along the ocean's shores is not sustainable, and 73 acres becomes 73,000 acres of wild, native, coastal habitats. In that dream I envision science-based sustainable angling and other less consumptive human recreational opportunities, feeding our souls and setting the tone for coexistence with this beautiful blue world. I see children discovering the sea, while learning of how things once were, and what we did to save the planet and ourselves. "Once upon a time . . . this was all condos." The six-year-old looks into the eyes of the sixty-year-old and says, "I can't imagine that. It's all so beautiful now." A man can dream—right?

CHAPTER TWENTY-ONE

Just One More Cast

Headwaters of the Mississippi River,
Flambeau and Chippewa Rivers, Northwoods of Wisconsin

There were no formerly heroic times, and there was no formerly pure generation. There is no one here but us chickens, and so it has always been: A people busy and powerful, knowledgeable, ambivalent, important, fearful, and self-aware; a people who scheme, promote, deceive, and conquer; who pray for their loved ones, and long to flee misery and skip death. It is a weakening and discoloring idea, that rustic people knew God personally once upon a time—or even knew selflessness or courage or literature—but that it is too late for us. In fact, the absolute is available to everyone in every age. There never was a more holy age than ours, and never a less.

~ ANNIE DILLARD, *FOR THE TIME BEING*

THE FIRST DAY

On my first morning on the Flambeau River, I was chock-full of antic-ipation, exhilaration, and questions. Would I be able to measure up; or would I screw it up? Could I cast an eleven-weight rod and a fly the size of a Cornish game hen for eight hours straight, or would my aged arms, shoulders, and back betray me? And if I was fortunate enough to cause a musky to follow my fly, would I do absolutely everything right, or would I make one of the many mistakes that will play on a loop through my mind for the rest of my life? There are so many things that can go wrong in musky fishing with a fly and only one way to get it right. I love a challenge.

I was honored to have been asked to be this year's guest at my dear friends Bob and Lisa White's annual Musky Madness event in Northern Wisconsin. And it was so nice to see Bob's smiling face as he picked me up at the airport in Minneapolis. We stopped by his house in Marine on St. Croix before driving on to the lodge outside Winter, Wisconsin.

The site for the lodge couldn't have been more beautiful with the lake just behind and tall trees all around. Legend and local history has it that this lodge was built by a Chicago gangster who was the only contemporary of Al Capone that he didn't have killed. Allegedly Capone stayed here on occasion, along with his "tommy gun"–swinging goons, which made me wonder if there was any special kind of fertilizer beneath the roots of the many large and healthy spruce trees on the property. Perhaps not everyone who got crossways of "Scarface" ended up "sleeping with the fishes."

In the morning we all woke to find one of Lisa's amazing meals waiting for us along with fresh hot coffee. There were various mugs to choose from and I quickly selected and filled a metal camper's cup with the words, "I'd Rather Be Fishing," and "Hayward, WI" written across its rounded face. Hayward, Wisconsin, is the self-proclaimed "musky capital of the world," and although I've never been there, I hear that they have a giant concrete musky likeness on the edge of town. I'm not too sure about kitschy-looking tourist stops, but I must admit that I'd kind of like to see it for myself. I immediately fell in love with this campy-looking mug and after the first sip of java over its narrow metal lip, I wanted one of my own.

The night prior, just after dinner, Bob announced which anglers were assigned to which guides, and I was more than pleased to see that I would be sharing the drift boat with my new friend, Tim Schulz. Among other things, Tim is an author, engineer, and college educator from Michigan's Upper Peninsula. He is also an all-around great guy who is brave enough to crack the kind of wholesome jokes that make you moan or chuckle while drifting down a river or sitting around a dinner table. Tim and I had communicated a few times via email, but this was our first time meeting in person, and I was happy that we'd get a day on the water together.

I was also thrilled to find out that our guide for that first day would be Gabe Schubert, whom I knew of by reputation, but also had never met. I don't remember much about any of the guides I've had in the Caribbean. They all blended together, competent, yet apathetic about my existence. I was a "sport" wanting to catch bonefish, and they would do what they needed to do in exchange for amazingly unattractive American dollars. (Why do other countries have beautiful images of wildlife, coral reefs, and mountains on their currency, and we have dead people?) Gabe was different. He was an unforgettable guide on an equally unforgettable river. And I for one will never forget my day on the water with this quiet, confident, deeply ethical man. I know I will never forget Gabe. If you're ever fortunate enough to be able to fish with him, do it.

When we launched Gabe's immaculate drift boat into the upper Flambeau River, the first thing I saw was a bald eagle perched on top of a tall spruce tree. I'm not sure that anyone else paid it much attention, but I don't ever want to find myself without a sense of awe whenever I see one of these majestic birds. They are the feathered poster children of what happens when we humans turn the knobs of nature without a clue as to the possible catastrophic outcomes of our tinkering. And they are examples of what acts of redemption we are capable of whenever we recognize the error of our ways and codify new behavior for "We the People." In my childhood they were absent. Now they are returning. I feel privileged every time I see an eagle. They give me hope.

The water was clear enough to see the rock and gravel bottom, and the current was quick enough to keep things moving at a pleasant but not urgent pace. I watched as Gabe worked the sticks, each together in unison, then one after another, then a back stroke or two where the river called for tempering, and ultimately returning to the easy, hand-and-wrist rolling rhythm of unified motion. It was artistic and almost mystical. I can't imagine him stranded on shore. It would be a sin.

Tim and I began casting toward each shoreline, port and starboard. I was casting from the bow and he was at the stern, and we were both simply and silently enjoying the first casts feeling of endless possibilities. We had barely rounded the first corner in the river when I cast into a bit of backwater along some downed timber and immediately received a vicious, swirling strike and strip-set the hook several times. Musky? Already? I had only made about ten casts—nowhere near the required thousand. But then I saw that I had caught a pike, and although a pike is not a musky, it was a nice start to the first day.

I've heard it said that anglers up here in musky country call pike "river whores" because "while a musky might flirt with you, a pike is always willing to go home with you." That made me smile, but I really love catching pike on the fly and wouldn't mind targeting some of those monsters I hear about in the Northwest Territories of Canada. I was grateful for my pike and thanked him as soon as we slipped the hook out and sent him home. I always thank the fish, either aloud or silently with my inner voice.

The river was hopeful, tinted in the color of autumn leaves, changing in mood from lazy to rambunctious. Gravel, grit, sand, stone, root, rock, and fallen timber—all in motion as one ever-changing swirling, churning, rolling reflection of the sun. It all came to my mind's eye as a singular experience. It was more symphony than song. An amalgam of earth, water, and sky all dressed up in trees of green, gold, yellow and red; each containing birdsong and the sound of wind and wave. A splash of suckerfish spun in the shallows. A good sign for musky fishers.

I was starting to get the hang of casting and retrieving the heavy fly in a manner that might ring the dinner bell for a flirtatious predator with the face of a duck and the teeth of a crocodile. Short, downward, halting strips that cause the fly to lurch forward, and then turn sideways, left and right, like a wounded sucker asking to be eaten. I liked it. I liked the rhythm of the process and the way it required an understanding of nature and the nature of my quarry. And I enjoyed the feeling of casting left, then right, forward cast, and back cast, in a methodical and peaceful manner—all the while hoping to provoke some violence. I could see how this kind of fishing could become an obsession.

We rounded a bend in the river and came upon a large, half-submerged rock projecting from the river off the starboard bow. Some idiot had spray painted it with the words, "Cam's Rock." With the exception of the graffiti left behind by "Cam," it was an idyllic spot along the river with nice runs twisting around plenty of submerged structure that felt like it held a musky or two just waiting to crush the next wobbling, wounded fish that wandered by. It looked like a place where we might get lucky, and as Gabe brought the boat ashore for lunch just upstream of "Cam's Rock" he mentioned that rumor had it that people like to wade out to the rock to "get lucky" together under a midsummer's moonlight. Apparently wolves aren't the only things howling at the moon in these woods.

I've noticed you can learn a few things about a guide or a person by the way they treat the ritual of lunch while fishing. None of it is "good" or "bad"—just interesting. My friend Ted Williams is all business, and for him eating and drinking is a waste of valuable fishing time. I can respect that and adapt by bringing quick snacks that I can have in between casts. My buddy Kirk Deeter has damn good taste in deli sandwiches and understands the value of an ice-cold Colorado Kool-Aid while floating the Yampa. I was to discover that Gabe Schubert has a poet's soul when it comes to food. He laid out a spread that included gourmet olives, cheeses, grapes, and apple slices, and the kind of baked goods that conjure images of cafés along cobblestone roads with the sound of Roma violins in the near distance. I found myself yearning for a glass of pinot grigio.

While we were sitting in the drift boat eating and watching the river flow, we chatted of life and fishing, which can sometimes feel like the same thing. Tim sat in the stern wearing a smile and a cotton slouch hat of enviable character and indeterminate color. In between bites of sandwich he'd say, "I just gotta feeling about Cam's Rock!" and "I think Cam's Rock is gonna be a lucky place for us." Then he added, "Steve, I think you're gonna get a musky just past Cam's Rock." And he kept saying this, off and on throughout lunch as if willing it to be so, might make it so. I was hoping there was some kind of magic in the old slouch hat.

After lunch, I offered Tim the bow but he said, "I'm liking it back here just fine" and so like Bogie and Hepburn, down the river we went. I looked back and watched Gabe at the sticks, rhythmically rolling his knuckles up-and-over the oar handles as if it were more of a dance than an effort. Just then, Gabe called out, "There's no bad casts here . . . it's all good water." Tim and I began casting our flies back and forth from bank to bank in hopeful anticipation of the unlikely.

That's about the time we passed Cam's Rock. I was casting to the left and away from the rock and Tim was casting to the right and toward it, since one place seemed as good as another. Almost immediately a big, emerald green musky grabbed hold of Tim's fly and began following it all the way to the boat like a toothy dog retrieving a wet sock. Tim was stripping the line as fast as he could, waiting for the fish to turn so he could set the hook, but it never did so at the last moment he strip set the hook as hard as he could, and the musky was on—sort of. It dug down and spun around as Gabe grabbed the net and in that moment the massive old fish jumped from the water, thrashing its head violently and so close to us that the river water was still dripping off our elbows when we realized it had thrown the hook and was free. We all moaned and laughed at the same time with the mixture of disappointment and joy. Tim took it all in stride, more grateful than disappointed.

It seems to me that you can tell a lot about an angler's character by the way they deal with losing a fish or being skunked. I could tell right away that Tim was a man of good humor, but now I saw he was also an angler of good character. Still, I do wish he had landed the fish. It was a beauty and from the point of view of a clueless novice, it seems to me that he did everything right. It just wasn't meant to be.

With a bit of expert coaching from Gabe, I was getting into the groove of casting those big flies on big rods, and as I relaxed my casting unfolded into a repeated, methodical, and relaxed kata that was beginning to feel natural and not contrived. For me, musky fishing felt like a wonderful gumbo of anticipation and acceptance. You knew that connecting with a fish was unlikely—but possible. It is in the possibilities that we find hope, and joy, and meaning. Like sculpture—in fishing the art often exists in the empty spaces between the clay or casts.

There is an alchemy of spirit that turns methodical into magical when you go out with the certainty of fishing but the uncertainty of catching a single improbable fish. When I think of some of my favorite angling days they never included catching batches of bluefish or truckloads of trout. They include fish like corbina, permit, Atlantic salmon, or musky where catching a single fish can make the day and catching nothing is often expected. Where is the adventure in any "sure thing"? Seeking the secretive can be far more rewarding than collecting the common.

This is not to say that there isn't any joy in doing something that is so beautifully predictable that it becomes tradition. My dad and I made a tradition out of catching a stringer full of bluegill that ended up crispy and delicious on a dinner plate. But there is value in pursuing something elusive, even if simply for the experience of the pursuit. Fish that aren't an "easy catch" all remind me of that pretty girl in high school who seemed so out of reach but who eventually said, "Let's dance."

As we meandered down the Flambeau, turn by turn and mile by mile, the sound of the oarlocks creaking rhythmically behind me, the sight of eagles perched in the trees to the front of me, the feel of my arms and shoulders doing their best to keep casting with the least amount of effort and the greatest degree of efficiency. . . . I began to consider the river that carried us and sustained so many living things—including musky. In a way, water seems like "God." Life as we know it cannot exist without water. It has no discernable beginning or end. It can take the shape of whatever contains it or break free and become uncontainable. "I am that I am!" Water declares. Water will be here long after the last human being is gone—I suspect. I'm just not sure what condition we will have left it in by the time we humans slip away like the dinosaurs who preceded us.

And what will become of us? Will we become potential fossil fuel for any visiting aliens who might be foolish enough to repeat our mistakes? Water changes form from liquid to vapor to solid ice. Its solid form is becoming ever more rarified, and if we're not careful Greenland will become green and Miami will become an artificial reef, albeit largely empty of life. I don't want that world. Do you? It is where "The Road" we are traveling is taking us, and everything else along with us. Murder-suicide. A pathetic crime.

Mile after mile of drifting through some of the most beautiful country imaginable culminated with a few last turns and a few final casts. We remained hopeful. At one point I cast my line toward a small cove along the left bank of the Flambeau and with the first strip of the fly the surface broke and the cylindrical back of a musky appeared just behind it and then a duck-faced monster bumped the fly and turned away without taking it—and my heart stopped with my breath. "Did I do something wrong?" I asked. Gabe was all business when he said, "No, it just didn't take it . . . cast again." I did cast again and there was another swirl in the river as the musky showed his presence as well as his reluctance to commit. We all moaned and Gabe said, "Keep casting!" I did. And with each hopeful, prayerful, yearning effort I reminded myself of what Gabe had taught earlier in the day. "Let the fish take the fly and give it time and room to turn. Say in your head, 'There's a musky!' and point your rod toward it so that it has a little slack to turn. When it turns, strip set the hook as hard as you can several times before you raise the rod tip. First, try to break the line, then try to break the rod." I cast to the spot and spots all around it and each time in my mind I said the words, "There's a musky," but sadly, there was no musky there anymore.

It seemed all too soon that we rounded the last bend in the river before coming to the takeout spot. I kept casting until the last moment when we had to pull the drift boat ashore and carry it a few yards at a time up the dirt road to the Forest Service gate where Gabe's truck and trailer were parked. Even as Gabe lined up the boat toward the ramp, he was generous with me as I noted a notch in the shoreline and said, "Gabe, mind if I take just one more cast?" He smiled. And he didn't mind. I cast and caught nothing, but still I was hooked on musky fishing.

It was with a great deal of respect and a bit of irony that Gabe Schubert has been given the name "Musky Jesus" by some of his compadres. It's a name that he doesn't much like but that seems to fit him so well and doesn't ring with even a hint of blasphemy. It's not just because of his long, loose tassels of hair, dark beard, bright smile, and easygoing nature. It's because he seems to perform minor miracles on the water with a modest, understated nature of a servant who embodies ethics when it comes to the things that matters. He is also a musky fly-tying genius—just my opinion and who am I? I'm just another apostle who is grateful to break bread and share some time fishing with him.

I can say this, when I was on the water with Gabe, I tried hard to not let him down. It just felt wrong. Like some sort of angling sin. I wished I had caught a musky that day—for Gabe. In the end, I did my best. Hopefully I did not let anyone down, including myself. All we can do in life is keep casting, keep trying, keep learning, keep forgiving ourselves and others, and never lose our sense of wonder and gratitude for an eagle on the wing or an artist at the oars.

THE SECOND DAY

Tony Stifter has one of the kindest hearts I've ever known, and, lucky for me, we became instant friends. I can't wait to fish with him again. The first thing he said was, "I'm not a guide, I just do this for Bob." My fishing buddy for the second day was Mike Sepelak of North Carolina who describes himself as a "hack writer, fly fisher, guitar player, photographer, footballer and old coot enjoying life." He's much more than that, of course. Mike's a nice guy with a cheerful nature and an easy laugh. I knew we were going to have a good day.

The plan of the day was for us to use Tony's jetboat to fish a lake and connecting tributary that led out to the Chippewa River. The night prior I overheard guide Russ Gontarek at the lodge talking about this spot and the likelihood of us connecting with a musky the next day. I was hoping he'd be proven prophetic in this instance. Russ is Bob and Lisa's next-door neighbor, a craftsman of beautiful boat oars, husband, father, musky guide, and good-hearted comedic relief for any potentially tense situation. I had met Russ before while visiting Bob and Lisa and instantly liked him. He was kind and lighthearted with an obvious love for his family, friends, and home waters, and I was hoping his predictions came true for either Mike or me.

It was just coming on to sunrise when we launched, and the east shore of the lake took on a golden aura as the tree-lined shores transformed from shadow to sunlight. Across the expanse of the lake's water a small tributary of the Chippewa emptied itself among semi-submerged fields of wild rice—the same rice that the Native Americans of this region have been harvesting and protecting for centuries. The Ojibwe people, also known as the Anishinaabe-Chippewa harvest the seeds of this aquatic wild grass that grows in the shallow calm waters of lakes, ponds, and deltas across Wisconsin, Minnesota, and southern Ontario. To this day these native peoples conduct the annual harvest in a sustainable way, collecting some of the seed while allowing the rest to fall into the water and regenerate naturally. They know that this is a vital part of the ecosystem and not a "one-and-done" crop. Besides humans, it is an important food source for waterfowl and other birds that live in or pass through these hallowed waters. The Ojibwe are caretakers of the environment, not simply takers from the environment. I'm not sure how to say, "sustainable" in Ojibwe.

As Tony guided the jet boat across the river and up the tributary, the air felt brisk and stinging in the way that numbs your face and fills your heart with the feeling of being truly alive. Some of the best things in life happen at first light. Love comes in many forms, and no matter the events of the day I am in love with mornings. And this morning we slid to a stop and engaged the trolling motor in a wide spot of the tributary just before it narrowed. Mike and I began casting from side to side, and it did not take long for me to feel the results of the prior day upon my aged back and shoulders. Whereas my day on the river with Gabe felt like a symphony of painless casting, the day on the lake with Tony was going to be more of a recital where every muscle ached and every joint creaked. I just wasn't at my best, but Tony was patient with my half-hearted casting. Nature keeps me humble, and my body is a part of nature.

Over the years I have discovered that I'm not a lake, pond, reservoir kind of guy as much as I am a river, stream, creek, and ocean surf angler. I'm in love with moving water, and while the calmness of a lake's surface reflects the autumn-painted maples magnificently, the silence and stillness feels haunting. And this was a beautiful lake, the shoreline dotted with the cottages of lucky homeowners and edged with wild rice that waved ever so slightly in the morning breeze. Still, I prefer movement and sound over stillness and silence.

For several hours Tony worked us carefully and thoughtfully across every inch of likely water. We did not count how many casts we had made but even if we had reached a thousand it didn't matter. Incredulously, like the waters of the tributary and the lake, movement was imperceptible if present at all. Even the lily pads seemed sleepy.

When lunch time rolled around I discovered that Tony is an avid carnivore. To say that Tony Stifter likes meat is like saying I like my morning coffee . . . an understatement of the worst kind. We had meat sticks, meat jerky, and meat on bread—and I think the bread was an afterthought. After trying out a "Wisconsin venison stick" that had cheese and cranberries mixed in for good measure, I smiled at Tony and said, "Don't pass on that colonoscopy, buddy." He smiled back and offered some more jerky. It was excellent jerky.

Periodically throughout the day Tony would reiterate that he was not a "professional guide." But I have never seen "a guide" do a better job of trying everything possible to put a "sport" on fish. We worked every inch of the tributary and much of the massive lake, but without result. And just before we had to pack it in I cast across a fishy-looking bit of water, made a quick strip of the line, and immediately felt a tug! I strip set the hook and felt my line being pulled backward and down and the rod tip bent and began throbbing. We all caught our breath, and that is when we saw the submerged tree branch I had caught—not a musky. Every time I pulled it flexed and then pulled back. It felt so promising, for a moment in time.

It wasn't long after that I stood on the dock watching the yellow-orange-red of the evening sky bleed into the yellow-orange-red of the autumn leaves. The boat was on the trailer, and it was time to go back to the lodge, but I wanted to grab the moment and let the colors burn into my memory. Tony came over, put his hand on my shoulder and smiled. He said, "I want you to come back and fish with me as my friend." I smiled back. As Tony walked toward the truck I took one last glance at the golden sunset.

What a gift this day had been. The lake did not give me a fish but that is something I had to earn anyway. But my new friend Tony had given me a day of light and laughter, moments and memories, and the sights and sounds of this beautiful historical landscape. This was gift enough. The ancient mystic Rumi was wise indeed as he danced in the streets of Aleppo singing, "When someone is counting out gold for you, don't look at your hands, or the gold. Look at the giver." Fish or no fish, this day was golden.

THE LAST DAY

My boatmate for the third and final day was Ron Hickie, a tall, youthful man of middle age from Chicago who like me refuses to dwell upon the passing years, knowing that the best years may be yet to come. He has a beautiful young family, a wonderful life, and a poetic, inquiring mind. We hit it off immediately.

Westin Their is, among other things, a fishing guide and sailboat captain whose loose tumble of hair might elicit envy from any balding man like me, and whose easy smile we should all emulate. Behind his casual nature and desire to be an established and respected "dirt bag," is the mind and spirit of a philosopher. Wes and Ron are both highly intelligent, extremely well read, and like me, open-minded seekers of greater understanding. Our conversations were as rich and diverse as these waters. And the morning began with a dreamlike drift down the Flambeau with more eagles in the trees and an osprey in the air. Things were looking up.

I should also mention that apparently, Ron has the musky mojo. He had been here previously and had caught a musky every time. And on this trip, he caught a musky on each of his first two days. Add to this the fact that it was Bob and Lisa White's "Musky Madness" that led to Ron meeting his lovely wife and starting that beautiful family, and it might seem as if he is somehow spiritually connected to these fish and rivers. He's a lucky man, and he knows it. I almost expected a bag of money to come floating down the river and attach itself to his fly. He's got the musky mojo.

The Marine in me found musky fishing to be like operating in a potential combat zone where the city appears abandoned, but you tread carefully and mindfully because you know "they're" out there—somewhere. There are hours of silent patrol, cast after cast, turn after turn of the river. But you can't let your guard down for a second because the moment you do all hell breaks loose, and in an instant, it's all over.

And that's how it was as Westin took us into a little backwater where the river was shallow and the submerged timber was ubiquitous. I was on the bow, Ron at the stern, and we were both casting and retrieving in a methodical, almost robotic manner just as we had done for the past hour of floating the river's main channel. I noticed a small cove between two areas of structure and cast to about four feet from the water's edge, made one strip of the line, paused, and watched as the water formed the shape of a torpedo that was aiming for the end of my tippet. Musky!

I had been rehearsing this moment for two days. I knew that when I felt the take I should hear the words in my head, "there's a musky" as I point the rod toward the fish. I knew that I needed to be patient and let the fish turn so that I can strip set the hook repeatedly and hard into the corner of its jaw, not the bony, toothy, front of its mouth. And I knew that I should only raise the rod tip after strip setting that hook solidly into the musky's jaw. I knew all this and rehearsed it again and again, but when the moment came I strip set immediately without letting it turn, raised the rod tip and watched in horror as a monster of a musky spit the fly and vanished into the dark waters of the Flambeau. What a clown! All I needed was the rubber nose and the floppy shoes.

I was disappointed in myself, and deep down inside I knew I had a long way to go to get the musky mojo. Ron would have landed that fish, and made it look easy. No matter. By the third day I had already become determined that I'd either catch one on this trip or keep returning to these Northwoods waters until I did. I was hooked.

After a quick lunch of sandwiches, chips, and bottled water we got back out on the river. I had moved to the stern, Ron at the bow and the river narrowed as we got closer to our pullout area. I cast to the right bank and Ron toward the left because it was all good water with lots of places for musky to lurk. While we cast and Westin rowed we discussed the vagaries of life, the blessings we've known, the hardships we've overcome, and our mutual love of being out in nature. And we discussed writing and literature from Ernest Hemingway and Jim Harrison to Cormac McCarthy. We discussed music and art and philosophy and poetry. We spoke of Rumi, Hafiz, and Ram Dass, and of the lessons we learn from nature. Everywhere I travel I find the same people with different faces . . . and I find some of the best people on Earth, when I'm out in nature.

We were almost at our pullout point when it happened. Ron was retrieving his line when he and Westin noticed a musky following the fly inquisitively right up to the boat and although he did everything he could do to illicit a strike, the fish drifted back into its original ambush position. Westin brought the boat back around and Ron began casting as we made another pass, and this time he felt the take, set the hook, and after a short tussle had a nice musky boatside. My new friend had managed to catch three musky in three days and it was a nice bronze-colored fish with a muscled body and emerald glistening sheen to its sides. I watched as it slid back into the river, kicked its tail, and swam off to the same notch in the shoreline where we found it. I was happy for my friend, even as I relived my own errors of that morning and the woeful memories of the one that got away.

No matter; it's fishing. We all have the opportunity to learn and grow through our mistakes. Through a combination of practice and persistence, I too can gain the musky mojo. There are so many things that can go wrong in musky fishing with a fly and only one way to get it right. It's kind of like writing. You just keep learning and adapting and trying until it all comes together. After all, if it were easy and predictable, why would we do it?

If uncertainty is the essence of adventure, then learning and growth are the essences of life. Life without change . . . becomes the death of a life. We breathe in; we breathe out. We exchange pieces of ourselves with the sky. Safeness and sameness are the last gasps of creativity; they are a pillow pressed tightly against the lips of creation. I won't be suffocated by safety or fettered by fear. I'll take my chances with both musky and madness. But I will not risk mere existence in a predictable life.

~——~

It would be fair for you to wonder why a story of America's salt waters begins in a freshwater creek in Texas and ends on a freshwater river in Wisconsin. The answer is simple. The story of Life on Earth is also the story of a water-covered planet, an oxygen-filled atmosphere, and a living star that feeds us all. Without these three things, almost nothing is alive. And the story of water is a circle and a cycle that never ends—it just changes. Whatever happens in the ocean changes the atmosphere; whatever happens in the atmosphere changes the ocean. And a bucket of paint spilled into a storm drain in Minnesota collectively changes the fate of a redfish in Louisiana.

If we were to follow the Mississippi River from its detergent- and fertilizer-filled dead zone in the Gulf of Mexico and through its delta with its vital but endangered saltwater marshes, and past the bayous all the way to its birthplace, we'd have quite a few different directions we might choose. Although the traditional origin of the Mississippi River is considered to be Lake Itasca in Northern Minnesota, this second largest watershed in North America is the culmination and commingling of waters that may fall as rain in Western Pennsylvania or snow in South Dakota. If we choose to follow the Mississippi up any tributary, our only problem might be which way we choose to go, and what we choose to forgo.

We could choose to meander east up the Tennessee River to the streams of the Great Smoky Mountains, or up the Ohio River all the way to my father's tiny brook trout streams in the Allegany. We might follow the Red River westward as it drains parts of Texas and Oklahoma or follow the Missouri River all the way to the Yellowstone where bison, elk, wolves, and grizzly bears live and struggle to keep living. But in this case, I decided to travel to the Flambeau and Chippewa Rivers, in the Northwoods of Wisconsin.

Every watershed resembles a tree with many twigs and branches at its beginning, a mighty trunk that extends for most of its length and then a network of roots at its delta. Like the trees, rivers can be healthy or unhealthy at any point along the way but what really causes its demise is what happens in its metaphorical canopy. And the thing is, almost every river flows into the sea.

The Mississippi is the lifeblood of the Gulf of Mexico, and its life is slipping away. Still, we can begin the process of saving the rivers and the seas, in a heartbeat. All it takes is the love of our original country, and the will to restore and protect as much of it as possible. In a way, it's a national defense issue where the only enemy is unrestricted growth, consumption, and a decided lack of forethought and maturity on the part of "We the People."

The Flambeau and Chippewa Rivers in the Northwoods of Wisconsin are the home of musky, pike, and small-mouthed bass, as well as gray wolves, black bears, and deep green forests. They are also some of the first waters to spill into the Mississippi River and flow out to form the Gulf of Mexico. All the water on Earth is all the water there will ever be on Earth. It just changes places and shapes, but it's all the same water. Sometimes it's part of a river or a raindrop, and sometimes it's part of a musky or me. It is all precious, if we believe life is precious, and I do. How about you?

After floating down that wild and wonderful river in the company of my fellow angling naturalists and warrior-poets, I refuse to believe that our best days are behind us and that some golden time once existed where humans were "god-like" and hope sprung eternal. Hope is an action verb. It is the vision of a better tomorrow, today. All we have is "Now," and as always in the present, we possess the power to choose more wisely, both individually and collectively. *"The absolute is available to everyone in every age. There never was a more holy age than ours, and never a less."*

We may well indeed ruin the world and end our own existence . . . but that too is our choice. Why do we search for other inhabitable planets with hopes of creating distant gardens while we turn the garden globe we've been given into an uninhabitable planet? It's far too easy to imagine a moon-like Earth. I prefer to imagine an Eden-like Earth where every choice we make individually and as a species begins with, "Is this healthy?"

In my dreams, I float down the Flambeau and Chippewa Rivers catching and releasing wild musky and small-mouth bass. And in those same dreams, I connect to wild redfish in the newly healthy Mississippi Delta, a once "dead zone," now alive, in the new world we imagined and created—together. Hope truly is an action verb. It is the vision of a better tomorrow, today. Dreams can come true if we choose to make it so and act accordingly . . . together.

Paradigm Shift—Our Last Chance to Avoid Silent Seas and Empty Waters

Moving from the Anthropocene (Age of Humanity), to the Naturaecene (Age of Nature)

Perhaps in the world's destruction it would be possible at last to see how it was made. Oceans, mountains. The ponderous counter spectacle of things ceasing to be. The sweeping waste, hydroptic and coldly secular. The silence.

~ CORMAC MCCARTHY, *THE ROAD*

ONE OF MY FAVORITE THINGS IN THE WORLD IS CASTING A LINE INTO the ocean's surf, just as the first lights of the day begin to glow. And I was doing just that on one early morning while standing next to two of my dearest friends, Aileen Lane and Kesley Gallagher. We were casting toward corbina that were riding in the swash in the hope of finding breakfast, while seals, sea lions, and dolphin swam behind the corbina, hoping for the same outcome. It was one of those magical moments you share with friends where no words are spoken—or necessary.

I looked down toward the sand being drawn away from my feet as the last wave receded, back toward its saline home. All around me were the featherlike antennae of sand crabs—the focus of the fishes desire and a big part of the reason that the fish, seals, dolphin, and anglers were there. I think we also came for the serenity and hopefulness of this place where ocean meets the land and the two worlds mingle, more than they collide.

During those times when there were no corbina and therefore nothing to cast to, I simply looked out at the tumbling waves, rolling seas, and frolicking sea lions. Everything around me was alive and thriving and it felt as if I were in the center of the circle of life. And as the breeze cooled the warm sunlight on my face, I closed my eyes and listened to the sound of the surf.

I began to image a lifeless ocean and an empty world where good food, clean water, and breathable air were scarce. I began to wonder, if there was no life in this ocean, would I have any reason to be here? And I began to imagine a "man-made-world" of synthetic everything and authentic nothingness. It was then that I thought to myself, "I don't want to live in such a world." Opening my eyes I saw the dolphin leaping, the seabirds searching, and the corbina swimming in the shallow swash. I could breathe again.

If you pay attention, and you should, you can see that things are changing rapidly, and not for the better. As an angler and a master naturalist, I know that the health of the ocean is reflective of the health and future of humanity. Even if you do not currently feel a passion for the seemingly cerebral concepts of environmental and social justice, it is my sincere hope that while you have traveled with me on these adventures, you have begun to understand that the fate of our oceans, seas, gulfs, bays, estuaries, rivers, and the tiniest of tributaries, is linked to our own fate. Everything is connected to everything. We need nature; nature doesn't need us.

I repeat these mantras often, because I want them to sink in like a tungsten-beaded Clouser in the surf. I want these realities to hook on to you and carry you forward across the currents and with every tide—of life. The key to everything that harms our quality of life and the lives of our progeny boils down to environmental and societal health.

The presence or absence of clean, non-acidic, healthy oceans is one way to read our report card. We are failing, and in short order the ocean will fail us too. Most of the oxygen we breathe comes from the photosynthetic life in the sea. Most of the life-giving water we depend upon comes from the sea. And the *climate* (not just the weather) that will decide if we live or die as a species, also, comes from the sea. What if our big blue planet becomes increasingly brown? What if future wars are not fought over fossil fuels, ideologies, or even power—but rather, over food, water, and places to live that haven't been rendered unlivable? Any dysfunctional mob can destroy things; it takes a healthy society to fix things.

At this moment in time, we face wars and rumors of war, anthropogenic climate change that is transforming into environmental and economic collapse, mass immigration, growing diseases and starvation, public health, and safety challenges, and the sixth mass extinction event in known world history. And absolutely all of this, was preventable and is changeable and, to some degree, reversible. Every serious challenge we face is the result of a dysfunctional human behavior issue. After all, we are almost all of the problem, and therefore we are almost all of the solution. It's up to us.

We've got a long way to go and a short time to get there. If we do not choose to move from the Anthropocene (the age of humanity) to the Naturaecene (the age of nature), I believe nature will do it for us. And nature isn't kind nor cruel . . . it is ambivalent to our existence. We must rise above our own apathy before it's too late—and it's almost too late.

I always find it difficult to take that last cast, snip off the fly, and walk away from the sea. It feels a bit like running away from home. Even as a child on the ocean with my father, this place and these waters have called to me and comforted me—when nothing else could. There's something gentle about the blueness of the water, the hush of the foaming waves as they ebb and flow—like the Earth breathing.

Just one final thought. In her book *The World Is Blue: How Our Fate and the Ocean's Fate Are One*, oceanographer Sylvia A. Earle said it well when she wrote, "Throughout the history of our species, the mostly blue planet has kept us alive. It's time to return the favor." Well . . . it is.

Acknowledgments

ONE OF THE GREAT JOYS OF THIS ADVENTURE HAS BEEN SHARING IT with some of the best people on Earth. I want to thank Bob and Lisa White, Chris and Betsy Wood, Kirk and Sarah Deeter, David and Cathy Blinken, Ted and Donna Williams, Aileen Lane, Kesley Gallagher, Preston Bean, Sue Kerver, Captain Greg Peralta, Mark Hieronymus, Captain Alan Corbet, Geoff Malloway, Captain William Townsend, Landon Rowlett, Captain Aaron Reed, Terry Gibson, Brandon Shuler, Gabe Schubert, Tony Stifter, and Westin Their for their friendship, guidance, and support. I am also grateful to my dear friends, Janice "Lil Red" Bowden Hardaway, Maggie Serva, Margarita Quihuis, Lillian Stokes, J. Drew Lanham, Kristen Mellitt, and Pam Uschuk, for their inspiration, support and kindness. Without each of these wonderful people, this work, and my life, would be so much the lesser.

I am deeply grateful to my editor and friend Gene Brissie of Lyons Press for taking the time to read my story, and then for choosing to bring it from the original manuscript to the completed literary work you now hold. And I appreciate the guidance and support of my production editor, Chris Fischer; my copy editor, Emily Natsios; as well as Joanna Beyer, Max Phelps, Emily Cable, and Maura Cahill at Lyons Press. They have made this long journey so much more pleasurable and meaningful with their professionalism, knowledge, and heartfelt dedication.

Most of all, I am grateful to my wife and best friend of forty years, Alice, our amazing daughter Megan, and her wonderful partner Nick, who together form our tight little family that we refer to as "The Regiment." And although I love my entire Regiment, I would be remiss not to single out my wife Alice, who has proofread and given constructive input to every word of everything I have ever written and published, including this acknowledgment. With a lifetime of dear family, friends, and fishing, I am a fortunate man indeed.

Selected Bibliography

Ackerman, Diane. *The Human Age: The World Shaped by Us*. New York: W.W. Norton & Company, 2014.

Ackerman, Jennifer. *The Genius of Birds*. New York: Penguin, 2017.

Ackerman, Jennifer. *Birds By the Shore*. New York: Penguin, 1996.

Ausubel, Kenny. *Dreaming the Future: Reimagining Civilization in the Age of Nature*. Chelsea Green Publishing, 2012.

DiBenedetto, David. *On The Run: An Angler's Journey Down the Striper Coast*. New York: itbooks, 2003.

Earle, Sylvia. *The World Is Blue: How Our Fate and the Ocean's Fate Are One*. Washington, D. C.: National Geographic, 2009.

Ebert, David, *Sharks of the World: A Complete Guide*. Princeton: Wild Nature Press, 2013.

Harari, Yuval Noah. *Sapiens: A Brief History of Humankind*. New York: Harper, 2015.

Kolbert, Elizabeth. *The Sixth Extinction: An Unnatural History*. New York: Picador, 2014.

Leopold, Aldo. *A Sand County Almanac: And Sketches Here and There*. New York: Oxford University Press, 1949.

Louv, Richard. *The Last Child in the Woods: Saving Our Children from Nature-Deficit Disorder*. Chapel Hill, NC: Algonquin, 2008.

McPhee, John. *The Founding Fish*. New York: Farrar, Straus and Giroux, 2003.

Miller, Matthew. *Fishing Through the Apocalypse: An Angler's Adventures in the 21st Century*. Guilford, CT: Lyons Press, 2019.

Monbiot, George. *Feral: Rewilding the Land, the Sea, and Human Life*. Chicago: University of Chicago Press, 2014.

Seabird Mortality Data: *US Fish and Wildlife Service, Alaska Seabird Die-off Factsheet*. September 2019.

Thoman, R. and J. E. Walsh. *Alaska's Changing Environment: Documenting Alaska's Physical and Biological Changes Through Observations*. Fairbanks: H. R. McFarland, Ed. International Arctic Research Center, University of Alaska, 2019.

US Global Change Research Program. *The Climate Report: The National Climate Assessment—Impacts, Risks, and Adaptations in the United States*. Brooklyn, NY: Melville House, 2019.

Weisman, Alan. *The World Without Us*. New York: Picador, 2007. Williams, Florence.

Williams, Florence. *The Nature Fix: Why Nature Makes Us Happier, Healthier, and More Creative*. New York: W.W. Norton & Company, 2017.

ADDITIONAL RESOURCES

Audubon Alaska https://ak.audubon.org/conservation/tongass-national-forest

American Salmon Forest: http://www.americansalmonforest.org

NOAA: https://oceanservice.noaa.gov

Scripps Institute of Oceanography: https://scripps.ucsd.edu/research/topics/
    coastal-ecology

U.S. Fish and Wildlife Service: https://fws.gov/

U.S. Forest Service, Tongass National Forest: https://www.fs.usda.gov/tongass/